THE
SAMSUNG
WAY

THE SAMSUNG WAY

TRANSFORMATIONAL MANAGEMENT STRATEGIES FROM THE WORLD LEADER IN INNOVATION AND DESIGN

JAEYONG SONG AND KYUNGMOOK LEE

New York Chicago San Francisco Athens London Madrid
Mexico City Milan New Delhi Singapore Sydney Toronto

1 2 3 4 5 6 7 8 9 0   DOC/DOC   1 2 0 9 8 7 6 5 4

ISBN: 978-0-07-183579-4
MHID: 0-07-183579-2

e-ISBN: 978-0-07-183580-0
MHID: 0-07-183580-6

Library of Congress Cataloging-in-Publication Data
Song, Jaeyong.
   The Samsung way : transformational management strategies from the world leader in innovation and design / by Jaeyong Song and Kyungmook Lee.
      pages cm
   ISBN 978-0-07-183579-4 (alk. paper) — ISBN 0-07-183579-2 (alk. paper)
1. Samsong Chonja—Management.   2. Electronics industry—Korea (South)—Management.   I. Lee, Kyungmook.   II. Title.
   HD9696.A3K7786 2015
   658.4'012—dc23
                                                        2014018891

McGraw-Hill Education books are available at special quantity discounts to use as premiums and sales promotions or for use in corporate training programs. To contact a representative, please visit the Contact Us pages at www.mhprofessional.com.

CONTENTS

Preface vii

Acknowledgments xi

PART ONE   TWENTY YEARS TO THE TOP 1

Chapter 1   Why the Samsung Way? 3

Chapter 2   How Did Samsung Become a
World-Class Corporation? 23

PART TWO   EVOLUTION OF THE SAMSUNG WAY 57

Chapter 3   Leadership and Governance
The Core of the Samsung Way 61

Chapter 4   The Evolution of Samsung's Management System 77

PART THREE   HOW DID SAMSUNG SUCCEED? 127

Chapter 5   Samsung's First Success Factor
Competency in Creation of Speed 131

Chapter 6   Samsung's Second Success Factor
Synergy Through Convergence 151

Chapter 7   Samsung's Third Success Factor
Evolutionary Innovation 173

PART FOUR   SAMSUNG-STYLE PARADOX MANAGEMENT
AND THE FUTURE OF THE SAMSUNG WAY 201

Chapter 8   Internal Co-opetition and Paradox Management 203

Chapter 9   The Future of the Samsung Way 223

Notes 257

Index 267

PREFACE

In the early 1990s, Samsung Group's products were at the top of many industries in Korea, but they were in the second or third tier in global markets. By then, the effects of major changes at home and abroad were seriously affecting the conglomerate. Democratization in the 1980s had ignited a labor movement that had led to soaring wages and the end of Korea's run as a low-cost production base. Moreover, Japanese manufacturers, Samsung's main rivals, had moved offshore to avoid the sharp appreciation in the yen that followed the 1985 Plaza Agreement. When their leading technology and brands in electronics were combined with low labor costs in Southeast Asia and China, Samsung's struggles in global markets were clearly visible. Finally, forecasts that the electronics industry would shift from analog to digital technology in the twenty-first century were amplifying long-term concerns.

In response to these major changes resulting from democratization, globalization, and digitization, Samsung Chairman Lee Kun-Hee unveiled his New Management initiative in 1993. The strategic blueprint completely transformed Samsung, allowing it to overcome the threat of competition and pave the way for its taking advantage of new opportunities. It included the lofty goal of improving Samsung's products and services to the point of excellence and making Samsung one of the leading global companies of the twenty-first century. In the days of analog, Samsung had lagged behind Japanese electronics companies, but Chairman Lee dreamed of Samsung's outdoing them in the digital age through aggressive, preemptive investments. The effort to achieve these audacious goals was summed up in Chairman Lee's directive to his senior executives: "Change everything except your wife and children."

Now, 20 years later, Samsung is one of the world's leading companies, holding the number one spot in key electronics businesses like mobile phones, televisions, memory chips, display panels, and rechargeable batteries. All elements of the company's operations, including corporate strategy, management systems, and core competencies, were realigned in accordance with the goals of the New Management initiative. As a result, Samsung now occupies the leading position in the global electronics industry. The company's transformation over the past 20 years and its rise to the forefront of the global corporate stage has set a compelling precedent for both Korean and foreign companies.

While a number of books have been written about Samsung's rise to the top and Chairman Lee Kun-Hee's role in its transformation, most of these books were written for the entertainment of the general public. Professional analysis and applications of theory from a management scholar's perspective on Samsung's strategy and its main strengths have been lacking. Moreover, several scholarly books on the subject lack in-depth, systematic analysis. Data about Samsung have also been difficult to acquire, and access to interviews has been challenging; thus, newspaper articles and publicly available data have often been the only materials available to management scholars. As a result, both foreign and Korean managers who wish to understand and benchmark Samsung's management system for their own companies have been unable to find information to aid them in their endeavors.

Under these circumstances, we have had the good fortune to be asked by the Samsung Economic Research Institute (SERI), a think tank of the Samsung Group, to conduct in-depth research into the sources of Samsung's competitiveness and to learn about its future plans. With SERI's cooperation, since 2004, we have interviewed more than 80 of Samsung's key executives, including CEOs, with most of them coming from Samsung Electronics. SERI also provided data about Samsung for examination and analysis. From 2008 to 2011, while serving as Samsung's academic advisors, we obtained a wide variety of information about the company. In 2011, as a result of this research, we published an article in the *Harvard Business Review* (*HBR*), in collaboration with Professor Tarun Khanna at Harvard Business School, on the factors influencing Samsung's success. This was the first case analysis of a Korean company to be published in *HBR*. Overall, during the past 10 years, beginning in 2004, in the process of conducting research and analysis, we have broadened our understanding of Samsung as a company, serving as academic advisors, educating executives, and writing research papers and case studies.

This book is the result of 10 years of careful research, during which the authors focused on Samsung's transformation and takeoff during the past 20 years since the New Management initiative. Among Samsung's many subsidiaries, we concentrated our efforts on the company's world-class electronics subsidiaries, particularly Samsung Electronics. This book presents Samsung's three major management paradoxes, along with an in-depth analysis of Samsung's distinctive competencies, and particularly the management system that Samsung built in the process of resolving these paradoxes and developing the Samsung Way. A broad picture of Samsung's future tasks is also included.

We believe that this book will be helpful for executives and employees who want to understand and benchmark Samsung's management system and its rise to the top. In particular, both corporations in advanced countries and latecomers in developing nations that want to catch up with front-runners can learn from Samsung's example. In addition, our analysis of Samsung's paradox management strategies and systems will provide many points of learning for management scholars and students.

We also believe that employees at Samsung, especially foreign employees, can understand or reevaluate Samsung's transformation, core competencies, key success factors, and management systems and mechanisms since the New Management initiative by reading this book. Our analyses and opinions may not necessarily be definitive, and they may differ from those of Samsung's employees. Yet since they are the views of outside experts, we believe that they merit attention and consideration. We hope that this book can help lay a cornerstone for further development of Samsung's strategies, management systems, and capabilities.

The book was written with interview support from Samsung's executives and employees, yet it is based on independent judgment and analysis. All of the content included herein represents the personal view of the authors, and does not represent Samsung's official stance.

Samsung's future depends on its employees. We sincerely hope that the company can overcome its external and internal challenges wisely, and further evolve and develop the Samsung Way by taking its unique paradox management system to the next level. We hope that the findings in this book can play some part in this process. We also hope that executives and employees at other companies, in particular non-Korean companies, as well as business scholars and students studying business administration all over the world, can understand Samsung better by reading this book.

Professors Jaeyong Song and Kyungmook Lee
Seoul National University

ACKNOWLEDGMENTS

We convey our deep appreciation to some 80 key Samsung executives who took time from their busy schedule for interviews with us over the past 10 years. Among these are Samsung's core executives, including Vice-Chairman Kwon Oh-Hyun (Vice-Chairman and CEO of Samsung Electronics, and head of Device Solutions), former Vice-Chairman Yun Jong-Yong (former CEO of Samsung Electronics), and former Vice-Chairman Lee Yoon-Woo (former CEO of Samsung Electronics). We also wish to thank President Yoon Boo-Keun (President and CEO of Samsung Electronics, and head of Consumer Electronics), President Shin Jong-Kyun (President and CEO of Samsung Electronics, and head of IT and Mobile Communications), and President Woo Nam-Sung (head of System LSI Business at Samsung Electronics), who are responsible for Samsung's major businesses. We also interviewed former President Hwang Chang-Gyu (former President of Semiconductor Business at Samsung Electronics), former Vice-Chairman Lee Ki-Tae (former President of Telecommunications Networks at Samsung Electronics), former President Lee Sang-Wan (former President of LCD Business at Samsung Electronics), and former President Chin Dae-Je (former President of Semiconductor Business at Samsung Electronics), who were the presidents of major businesses at Samsung Electronics in the 2000s. We also met the CEOs of other Samsung affiliates, including former President Son Wook (former President of Samsung Advanced Institute of Technology, Samsung Human Resources Development Center, and Samsung SDI), former President Lee Soo-Chang (former President of Samsung Fire and Marine Insurance), former President Her Tae-Hak (former President of Samsung Everland), and President Choi Chi-Hun (President of Samsung C&T Corporation).

Other executives who also readily spared time for interviews included who were those responsible for management functions (including R&D, HR, marketing, and management innovation), including President Hong Won-Pyo (head of the Media Solutions Center at Samsung Electronics),

President Won Gee-Chan (President of Samsung Card), Executive Vice-President Shin Tae-Gyun (Executive Vice-President at Samsung Human Resources Development Center), Executive Vice-President Gee Wan-Goo (head of the Corporate Business Innovation Team at Samsung Electronics), Executive Vice-President Gil Young-Joon (head of the CTO Office at Samsung Advanced Institute of Technology), Executive Vice-President Jung Eun-Seung (President of the Semiconductor R&D Center at Samsung Electronics), Executive Vice-President Kim Chang-Yeong (President of the DMC R&D Center at Samsung Electronics), Executive Vice-President Lee Sun-Woo (head of Samsung Electronics Europe Headquarters), Executive Vice-President Jeon Yong-Bae (Executive Vice-President at Samsung Fire and Marine Insurance, and former head of the Corporate Management Support Team at the Corporate Strategy Office), former Executive Vice-President Eric Kim (former head of global marketing at Samsung Electronics), former Executive Vice-President Chung Kook-Hyun (former head of the design strategy team at Samsung Electronics), Executive Vice-President Park Hark-Kyu (head of the administration team of Mobile Communications at Samsung Electronics), Senior Vice President Chung Kweon Taek (head of human resources and the Organization Research Department at Samsung Economic Research Institute), senior Vice-President Kim Jae-Yun (head of Industry and Strategy Department I at Samsung Economic Research Institute), and Executive Vice-President Kim Hak-Sun (President of Samsung Display Research Center). For the book's major case studies, that is, Samsung Electronics' semiconductors, mobile phones, TVs, and displays, senior executives, including the presidents, were interviewed. We would like to express gratitude to those whose names are not mentioned here.

This book is the product of the authors' more than 20-year journey as business scholars. Since we met as doctoral students at the University of Pennsylvania's Wharton School of Business in the early 1990s, we have maintained close ties as scholars, colleagues, and coauthors. We would like to thank all the people who gave us valuable lessons. We wish to convey particular appreciation to our colleagues at Seoul National University Business School. We further wish to thank the research assistants in the master's and doctoral programs at Seoul National University Business School, who have assisted with research and writing on Samsung since 2004.

The first author of this book, Professor Song Jaeyong, would like to express his deep appreciation to Professor Cho Dong-Sung, who led him to the field of strategy, and the respected teachers who gave him guidance and encouragement. Professor Song dedicates this book to his mother, who devoted all her life to calligraphy and set an example for her children, and his wife, Kim Soomi, whose dedicated support has helped him in writing books and papers. He also sends thanks to his daughter, Song Youjin, who provided encouragement and hopes to follow him as a professor of business administration.

Professor Lee Kyungmook, the second author of this book, sends deep gratitude to Professor Shin Yoo-Keun, who guided him in master's and doctoral courses, as well as his other respected teachers. Professor Lee would also like to thank his late parents and his parents-in-law, who have cared for him as if he were their own son. He also wants to thank his wife, Kim Sooyoun, who helped him focus on research while raising their three beloved children, Sanghyun, Hyesoo, and Hyein.

THE
SAMSUNG
WAY

TWENTY YEARS TO THE TOP

I n Part One, we suggest that there is a need to analyze Samsung-style management, or the "Samsung Way," and examine Samsung's growth and transformation. Chapter 1 explains Samsung's remarkable business performance since the 2000s and discusses the three paradoxes inherent in the Samsung Way that made this possible. We argue that an in-depth analysis of Samsung's competitiveness should focus on the three paradoxes. Chapter 2 covers Samsung's growth and transformation. The company's history, from its foundation to the present, is summarized, and the "New Management" initiative that enabled Samsung to shift from quantitative growth to upgrading quality, transforming itself into a world-class company, is analyzed in depth.

CHAPTER 1

WHY THE SAMSUNG WAY?

1

Samsung Takes Off to World-Class Status

The birth of a world-class corporation is a phenomenon that is typically observed only in advanced nations. In the late twentieth century, as developing nations began to experience economic growth, a multitude of big corporations emerged, but they were not qualified to be considered world-class corporations. Samsung, however, was the exception, as acknowledged by management scholars and media all over the world. Samsung's success is further illustrated by the fact that in 2014, the company was ranked 21st on *Fortune*'s "World's Most Admired Companies" list. Today, every move that Samsung makes is closely scrutinized by the global media, and prominent academic journals—including the *Harvard Business Review*—have analyzed the factors behind Samsung's success.

In 2013, the annual revenue of Samsung Electronics, the flagship company of the Samsung Group, amounted to 228 trillion Korean won (about US$201 billion), surpassing those of Hewlett-Packard, Siemens, and Apple. Samsung Electronics thus held the title of the world's largest electronics and information technology (IT) company for the fourth consecutive year, beginning in 2010. In addition, its operating profits exceeded 36 trillion won (about US$34 billion), making Samsung Electronics the world's best-performing manufacturer in terms of profit. Samsung Electronics has held the world's number one spot in the memory chip industry for the past 21 years, and in the television industry for 8 consecutive years. In 2012, it overtook Nokia to become the top company in the mobile phone industry as well.

Outside of Korea, Samsung is mainly known as an electronics company, but it is actually Korea's largest conglomerate. It has subsidiaries in the heavy chemical industry, the shipbuilding industry, the financial sector, and the service sector. Until the 1980s, Samsung's main focus was on Korea's domestic market, but with the ascendancy of Chairman Lee Kun-Hee, the second-generation owner and manager, the company began to experience dramatic growth (see Figure 1.1). In 1987, the year Chairman Lee took over, the total revenue of Samsung Group was 10 trillion won, but by 2013, this figure had increased 41 times, to 410 trillion won (US$376 billion). Samsung's market capitalization had increased 300-fold, from 1 trillion won to 318 trillion won (US$301 billion) as of April 3, 2014. Some 25 years after Chairman Lee's accession, Samsung's exports had increased 25-fold, while its share of Korea's total exports rose from 13 percent to 28 percent. In 2012, Samsung held the world's largest market share in 26 products, including dynamic random access memory (DRAM) chips, flash memory, mobile application processors, digital televisions, organic light-emitting diodes (OLEDs), mobile phones, monitors, rechargeable batteries, and drillships.

Samsung's advances in the area of intangible assets are also dazzling. In 2013, Samsung registered 4,676 patents at the U.S. Patent and Trademark

Figure 1.1   *Trajectory of Samsung Group's Performance*

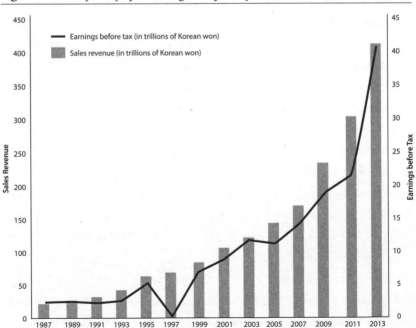

Office. Since 2006, Samsung has continuously placed second in patent registrations in the United States, surpassed only by IBM. In 2013, Samsung was also ranked second by the Boston Consulting Group, a global management consulting firm, in its survey of the most innovative companies, up from 26th in 2008.

The company's brand value has also risen steadily since 2000. Samsung was ranked eighth by *Bloomberg Businessweek* and Interbrand's 2013 Global Brand Rankings. In that year, Samsung placed higher on this list than Japan's highest-ranking company, Toyota, becoming the highest-ranking non-American company. Samsung's design capabilities are also considered to be among the best in the world. In 2013, Samsung Electronics received nine Industrial Design Excellence awards, which were co-hosted by the Industrial Designers Society of America and *Bloomberg Businessweek*. In total, it received the most awards of any company that year.

With such powerful technology, brand power, and design capabilities, Samsung Electronics was able to successfully implement differentiation strategies based on premium products. Until the mid-1990s, it had been a little-known original equipment manufacturing (OEM) firm and a second-tier company that focused on lower-priced products. But today, Samsung Electronics is a world-class corporation that sells televisions, mobile phones, and memory chips at higher prices than most competing firms.

Samsung's rising stature can also be seen in its strategic alliances. Samsung Electronics has forged strategic ties with leading global companies like IBM, Sony, Microsoft, Intel, Qualcomm, and Hewlett-Packard. While it had previously allied with global companies as a subordinate partner because of its lack of technology, brand equity, and marketing, Samsung now partners either on an equal footing or as the leading partner.

Paradigm Shifts in the Domestic and Foreign Environments and Samsung's Takeoff

At the time of Chairman Lee's accession in 1987, Samsung was Korea's unequivocal leader in most of the industries it had entered. However, this dominance was limited to the small domestic market. The Samsung name was almost unknown outside Korea. In terms of product quality and management style, Samsung lagged far behind the global leaders in the same industries. For a long time, quantity was the priority, and the company pursued diversification for its own sake, often into unrelated business areas where it lacked the necessary core competencies.

Chairman Lee was very concerned about Samsung's lack of competitiveness in the global marketplace. He proposed drastic changes in the form of the New Management initiative in 1993. Chairman Lee described the environment when he declared the New Management initiative in 1993, saying:

> An age is coming where the number one can fall to the bottom and the bottom becomes number one. If we fail to become first class, and fail to make swift movements in a situation where the competitive landscape is being reorganized completely, we will have to be satisfied with second- and third-tier status permanently.

Globalization, democratization, and digitization, the trends that were emerging in the 1990s, encouraged Chairman Lee to take such bold initiatives. On the one hand, with the end of the Cold War, world markets were rapidly integrating into a single global market. More important for Samsung, however, the sharp appreciation of the yen after the 1985 Plaza Agreement accelerated Japanese foreign direct investment in East Asia. As a result, Samsung faced much tougher competition from Japanese electronics companies that combined their newly gained low manufacturing costs with robust technologies and brands. To make matters worse, after the democratization of Korea in the late 1980s, local wages had increased sharply; thus, Korea was no longer a viable low-cost manufacturing base. Chairman Lee felt that in the twenty-first century Samsung would not be able to compete solely on the basis of low cost. He believed that its R&D, marketing and branding, and design capabilities needed to be substantially upgraded to enable the company to survive in the new business environment.

Meanwhile, with the increasing use of personal computers, the Internet, and mobile phones, digitization was fast becoming a fact of life. Chairman Lee viewed these paradigm shifts toward digital technologies as a golden opportunity to get ahead of Japanese electronics giants like Sony and Matsushita, leaders in the manufacturing of the then-popular analog technologies. These companies were reluctant to adopt disruptive digital technologies because of their strong positions in their industries. In the era of analog technologies, cumulative knowledge and experience were important. As a result, latecomers had tremendous difficulty catching up with the incumbent leaders. However, in the digital era, new types of competencies were required. The rules of the game were creativity, speedy adaptation, and technological convergence. With its early entry into the digital electronics market, Samsung's disadvantage as a latecomer in the analog era all but disappeared. While leaders of analog technologies such as Sony stuck to their products, partly because of the success trap and partly because of fear of cannibalization, Samsung aggressively invested in digital technologies, changing its strategy and management system dramatically. As a result, the company was soon far ahead of the analog leaders who had refused to accommodate the new rules of the game in the digital era.

Under Chairman Lee's leadership, Samsung's transformation to cope with such paradigm shifts involved three movements: (1) the declaration of the Second Foundation immediately following Chairman Lee's accession in 1987, (2) the ascent of Samsung's DRAM chips to the global number one position in 1992, and (3) the introduction of the New Management initiative in 1993. The latter two crystallized Samsung's goal for globalization in the Second Foundation. Samsung promoted massive investments and grew to become number one in the world in DRAM. Based on the confidence it developed through this success, Samsung invested aggressively in thin-film-transistor liquid-crystal displays (TFT-LCDs), mobile phones, and automobiles. The New Management initiative that Chairman Lee embarked on in June 1993 was an effort to spread the DNA of the semiconductor business throughout the entire Samsung Group.

The objective of Chairman Lee's New Management initiative was to turn Samsung into one of the world's best companies in the twenty-first century, especially in emerging digital products. To this end, the management paradigm itself needed to be transformed from a traditional quantity-dominated one to a quality-dominated one. Chairman Lee clearly understood that enhancing the quality of a company's products and services always goes hand in hand with enhancing the company's intangible resources like technological competence, brand power, and design. The New Management initiative was intended to strengthen the company's competitiveness by building up the R&D, marketing, and design capabilities in its core businesses, especially in the emerging market for digital products. The initiative was a form of "creative destruction" that Samsung had to undergo if it was to become world-class. It is no exaggeration to say that most of Samsung's core competencies and current managerial systems are the result of the New Management initiative.

The Asian currency crisis that hit Korea in late 1997 inflicted new hardships on Samsung, forcing it to restructure its business and its workforce. Nonetheless, Samsung emerged stronger. The sense of crisis—that Samsung must change if it was to survive—along with quality-focused management, provided the cornerstones of the New Management initiative. The program rapidly gained support among Samsung's employees.

Against this backdrop, Samsung was able to promote massive restructuring. More important, Samsung succeeded in introducing management systems that would attract core talent, deploying performance-based compensation, and inducing internal competition, with relatively little resistance from employees. These management systems introduced in the wake of the currency crisis remain essential to Samsung's current management system.

The outcomes of the New Management initiative were astounding. Since 2004, when Samsung Electronics recorded a profit of more than 10 trillion won (nearly US$9 billion) for the first time, its operating profits have consistently been higher than the sum of the annual operating profits of Japan's five major electronics companies, including Sony and Panasonic.

During the global financial crisis that began with the collapse of the U.S. investment bank Lehman Brothers in the second half of 2008, Samsung again transformed the crisis into an opportunity. The "smartphone shock" led by Apple coincided with the financial crisis. Under Chairman Lee's leadership, Samsung successfully overcame these crises and greatly increased its market share in most of its core business areas. For example, in 2013, Samsung's market share in the global smartphone business was 32.3 percent, while Apple's market share had shrunk to 15.5 percent. How did Samsung manage to turn crises into new opportunities over the past two decades, thus establishing itself as a world-class corporation? This question is addressed in this book.

The Samsung Way as the Basis for Samsung's Competitiveness

Successful companies generally have their own set of management principles or systems. When their approach delivers growth over a long period of time, the principles or system come to be known as the company's "Way." Thus, we now hear about the "GE Way" and the "HP Way" in business schools. Likewise, Toyota's ability to achieve record success even in Japan's notorious long-term recession has brought attention to the "Toyota Way," which is the title of a best-selling business book written by Jeffrey Liker of the University of Michigan.[1]

Academic discussions of management systems often divide them into three categories: American, Japanese, and German. The U.S. style features frequent business restructuring and performance-based evaluation and pay. The Japanese version emphasizes harmony and lifetime employment with seniority-based salaries. The German system features consistent labor-management cooperation and employee participation in strategic decision making.

Korean firms have mainly employed U.S.- and Japanese-style management systems. These models are regarded as being more appropriate for Korean businesses. This is because Korea, like the United States and Japan, industrialized within a short period of time despite being a latecomer to the Industrial Revolution. In addition, Korea's geopolitical and historical links to both countries encouraged Korean firms to adopt their systems. In the 1970s and 1980s, when continuous improvement and quality management were being emphasized, Korean firms mainly imitated the Japanese style of management. In the 1990s, when corporate reengineering and restructuring became a central issue, Korean companies shifted toward the American model. In particular, since the 1997 Asian currency crisis, Korean firms have strongly embraced U.S.-style governance and management practices that give priority to shareholder interests in the name of adopting global standards.

However, the increasing diversity and complexity in the business environment are calling for more flexibility. Japanese and U.S. companies do not necessarily adhere to their "national" management styles any longer. The Japanese automaker Nissan, for example, has adopted Western-style restructuring under a foreign CEO, whereas Toyota has maintained its traditional management system.

Companies that hope to become global pacesetters naturally strive to have a management style that suits their own characteristics. In the knowledge-based economy, intensifying global competition and the increasing prevalence of "winner-takes-all" economies have made it impossible to gain a sustainable competitive advantage through imitation. In an essay submitted to the *Frankfurter Allgemeine Zeitung* in 1994, Chairman Lee Kun-Hee stated:

> In the past, it was believed that there is a single exemplary and standardized management system. Today's global leaders, however, have shed this old way of thinking and tend to employ their own unique management style. In other words, it has become meaningless to divide management styles into Japanese, American, or European ones. The management of the future, where every business will have its own management style, will mean a revolt against the traditional concept of management.

Chairman Lee's remarks highlighted what Samsung needed to do under the New Management initiative to become a global business group, as well as its need to secure a sustainable competitive advantage through proprietary, quality-driven assets. Samsung had to establish unique core competencies and practices that would create unmatchable customer value and competitiveness. This led to the establishment of the Samsung Way.

The Three Paradoxes of Samsung's Management

According to the theory of competitive strategy suggested by Michael Porter, who put forward several popular theories on strategy in the late twentieth century, firms should select and focus on only one of the following competitive strategies: differentiation, low-cost leadership, or focus. Differentiation and low-cost leadership require different resources and organizational cultures. Porter argued that if a company chooses a strategy of pursuing multiple competitive advantages, such as differentiation and low-cost leadership, it risks falling into a "stuck-in-the-middle" state, achieving neither type of advantage.[2]

Porter's generic competitive strategies were first introduced in 1980 and were widely used in corporate strategizing in the late twentieth century. However, in the early twenty-first century, as the world began to shift to an information-based economy, traditional borders between industries became blurred as a result of the convergence effect, and the era of global hypercompetition began. Companies that aspired to become global leaders could no longer follow the traditional maxim that firms should rely on only one source of competitive advantage. In order to become a leading company in a hypercompetitive global marketplace, the pursuit of multiple, potentially conflicting sources of competitive advantage became necessary.

In the new knowledge-based economy and the era of global hypercompetition, ambitious companies began scrambling to adopt strategies that allowed the simultaneous pursuit of multiple conflicting management goals or elements that would provide a competitive advantage. Some of these conflicting goals include differentiation and low-cost leadership, creative innovation and efficiency, economies of scale and speed, and global integration and local responsiveness. Leading companies like Apple and Toyota succeeded admirably in securing multiple competitive advantages.

Accordingly, so-called paradox management arose as a new field of research for management scholars. Paradox management refers to a management style in which seemingly contradictory goals, such as differentiation and low-cost leadership, are pursued simultaneously.

Samsung went from being a no-name company in the global market of the early 1990s to a world-class corporation in the second decade of the new millennium because of the success of its style of paradox management after the New Management initiative. Samsung achieved multiple competitive advantages simultaneously. For example, Samsung Electronics' memory chip division recorded significantly lower costs than its competitors. In addition, Samsung achieved differentiation by releasing the newest and best-quality memory chips before its competitors and providing customized solutions for each of its customers. Thus, beginning in 1992, Samsung has retained the number one spot in the memory chip industry for more than 20 years. Recently, the market share gap between Samsung and its competitors has widened even more.

Chairman Lee emphasized the importance of paradox management in his New Management as follows:

> World-class companies and long-lived companies are strong in "paradox management" that harmonizes conflicting factors. Because I have emphasized quality management while advocating New Management, many believe that this means Samsung is giving up on quantity management. Such thinking is like driving a car without seeing the traffic coming down the opposite lane. A company that does not harmonize seemingly conflicting factors will find it hard to become world-class.[3]

Closer investigation of the Samsung Way reveals conflicting phenomena and disparate characteristics within Samsung's unique management system. In this book, we call these the *paradoxes of Samsung's management*. The management paradoxes that are evident at Samsung can be summarized as follows. First, Samsung's management processes are very speedy, despite the fact that it is a large, diversified organization. Second, Samsung is highly specialized and competitive in its core business areas while also being extremely diversified and vertically integrated. Third, Samsung has successfully mixed and matched American and Japanese management systems, which were formerly viewed as incompatible.

These three paradoxes form the foundation of the Samsung Way. They are worthy of attention by management researchers because they surpass or even defy the typical conventions and principles presented by mainstream management scholarship, which is largely based on research on Western corporations. Samsung's great success has made it a world-class corporation. Such success is difficult for competitors to reproduce. Skillful internal balancing of these paradoxes was necessary to accomplish this. Accordingly, an understanding of Samsung's paradox management is crucial in any investigation of the Samsung Way. The three paradoxes are discussed in more detail in the following sections.

Large but Speedy

Samsung Group is currently Korea's largest conglomerate, with 75 affiliate companies in diverse industries. It has a labor force of 500,000, including everything from PhDs to ordinary laborers. Its geographical scope is also immense: it has nearly 600 facilities in 63 countries performing a variety of functions, including R&D, product design, production, and procurement. Even on its own, Samsung Electronics, Samsung's main subsidiary, is an enormous company.

Compared to smaller organizations, larger organizations are generally thought to be slower in making and executing decisions. As an organization grows, information flow and decision making are likely to slow, and conflicts of interest between affiliates or divisions are likely to increase. Thus, large organizations have an increased need for control and coordination. Management in such companies often focuses on administrative issues and bureaucratic control, which slows operations. Traditionally, management research has held that large, highly diversified conglomerates like Samsung will have complex decision-making structures and administration processes, making quick decision making and execution more difficult.[4]

However, the speed of Samsung's decision making and execution surpasses that of its rival Japanese electronics companies. For example, in memory chips, one of Samsung's core business lines, Samsung controls the entire value chain from development to product release, launching new chips an average of 1 to 1.5 times faster than its competitors. In the smartphone industry, which Samsung entered after being hit by the Apple shock, the company became a world leader in only four years. Samsung's speedy development capabilities allowed it to develop Android-operated smartphones faster than any other mobile phone manufacturer in the world.

Samsung's speed is especially noticeable in its decision-making processes. Even during economic downturns, Chairman Lee has made quick and resolute decisions about large-scale investments in areas such as semiconductors and LCDs. This led Samsung to defeat its Japanese competitors, who were slow in making decisions and passive when it came to investing during recessions. As professional managers, Samsung's CEOs and division heads make operational decisions on the spot. Large-scale investment decisions that involve hundreds of millions of dollars are made equally quickly.

For Samsung, speed is a strategy in and of itself. Samsung's "premium-price" strategy was bolstered by new product development based on time-to-market speed. The speed of distribution and flow of raw materials and information was enhanced through innovation in the IT process, such as the construction of world-class global supply chain management and enterprise resource planning systems. Recently, because of its speed in making and executing decisions, Samsung has successfully transformed itself from a fast follower to a market leader. Samsung's speed is a powerful competitive weapon and a notable strength of its paradox management strategy.

Diversified but Specialized

Since its establishment as a corporation, Samsung has continuously diversified. Currently, Samsung's business domain encompasses a very broad spectrum of industries, including light to heavy manufacturing industries and a wide range of services. Its interests include semiconductors, chemicals, construction, shipbuilding, defense machinery, building security management, hotels, advertising, fashion, investment banking, insurance, and theme parks.

Conglomerates that pursued unrelated diversification were common in advanced nations until the 1980s. However, after the 1980s, because of inefficiencies in resource distribution and management processes, conglomerates generally became less competitive than specialized companies devoted to particular businesses.[5] This was especially true in advanced nations where capital markets were well developed. Past research has indicated that the performance of conglomerates that operate in unrelated domains has fallen behind that of focused companies that are devoted to one or two specialized domains or that operate in a number of related domains. As a result, in the U.S. stock market, for example, a "conglomerate discount" is widespread.

Since the 1990s, leading businesses in advanced countries have focused their resources on the areas in which they are most competitive. In addition, withdrawal from noncore businesses or otherwise low-value-added activities has become common; this may be done through strategic alliances, outsourcing, or selling off or liquidating assets. During this process, the level of vertical integration in the internal production of parts, materials, and finished products has also decreased.[6]

Samsung, however, has defied this trend and consistently provided successful performance despite its highly diversified and vertically integrated business structure. Samsung currently holds the global top or runner-up spot in many fields, including multiple IT and electronics businesses and the shipbuilding industry. The source of Samsung's competitiveness has traditionally been massive amounts of investment that enabled the company to achieve economies of scale and take its manufacturing competitiveness to unprecedented levels. In addition, Samsung has improved its soft capabilities (for example, innovative technology, brand power, and design capabilities), thus strengthening its competitiveness in its core businesses in terms of intangible assets. Remarkably, not only has Samsung overcome the problems common to diversified and vertically integrated systems—including lack of strategic focus, bureaucratic inefficiency, and decreasing competitiveness resulting from the dependence of less competitive subsidiaries on stronger ones—but it has also leveraged the advantages of this system to create a convergence synergy through systematic cooperation among related subsidiaries and divisions. The company's global competitiveness has continued to increase as a result.

Samsung may seem similar to GE in that it owns many businesses that perform well in global markets, but it differs in that its achievements were accomplished through greenfield investment rather than through mergers and acquisitions. This was possible because Samsung not only shared its "success DNA" internally but also quickly spread it to new businesses.

Samsung currently competes with the world's best companies in diverse product groups. Its competitors include Apple, Nokia, Motorola, HP, Intel, Micron, Sony, and Dell. Most of these competitors focus on products in one specialized area or business. An important aspect of the paradox of the Samsung Way is that Samsung, a highly diversified and vertically integrated company, has a competitive edge over highly specialized global companies.

Japanese and American Management Styles Combined

Samsung's management style is a hybrid of the best from the Japanese and American approaches to management. The company has used its excellent learning capabilities to optimize the best aspects of both management styles for many years. In the past, Samsung benchmarked Toyota and GE almost equally in order to learn from their success. The semiconductor division of Samsung Electronics, for example, is probably the most Americanized division within Samsung, yet it sent hundreds of employees to Toyota every year to learn from Toyota's best practices.

Generally, Japanese management is characterized by a market share orientation, unrelated diversification, vertical integration, emphasis on manufacturing competitiveness and operational efficiency, strict organizational discipline, emphasis on employee loyalty, internal and seniority-based promotion and rewards, and participation of both workers and shareholders in management.[7] The American management style, on the other hand, emphasizes profits and revenue, focusing on relevant industries and frequently restructuring businesses and products. American companies also tend to outsource manufacturing or move it abroad, with the result that their core competencies are soft capabilities or intangible assets such as technological innovation, brand marketing capabilities, and design capabilities. Compared to Japanese companies, American businesses are typically more centralized, and because they value core talent with differentiated competencies more than the loyalty of executives and employees, they depend more on external labor markets than on internal cultivation of employees As a result, short-term employment, promotions based on thorough assessments, and employees who specialize in a particular area are common in U.S. workplaces.

Samsung's vertical and horizontal diversification, emphasis on manufacturing competitiveness and product quality, open competitive recruitment for entry-level positions, intensive employee training to develop a standardized workforce, strict organizational discipline, and emphasis on organizational loyalty all resemble Japanese-style management. However, Samsung's management style also resembles American-style management in many ways. Samsung headquarters' strategies and personnel policies exemplify this similarity. Frequent restructuring, emphasis on soft capabilities (technology, brand, and design), talent recruitment, excellent performance-based compensation, and risk-taking CEOs are all evident in Samsung businesses. These are all characteristic of American management.

According to management scholars and economists like William Ouchi, Paul Milgrom, and John Roberts, the Japanese management style is essentially incompatible with the American one. These scholars claim that attempting to reconcile Japanese and American management styles in a single organization will be counterproductive and will have negative effects on the firm's profitability and competitiveness. For example, maintaining organizational loyalty and active participation of employees is difficult in an organization where restructuring occurs frequently.

Yet Samsung manages to combine the two styles successfully. In fact, Samsung takes the combination of management styles one step further by successfully modifying Japanese and American management styles to reflect Korean and Confucian culture. Samsung's own distinctive values and culture are also added to the mix. In essence, Samsung has created its own unique hybrid management system that consistently produces excellent results.

Organization of the Samsung Way

When seemingly contradictory strategies are practiced within the same company, that company might naturally be expected to lose its competitiveness and succumb to conflict and chaos. How, then, did Samsung transform a management paradox into a source of competitive strength?

In this book, we conduct an in-depth analysis of how Samsung successfully overcame the obstacles inherent in its paradox management and built on that management, the process by which Samsung evolved into a world-class corporation, and the origin and characteristics of the Samsung Way, which developed in the process. We also conduct a detailed investigation of how Samsung (especially Samsung Electronics) overcame the disadvantageous business environment in newly industrialized Korea and the financial crisis of the late 1990s to become a globally successful corporation in the twenty-first century. We focus on the radical transformation of Samsung that has taken place over the past 20 years since Chairman Lee began the New Management initiative. These in-depth analyses are based on interviews and documents, both internal and external. This book provides answers to the following questions:

- What changes did Samsung experience during the radical transformation that followed the New Management initiative? What were the main causes of its successful transformation?
- What role did Chairman Lee's leadership play in Samsung's rise to the top?
- What is the essence of Samsung's unique management system? More specifically, how did the configuration of its management system, including such elements as strategy, human resource management, management control, and culture and values, change after the New Management initiative? How do these elements fit together internally?
- What are the core competencies that Samsung achieved during its transformation? How were these core competencies developed, and how have they operated as a source of sustainable competitive advantage?

- How has Samsung overcome the three major management paradoxes discussed earlier? How did it prevent these paradoxes from becoming a source of conflict, leading to a loss of competitiveness? How did it leverage them to gain a sustainable competitive edge unmatched by its competitors? What is the essence of the firm's paradox management that led Samsung to become a globally competitive corporation?
- How should Samsung develop the Samsung Way so that it can rise even further in the business world? What are the challenges that Samsung faces in sustaining the Samsung Way?
- What can other corporations learn from the Samsung Way? What characteristics or principles of the Samsung Way can other corporations benchmark and adopt?

This book has four parts and nine chapters (see Figure 1.2). Chapter 2 outlines the history of Samsung's growth, focusing on the New Management initiative. In order to understand Samsung's rapid transformation and progress after the New Management initiative, one must first understand what Samsung was like before New Management. To this end, we describe Samsung's management system in the 1980s and early 1990s, focusing particularly on the success of the memory chip business, which sparked the New Management initiative. This is followed by an in-depth analysis of the New Management initiative, which provided the momentum for Samsung's change in focus from increasing quantity to improved quality.

Part Two of this book investigates the main factors that make up the Samsung Way: leadership and governance, strategy, HR management, management control, and culture and values. In Chapter 3, we focus on leadership and governance, analyzing Chairman Lee's revolutionary vision and insightful leadership. Samsung's Corporate Strategy Office, which is the group's headquarters, and its capable professional managers also played an important role in the company's rise. Accordingly, we discuss the division of roles among family owner-managers and professional managers in Samsung's corporate governance.

Figure 1.2 *The Samsung Way and the Structure of the Book*

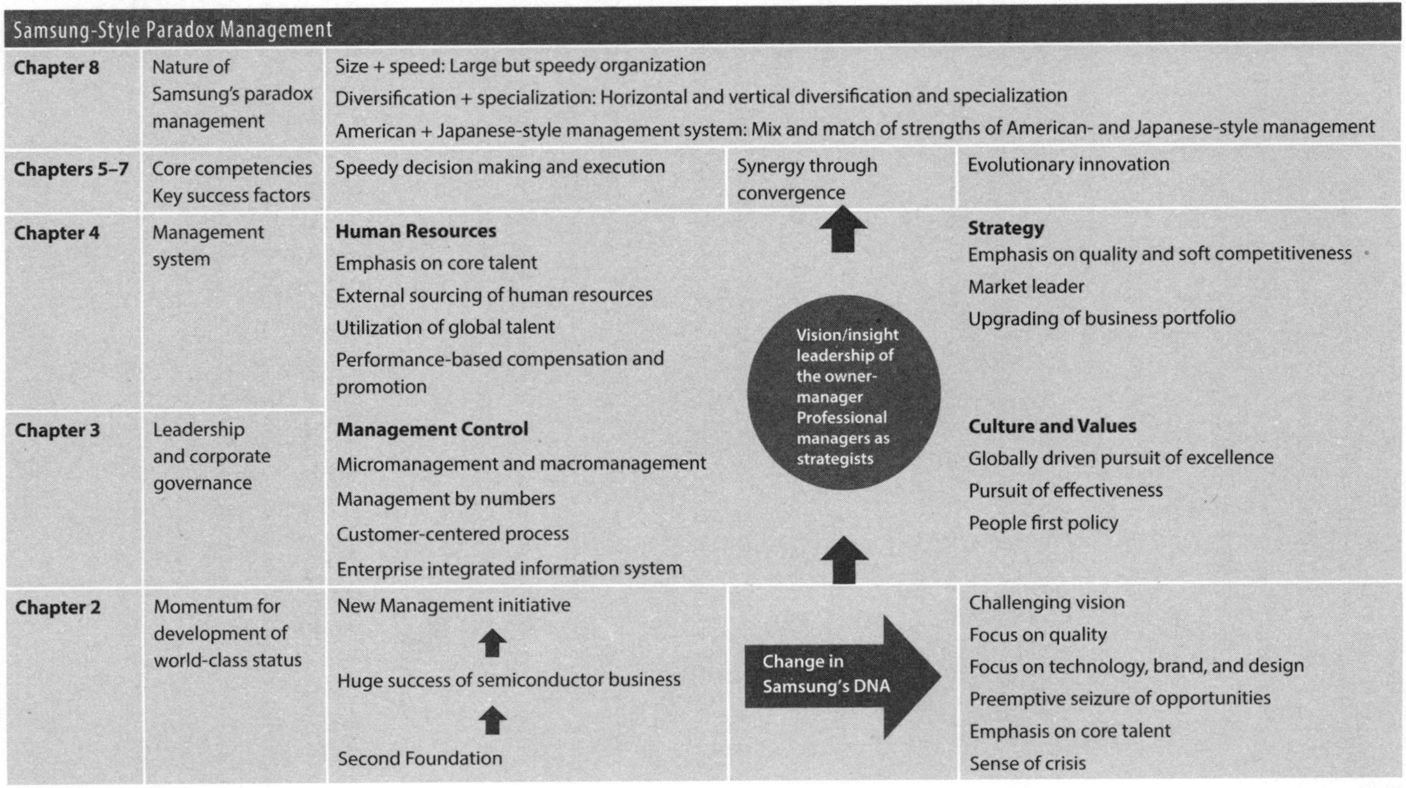

Samsung-Style Paradox Management

Chapter 8 — Nature of Samsung's paradox management
- Size + speed: Large but speedy organization
- Diversification + specialization: Horizontal and vertical diversification and specialization
- American + Japanese-style management system: Mix and match of strengths of American- and Japanese-style management

Chapters 5–7 — Core competencies / Key success factors
- Speedy decision making and execution
- Synergy through convergence
- Evolutionary innovation

Chapter 4 — Management system

Human Resources
- Emphasis on core talent
- External sourcing of human resources
- Utilization of global talent
- Performance-based compensation and promotion

Strategy
- Emphasis on quality and soft competitiveness
- Market leader
- Upgrading of business portfolio

Chapter 3 — Leadership and corporate governance

Management Control
- Micromanagement and macromanagement
- Management by numbers
- Customer-centered process
- Enterprise integrated information system

Culture and Values
- Globally driven pursuit of excellence
- Pursuit of effectiveness
- People first policy

Center: Vision/insight leadership of the owner-manager / Professional managers as strategists

Chapter 2 — Momentum for development of world-class status
- New Management initiative
- Huge success of semiconductor business
- Second Foundation

- Challenging vision
- Focus on quality
- Focus on technology, brand, and design
- Preemptive seizure of opportunities
- Emphasis on core talent
- Sense of crisis

Change in Samsung's DNA

In Chapter 4, we illustrate the changes in strategy, HR management, management control, and culture and values that came about after the New Management initiative. These key elements, along with leadership and corporate governance, make up Samsung's management system. We also describe the distinguishing characteristics of these elements in detail. This is followed by an analysis of the evolution of Samsung's management system after the New Management initiative.

Part Three presents our assessment of the core competencies that were built during Samsung's rise after the New Management initiative. Samsung's core competencies, which are the source of its competitive advantage, are identified as follows: the achievement of high-speed decision making and execution (Chapter 5), the creation of synergy through convergence (Chapter 6), and evolutionary innovation (Chapter 7). Through case studies and theoretical analysis, we explain how each core competency was created in Samsung's paradox management system, the organizational culture that underlies these core competencies, the infrastructure and mechanisms by which Samsung achieves its core competencies, and how such core competencies lead to Samsung's competitiveness.

Part Four is an analysis of the resolution of the Samsung Way's three major paradoxes. The future and sustainability of the Samsung Way are also discussed. In Chapter 8, we outline the main characteristics and structure of the Samsung Way in a manner that will be useful for companies that are seeking to benchmark and learn from Samsung's success. Finally, Chapter 9 looks at the external and internal fit of the Samsung Way to determine its sustainability. In addition, we analyze and suggest solutions to Samsung's main challenges for the future. The authors' opinions concerning how Samsung should maintain its position as a world-class corporation and how the Samsung Way should continue to develop with respect to paradox management are presented in this chapter. Finally, we conclude by suggesting what other corporations can learn from the Samsung Way.

CHAPTER 2

HOW DID SAMSUNG BECOME A WORLD-CLASS CORPORATION?

2

Samsung was founded just before World War II as a small company trading in groceries and other goods. By the second half of the twentieth century, Samsung was at the forefront of Korea's transformation from a poor and underdeveloped nation to an economic success story.

The first section of this chapter traces Samsung's development over the past 75 years. The second section focuses on Samsung's semiconductor business, which became the template for the New Management initiative.

The History of Samsung's Growth

Samsung's history can be divided into four periods (see Table 2.1): foundation (1938 to mid-1950s), expansion (mid-1950s to late 1960s), leading domestic company (late 1960s to late 1980s), and global leader (late 1980s to the present).

Founding and Establishment of the Management System (1938 to Mid-1950s)

Samsung was established in 1938 in Daegu, Korea's third largest city, in the southeast part of the nation. It began as a trader and distributor of, among other things, vegetables and dried seafood. Even in those early days, however, Samsung had ambitious ideas, and their legacy still guides the company today. The company's founder, Lee Byung-Chull, set forth three principles for the management of his company: "contribution to the nation through business," "people first," and "pursuit of rationality." These principles came into existence after Samsung experienced and learned from the numerous challenges and hardships that it faced at the time of its founding.

Table 2.1   Samsung's History of Change

	Samsung's Growth Stages		Major Events at Samsung
1938–mid-1950s	Foundation and establishment of Samsung's management system	Small and midsized company (foundation and formation of core businesses)	Entry into manufacturing (1953–1954)
Mid-1950s–late 1960s	Growth into a large company	Large company (initial stage as a business group)	Diversification (electronics, heavy industry, and chemicals) Beginning of open competitive recruitment for entry-level positions
Late 1960s–late 1980s	Emergence as Korea's leading company	Large business group (upgrading of the business portfolio)	Commencement of the semiconductor business
Late 1980s–present	Emergence as a world-class company	Global business group	New Management initiative (1993) Restructuring (late 1990s) Global number one products (in electronics, shipbuilding, heavy industry, and chemicals)

Today, "contribution to the nation through business" has taken on new meaning, as Samsung has become a global firm. "People first" and "pursuit of rationality" also remain important elements of the company's unique style of management. Lee Byung-Chull was an especially strong believer in the importance of bringing talented people to his company, a principle that is still in place at Samsung today.

I have never put the company seal on a check myself, or directly purchased anything for the company. I believe it is my job to find and nurture people who can do these jobs. I would say that I have spent 80 percent of my life looking for and training talented people.

—*Samsung founder Lee Byung-Chull*

"Pursuit of rationality" refers to Lee's belief that Samsung's business must always depend on rational analysis and use rational methods, rather than relying on luck or the arbitrary decisions of a manager. Lee Byung-Chull required his staff members to review matters that he himself had already reviewed, and commenced business only after he was fully prepared.

Growth into a Major Corporation in Korea (Mid-1950s–Late 1960s)

During this period, supported by the Korean government's export promotion and import substitution policy, Samsung grew into a large company. In the early 1950s, the company began manufacturing with the launch of CheilJedang and Cheil Industries. The main products of CheilJedang were sugar and flour, while the main products of Cheil Industries included woolen fabric and chemical fibers. Samsung used the capital it acquired from these firms to purchase Ankuk Fire & Marine Insurance in 1958, thereby entering the financial services industry. In the 1960s, the company expanded into life insurance, distribution, papermaking, and media.

As it expanded, Samsung recognized the need for a management system that could deal with its increasingly complex business operations. To this end, Samsung introduced management methods and systems from Japanese companies, and adapted them to Korea's particular circumstances.

Samsung's first significant change was the introduction of "open competitive recruitment" in 1957. Samsung publicly recruited school graduates in the spring and fall and selected appropriate individuals as entry-level hires. They were brought into Samsung at the same time and the same rank. By doing this, Samsung abolished its previous practice of ad hoc hiring and recruitment through personal connections so that it could gain access to a continuous stream of incoming talent. Samsung was the first Korean company to adopt this approach, and it later provided the foundation for a fair and systematic management of human resources, as well as the systematization of overall management.

Another major addition was the creation of a secretariat as a professional staff organization in 1959. Initially, the secretariat supervised protocols for

Lee Byung-Chull and helped plan new ventures. In the early 1960s, it took on finance and auditing functions, and it later came to oversee personnel tasks. It acted as a de facto headquarters for Samsung Group under a variety of names, including the Corporate Restructuring Office, Strategic Planning Office, and Corporate Strategy Office. The secretariat's responsibilities included conducting internal audits, deciding whether to expand into new industries, and approving large investments in existing businesses. It also coordinated and integrated affiliated companies to create synergies. Moreover, it nurtured promising executives and decided on top managerial appointments, while developing the corporate culture and management methods that would prevail at Samsung.

Becoming a Domestic Leader (Late 1960s–Late 1980s)

Most of the key businesses that are leading Samsung's growth today originated during this period. Starting with the birth of Samsung Electronics in 1969, Samsung invested intensively in its electronics business into the early 1970s. When the Korean government turned its attention to heavy industry and chemicals in 1973, Samsung expanded into petrochemicals, construction, and shipbuilding. It also began its forays into hotels and advertising.

In the 1980s, Samsung moved into high-tech industries, including semiconductors, aviation, computers, and telecommunications. During this period, Samsung completed the vertical integration of its electronics industry and saw its semiconductor business turn a profit, laying the foundation for its eventual global leadership in this area. This period also saw the establishment of the Human Resources Development Center, the Economic Research Institute, and the Advanced Institute of Technology, which act as supporting learning organizations for headquarters.

Samsung's increasing size made centralized command less practical, and in the mid-1970s, Samsung was restructured into divisions. Samsung's management control system was also upgraded further into a major differentiating factor for the company. This management control system began with audits of accounting and expenses at Samsung affiliates, then expanded to cover a wide range of management issues, including cost analysis, business evaluations, and strategic planning. Samsung's oversight proved so thorough and meticulous that the group was nicknamed "Well Managed Samsung."

Another pillar of Samsung's management system that was introduced at this time was its advanced human resources management. Three basic principles, "fairness," "the right person for the right position," and "reward good work and punish misbehavior" were practiced consistently. Since Korea's corporate culture at the time was often plagued by the formation of rival factions, this served to further distinguish Samsung from its peers. Samsung's management control system, which was based both on a dedicated staff organization within affiliates and on the group secretariat, was put firmly in place during this period. Under this system, Samsung pursued both optimization of divisional performance based on decentralization and groupwide goals through the coordination of group headquarters. Its auditing system, which is well known for its rigorous approach to any improprieties, was also further developed.

Samsung divided itself into divisions in 1975 to empower each division and make it responsible for its own performance. The heads of the divisions were given considerable independence, making them effectively like CEOs. New businesses were typically established by forming a new legally independent company; in many cases, Samsung did not own the entire new firm, allowing it to publicly trade its shares. This differs substantially from the example set by American companies like GE, which either created a new division for a new business or established an affiliate in which it had a 100 percent stake.

Becoming a Global Corporation (Late 1980s–Present)

The ongoing fourth phase of Samsung's growth has been led by Lee Kun-Hee (Lee Byung-Chull's third son), who took over when the elder Lee died in 1987. During this time, Samsung moved from being a top local firm to becoming a world-class company. This period can be further divided into four subperiods.

During the first five years of his term, Chairman Lee established a new vision of Samsung as a world-class business and declared a "Second Foundation" for Samsung. Lee set his sights on transforming Samsung into a world-class corporation. To this end, Samsung integrated its electronics-related businesses, expanded its heavy industry and chemical businesses, strengthened its financial and service arms, and accelerated its entry overseas. It also ramped up its efforts to nurture global-level talent and increased its information technology (IT) capabilities. To accomplish this, Samsung developed technology-centered management that helped it become the world's largest producer of memory chips.

The second period began with the introduction of the New Management initiative in 1993 and ended with the 1997 Asian currency crisis. Chairman Lee declared that Samsung's management priorities must shift from a focus on quantity to a total embrace of quality. Lee introduced radical measures like a 7 a.m. to 4 p.m. workday for office employees and a "line-stop system," that allowed any employee to completely stop an assembly line if he or she discovered any defects. Employees came to accept initiating and embracing change as an integral part of their duties. The New Management initiative brought about a sea change in Samsung's vision, strategies, HR policies, management control, and organizational culture. Samsung also pursued globalization in earnest at this time, establishing headquarters and manufacturing complexes overseas and developing concerted campaigns to increase its brand recognition. As a result, Samsung was able to transform itself into a producer of world-class products in multiple categories.

The third period was the five years beginning in 1998. Armed with the lessons of the New Management initiative, Samsung was able to use the Asian currency crisis as an opportunity to pursue large-scale restructuring. It announced "Digital Management" in line with the paradigm shift from analog to digital in the electronics industry, and it adopted policies like performance-based pay and promotion. Global operations were strengthened, with more aggressive entry into emerging markets. As a result, Samsung emerged as a strong competitor in the digital era, increasing its global status.

The fourth phase stretches from 2003 to the present, and proved to be a period in which the New Management initiative reached its full potential as the driver of Samsung's spectacular success. Chairman Lee also presented a new vision at this time, leading to further change. Samsung invested heavily in marketing, design, branding, R&D, and software development to strengthen its competitiveness. Beginning in 2006, Samsung strove to create new markets through technology convergence and released groundbreaking memory chips and digital TVs. In the 2010s, in search of new growth engines, Samsung further diversified into a few select industries, including biotechnology, pharmaceuticals, and medical equipment. To achieve success in these areas, Samsung has made vigorous efforts to transform itself into a more flexible, open, and creative organization and become a genuine market leader under Chairman Lee's new vision of "Creative Management."

Chairman Lee Kun-Hee Leads Samsung's Transformation

Chairman Lee Kun-Hee has spearheaded Samsung's dramatic transformation since his ascension in 1987. In this section, we analyze how Samsung's semiconductor business became the template for the New Management initiative. And then, we elaborate the New Management initiative that enabled Samsung to shift from quantitative growth to upgrading quality, transforming itself into a world-class company.

The Second Foundation: A Vision for a Global Company

In March 1988, four months after he was installed, Chairman Lee Kun-Hee led the celebration of the 50th anniversary of Samsung's founding and plotted a course that would define his tenure.

Samsung's Vision of Becoming a World-Class Company

Shortly after assuming control, Chairman Lee initiated a "Second Foundation" for Samsung, setting his sights on changing Samsung from a leading Korean business group into a world-class company in the twenty-first century. Lee had begun to entertain this goal when he was still vice-chairman. At the time, the twenty-first century and global leadership were not yet on most people's minds, let alone the focus of Samsung's employees. Chairman Lee realized that a massive campaign would be needed to broaden his employees' perspective, as Samsung could no longer be content with maintaining its position as Korea's largest enterprise. He envisaged full-fledged organizational innovation and a new vision that could drive Samsung forward to become a world-class company.

Chairman Lee argued that Samsung needed to revamp its ideas and values and renew its management philosophy. The three founding tenets, "contribution to the nation through business," "people first," and "pursuit of rationality" had made Samsung a national leader, but they would not be good enough to enable it to join the ranks of the global elite.

"Contribution to the nation through business" was too limited and nationalistic for a company with global ambitions that intended to contribute to people's lives all over the world. "People first" made Samsung seem like a company in which only the smartest and most skilled employees were appreciated and encouraged to succeed. "Pursuit of rationality" made Samsung seem hesitant about seizing opportunities. Thus, Chairman Lee championed "autonomous management," "respect for humanity," and "focus on technology" as the new ideologies of the Second Foundation. In the field, he encouraged employees to embrace change through the principles of "seizing opportunity first," "changing one's ways of thinking," and "concentrating on business-level key success factors."

In the wake of the Second Foundation, Samsung sought to change its corporate culture. The company needed to reinvent its existing conformist and monolithic culture, developing a younger and more dynamic one in which managers and employees could have a large measure of autonomy. To this end, Samsung introduced radical reforms in top management, including changing the roles of the chairman and the secretariat by delegating some of their power to the affiliates' CEOs. These new changes helped Samsung promote employee autonomy and respect employees' individuality based on the belief that "good products come from the fingertips of our employees and partners." At the same time, Samsung revamped its work environment and its welfare and benefits systems. In March 1993, on the fifth anniversary of the Second Foundation, Chairman Lee announced Samsung's new ideology and ethos to reflect the changing demands of the era, as shown in Table 2.2.

Table 2.2   *Ideology and Ethos*

Management Ideology	Samsung Ethos
Devote our human resources and technology to create superior products and services that contribute to a better global society	1. Be with the customer 2. Challenge the world 3. Create the future

Employees Hesitate

In pushing for globalization, Chairman Lee repeatedly said, "A new century is coming, and with it many new changes. Samsung cannot survive as anything other than a world-class enterprise. If we stay the same, we are doomed." Despite this warning, Lee's new visions were often met with resistance. Samsung's corporate culture continued to be characterized by selfishness, authoritarianism, and conformity.

Samsung's employees did not embrace the chairman's new global vision quickly. The company's affiliates were still obsessed with sales volume and growth, resulting in a focus on achieving short-term quantitative targets. Qualitative factors such as added value, synergy, and long-term competitiveness were pushed aside.

At a meeting in New York in November 1991, Chairman Lee criticized the obsession with quantity, saying:

> In response to my emphasis on technology, managers simply increased the number of both R&D employees and R&D projects recklessly, without considering R&D efficiency. We have focused too much on technology for appearance's sake.

However, this reproach produced only temporary tension and failed to bring about lasting change. Unlike the chairman, whose ambitions were for a world-class company, Samsung's employees continued to be satisfied with being at the top of the domestic market. Moreover, despite the chairman's new emphasis on autonomy, the secretariat continued to intervene in the affiliates' affairs. Samsung's management control system, with its focus on micromanagement, had once been one of the company's strong points, but it had now become a drag on its drive to embrace change.

Frustrated by the lack of progress, the chairman confided to those close to him in late 1992, "I have tried to convey my beliefs in my inauguration speech and in five of Samsung's New Year's speeches. But nobody remembers what I said."

Moreover, the new chairman was asking Samsung's employees to abandon the organizational heritage that had previously led them to success. In effect, structural inertia that favored previous customs was preventing Samsung from embracing disruptive change. At the same time, the CEOs of most of the affiliates had already worked at Samsung for longer than the chairman (who was in his forties at that time). They thought they knew how Samsung should be managed better than the chairman did, thus thwarting attempts at change.

Semiconductors: A Template for Samsung's Reform

Chairman Lee concluded that another approach was needed if his Second Foundation was to become entrenched. He turned to the success of Samsung's successful semiconductor division as a template for the whole company.

Samsung had entered the memory chip business in 1983. Entering this business was a big step for Samsung. The company was a latecomer that completely lacked knowledge and experience in this area, but it dramatically narrowed the technology gap with the industry's top firms in four or five years. By 1992, Samsung was the world's largest company in the dynamic random access memory (DRAM) business, and it became a leader of the global memory chip industry the next year. The capabilities and experience acquired during this process have served as the basis for the New Management initiative.

Management System for the DRAM Business

Samsung underwent major changes in its management system while nurturing its semiconductor business (see Table 2.3). By its nature, producing memory chips requires massive amounts of investment in equipment and high levels of technology, meaning that Samsung could not simply extend its existing business practices to this area. The company was thus compelled to start from scratch in this fundamentally different business. Though developing a

Table 2.3   *Changes in Samsung Management Introduced by the Semiconductor Business*

Management System Prior to the Semiconductor Business	Keys to Success	Management System After the Semiconductor Business
Owner management	1. Challenging vision	Owner management + professional management
Quantitative growth	2. Bold and speedy decisions	Market leader
	3. Emphasis on technology	
General talent Seniority system Internal promotion	4. Core talent	Core talent Performance-based system Hiring from outside
	5. Sense of crisis	
Micromanagement	6. Speed	Market preemption

competitive semiconductor business posed many difficulties for Samsung, the nature of the business also gave Samsung an opportunity to introduce fundamental changes.

First, the semiconductor operation allowed the new chairman to depart from his father's style of involving himself in the minor details of business. Instead, Chairman Lee presented a challenging vision and made bold decisions on investments, while stoking a sense of crisis throughout the entire organization. As the CEOs of affiliates were given responsibility for their daily tasks, Samsung was able to strike a balance between the owner-manager and the professional managers.

Second, the semiconductor business also permitted Samsung to make drastic changes in its overarching strategy. Previously, Samsung's strategy had emphasized market share growth at home and price competitiveness overseas. In memory chips, however, Samsung set out to become the global market leader from the start, because the company could not survive as anything less than a world-class business.

Third, the semiconductor business provided Samsung with a chance to reform the way it treated its workforce. In semiconductors, a disproportionate share of the value comes from a small number of people, the "geniuses who can feed 100,000." While the company continued to nurture talent organically, it also increasingly recruited talent from outside. Compensation and promotion were based on performance and contribution, rather than on seniority.

Fourth, even as it maintained its traditional strength in price, Samsung introduced new methods for faster development and release of products. These included concurrent engineering, parallel development, advanced development of next-generation technologies, and clustering, as will be explained later in this book.

Fifth, the semiconductor business gave Samsung an opportunity to revamp its core values and culture. Since its viability as a memory chip manufacturer was dependent on its being the world's number one, Samsung's semiconductor business was in crisis from the beginning. This sense of crisis would later spread throughout Samsung. The fierce global competition and frequent changes in technology and market trends that characterized the memory chip business forced employees to discard old practices and embrace new ones. This included introducing a horizontal communication system among skilled workers, rather than Samsung's traditional top-down structure.

Keys to Success in Semiconductors

Six factors contributed to Samsung's success in semiconductors.

Challenging Vision   When Samsung entered the memory chip business, there was little domestic demand for DRAMs, let alone any domestic competitors or technology. Samsung thus had no choice but to target global customers and to compete with global companies. This meant that Samsung's vision and management style in the memory chip business had to completely depart from the past.

Simply surviving in an industry that was already crowded with world-class firms would be challenging. However, Samsung did not temper its expectations to accommodate the inexperience of its workforce. Instead, it intentionally set ambitious targets in product development, product line construction, yield rates, and sales. Samsung's employees did not disappoint. Early on, Samsung challenged itself to make a 64K DRAM, a breakthrough that few companies had achieved. Samsung soon went on to build a fabrication plant in only six months that quickly reached 90 percent yields. The new division's confidence grew with each success.

Bold and Speedy Investment Decisions   The memory chip business is a risky business because of its rapid pace of innovation and massive facility investment requirements. DRAM manufacturers must be willing to make astronomical investments boldly and rapidly. This was a huge departure for Samsung, which had grown up as a risk-averse company. Thus, when its competitors balked at making new investments because of poor economic conditions or the notoriously frequent downturns in the cyclical memory chip business, Samsung took risks by making preemptive investments. Lee Kun-Hee (at that time a vice-chairman at Samsung) took full responsibility for any failures in advance, enabling Samsung to make bolder bets than its competitors.

Emphasis on Technology   As Samsung shifted its focus to high tech in the 1980s, its management placed an increasingly high value on state-of-the-art technology and on the talented engineers who produced it. Semiconductor engineers in their forties thus became the CEOs of divisions, an unprecedented step for Samsung. Some of these engineer-managers included Lee Yoon-Woo, Chin Dae-Je, Hwang Chang-Gyu, and Lim Hyung-Kyu, all legendary semiconductor engineers.

Chairman Lee himself stressed "technologically aware managers" and "management-aware technologists." Intimately familiar with the fine points of semiconductor technology, Lee often engaged in technical debates with his work teams, playing a major role in selecting the cell structure and wafer size of Samsung's new semiconductors. Lee also played a major role in appointing the aforementioned engineers as Samsung CEOs.

Core Talent   In technology, and particularly in semiconductors, one genius can be worth 100 ordinary technologists. Samsung learned this truth in building its semiconductor business, then used it to guide the company's overall personnel management in the 1990s.

In the semiconductor business, Samsung's main competitors were global firms rather than Korean firms. These organizations had the resources and ability to attract the best and brightest people in science and technology. Faced with the need to build its own world-class workforce, Samsung needed a better way to procure talent than its existing open competitive recruitment system. Samsung's hiring managers thus became willing to go anywhere in the world to identify and recruit promising engineers. As part of this change, Samsung abandoned its tradition of promoting exclusively from within and providing seniority-based compensation in favor of recruiting core talent from outside, choosing the best people, and providing generous compensation based on competence and performance.

Sense of Crisis   Samsung's semiconductor business began, and continues to this day, with crisis. For the first three or four years after it entered the business, the operation endured massive losses that put the entire Samsung Group at significant risk. The high-stakes nature of the semiconductor business thus induced a continuous sense of crisis among employees. Memory chip production requires multibillion-dollar investments if it is to be profitable, even though these investments do not guarantee success. Memory chip prices are also very volatile and fall rapidly soon after a particular chip's market launch. Even if profit is realized, most of it must be reinvested for production of the next generation of products. Semiconductors thus proved ideal for inducing a sense of crisis throughout the whole of Samsung.

Speed   Speed is a critical factor in the memory chip business. It provides the basis for competitiveness in all areas, ranging from investment to innovation to development and production. The tendency toward rapidly falling prices of memory chips means that being first can provide disproportionate rewards. The most competitive firms succeed because they can develop technologies and production systems faster than their competitors. In the 1980s, Samsung, though a latecomer to the industry, adopted a strategy of being a "fast follower," using speed as its means of catching up with the industry leaders.

Samsung devoted all its resources to increasing its business speed by using concurrent engineering (a process that shortens the time required for development, design, and production) and co-locating R&D and production facilities within the same geographical area. As a result, speed became a core competency of Samsung's semiconductor business.

Samsung's emphasis on speed led to dramatic changes in the company's traditional hierarchical culture. Entering the semiconductor business helped Samsung abolish unnecessary bureaucracy and formalities, while encouraging open discussions that helped it maximize efficiency. Field managers also gained the authority to make decisions on their own.

The New Management Initiative

The New Management initiative began when the semiconductor division experienced great success even though the rest of Samsung was failing to completely embrace the change that Chairman Lee desired. Lee felt an acute need to communicate a clear and vivid vision for Samsung as it approached a new century.

The New Management Declaration

In 1993, Chairman Lee declared and diffused his New Management initiative through a series of meetings with his executives that were held in major overseas locations in the United States, Japan, and Europe.

The Los Angeles Meeting   In February 1993, Chairman Lee convened an emergency meeting of the CEOs of Samsung's affiliates in Los Angeles. Before the meeting, Lee and his executive team visited electronics retailers in the Los Angeles area to see how Samsung products were displayed at retail stores. They found that Samsung products were abandoned in a corner, ignored by customers, and gathering dust.

Chairman Lee then lined up an array of Samsung's products and competitors' products to compare their design and quality in front of his executives. In particular, he compared the interior of Toshiba's videocassette recorder with that of Samsung. The difference in quality was immediately visible, despite Samsung's status as a well-regarded brand back home.

"These products do not deserve the name of Samsung," Chairman Lee declared. "Why do we allow the name of Samsung to be on products that gather dust in stores? Unbelievably, some of our products in the stores were broken or nonfunctional. This amounts to cheating our shareholders, our employees, the Korean people, and the country."

He added, "The old Samsung came to an end in 1986. I have felt a sense of crisis for 15 years now. Now is not a time to just say we will do better. Now is a time to do better or die. Our products are still far from catching up with those from advanced countries. We must get rid of a second-place mindset. If we are not the world's number one, we will not survive."

The Frankfurt Declaration   The next month, Chairman Lee met in Tokyo with 46 CEOs of Samsung Group to establish strategies that would boost Samsung's competitiveness. Just as he had done in Los Angeles, Lee and his fellows carefully examined the production and retailing sites of Japanese electronics firms and compared them with Samsung's.

On June 4, 1993, the chairman engaged in candid discussions with Japanese consultants to Samsung Group. His talks with these advisors convinced him that the instructions he had given since his inauguration were not trickling down to Samsung's production sites.

Moving on to Europe, Chairman Lee reaffirmed Samsung's critical situation a few days later. In Frankfurt, Germany, Lee watched a program on Samsung's in-house television network, Samsung Broadcasting Center (SBC). He was shocked to see that the washing machine lids being fitted on Samsung's assembly line did not close tightly. However, Samsung employees crudely cut them by hand until they fit and sold the washing machines to customers.

Lee was astonished at his employees' lax attitude toward customers. He then realized that Samsung's problem was much more than a production issue. Simply reducing the defect rate and implementing measures to raise quality would not be good enough to eradicate what had become common practices in all of Samsung's departments and divisions. Samsung had to remove the problem at the roots to allow healthy growth to return.

Chairman Lee then summoned his senior executives to Frankfurt for a seminal meeting. What emerged was the announcement of the New Management initiative, in the form of the Frankfurt Declaration, released on June 7. On June 13 and 14, Lee delivered four lectures to about 100 of Samsung's top managers. He then further spread the New Management gospel at meetings in London, Osaka, and Tokyo, briefing 1,800 executives and employees. Over a period of some three months, Lee delivered 48 lectures in some 350 hours of speaking. The lecture notes alone were 8,500 pages long.

The core of Lee's New Management initiative was the transformation of Samsung from a quantity-driven company to a quality-driven company in terms of its mindset, systems, and practices. Chairman Lee firmly believed that Samsung could become a world-class company in the twenty-first century, but only if it put quality first. At the same time, he insisted that nothing could change unless each employee at Samsung understood and internalized the belief that "change should begin with me."

Implementation

Two months after the Frankfurt Declaration, Chairman Lee ordered Samsung Group's secretariat to quickly produce a book that would explain the New Management initiative so that all employees could understand the need for change and would motivate them to move in one direction. To rapidly inculcate the values and ideas of the New Management initiative, the secretariat established the Office of New Management to handle the publishing of books and the delivery of lectures explaining Chairman Lee's philosophy, allowing New Management ideas to spread to all affiliates.

Map of New Management   Figure 2.1 gives a systematic view of Samsung's vision of being "a world-class company in the twenty-first century that contributes to the development of human society" as set forth in the New Management initiative. The figure shows the process of change being pursued under this initiative. Samsung employees were encouraged to reflect on

Figure 2.1   *New Management Action Plan*

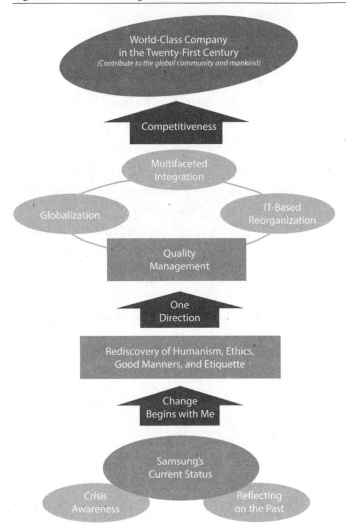

Samsung's crisis at the end of the century, and on Samsung's existing quantity-driven management practices. By doing this, they were to gain awareness of their current position and internalize the will to change. The changes needed to overcome the crisis would be based on the four bedrock values of the Samsung Constitution—rediscovery of humanism, ethics, good manners, and etiquette—and on "change begins with me." Change that was not based on the Samsung Constitution could be only temporary and incomplete.

Vision: A World-Class Company   In his declaration of the New Management initiative, Chairman Lee defined a "world-class company" as "a company that contributes to society by providing the most competitive goods and services to customers based on high-quality talent and technologies." More specifically, he explained, "A world-class company is a healthy organization whose members have strong mutual ties and attachment. It is characterized by vitality and abundance, where autonomy and creativity are alive." He further added, "A world-class company communicates a position of strength to its competitors. It is respected in its industry and loved by its customers." Becoming a world-class company, Chairman Lee believed, would benefit everyone, from employees, shareholders, and suppliers to customers and the community in general.

Quality-Driven Management   Chairman Lee believed that hiring talented people to produce inferior goods would be a profound loss to society. Samsung, he said, should provide goods and services of the highest quality based on quality-driven management. Two of Chairman Lee's remarks at the time illustrate his commitment to Samsung's quality-driven transformation.

> What I stressed after my inauguration as chairman was that Samsung should pursue qualitative growth. Samsung will be unable to survive unless it breaks quantity-oriented thoughts and practices that have lasted for 50 years.
>
> Moving our focus from quantity to quality is akin to departing from 5,000 years of history in Korea, and from five decades of history at Samsung. This transformation requires nothing less than total commitment.

What About Quantity?   In exhorting his employees to make quality paramount, Chairman Lee said,

> I say the weight of quantity to quality at Samsung should be zero to ten. Not five to five, or three to seven. Quantity should be sacrificed for quality. Samsung is willing to stop production lines if that is what it takes to raise the quality of our products, services, people, and management.

Samsung's managers, however, were initially slow to grasp the full import of the chairman's message. Stopping production lines in particular seemed unthinkable, as it would lead to losses beginning the moment a stoppage occurred. Some argued that even though Samsung was not a market leader in any category, the company had still achieved the highest global market share in items like microwaves and cathode-ray tubes. Obsessively focusing on quality, these managers reasoned, would be tantamount to giving up the market share that Samsung had achieved. Others argued that improvements in quality would arise naturally from quantitative growth.

Chairman Lee, on the other hand, asserted that quantitative growth would follow naturally from quality improvement. At a meeting held on July 14, 1993, in Osaka, Japan, he stressed that an obsession with quantity would be meaningless in the postindustrial society of the twenty-first century, saying, "Under quality-driven management, defects will decrease, product quality will improve, efficiency will increase, and then eventually production volume will increase as well. Quality-driven management will thus lead to quantitative expansion. Currently, Samsung is just producing poor-quality goods in mass quantities. Under our current system, we can increase production, but the end result is decreasing market share and increasing losses."

Product Quality, People Quality, and Management Quality   Products were not the only focus of the quality-first push. Employees and managers were to be part of the solution as well. Higher-quality employees would lead to higher-quality management, which would in turn lead to higher-quality products. Chairman Lee noted:

> A company is evaluated by customers in the market every day. Businesses thus have to value and respect their customers, and provide quality goods and services that reflect their opinions.

As part of this drive for quality, Chairman Lee emphasized "creativity, strategy, and management." As the twenty-first century was sure to bring diminishing returns from imitating others, he sought creative employees who could think for themselves. Henceforth, Samsung's employees had to be equipped with the insight to seize opportunities faster than others and the ability to turn a crisis into an opportunity. To this end, Chairman Lee sought out the most talented people, and rewarded them based on their competence.

Regarding the quality of management, Chairman Lee required senior managers to engage in businesses only after they fully understand those businesses' core "concept of business," or business-level key success factors. As each industry has different concepts or success factors for sales, purchasing, and management, managers have to develop a customized business philosophy and seek out unique factors that can lead to success. Chairman Lee also highlighted the vast gap between the leaders of the world's industries and the second-best players, and urged Samsung to pursue market preemption, develop speedy decision-making and execution systems, and focus on industries where it could be the world's number one.

Globalization, IT-Based Reorganization, and Multifaceted Integration   The three core tasks for the New Management era would be globalization, IT-based reorganization, and multifaceted integration. Globalization and IT-based reorganization would take precedence as part of Samsung's drive for world-class status in the twenty-first century, while multifaceted integration would differentiate Samsung from other companies.

Chairman Lee highlighted the limitations of doing business within the small Korean market and the need for globalization if Samsung was to become a world-class corporation. To this end, Samsung needed to have a workforce with local expertise around the world that could develop and execute market-entry strategies that were suitable for each region. In the process, Samsung could pursue coexistence and co-prosperity with its communities as a respected corporate citizen. This required a global mindset and a global management system.

In implementing IT-based reorganization, Samsung needed to bolster its speed and its intangible competitiveness if it was to become a world-class company. Chairman Lee emphasized that employees needed to become adept at computer software, including computer-aided design (CAD), computer-aided manufacturing (CAM), and computer-aided engineering (CAE) software, to expedite its design, manufacturing, and engineering capabilities. He also insisted that Samsung needed at least 20,000 software developers, along with a global information network for all Samsung employees.

Finally, Chairman Lee believed that multifaceted integration among infrastructure, facilities, functions, technologies, and software would be the unique source of Samsung's competitiveness in the twenty-first century. When related facilities and functions are located in one place, employees from diverse business departments can easily meet one another and share ideas that can provide the seeds for future competitiveness. Multifaceted integration can involve the development of multimedia products, integration of distribution channels, and diversification into businesses that help promote one another. To maximize convergence, Chairman Lee maintained, it was crucial to establish production complexes where all related business departments, such as R&D and manufacturing, are agglomerated.

The Samsung Constitution   Perhaps the most pressing issue in the New Management initiative was the recovery of Samsung's humanity and integrity. Lee asserted that high-quality goods and services can be produced only by people of equivalently good character. Based on this belief, he declared that the company must rediscover humanism, ethics, good manners, and etiquette as the bedrock values of the Samsung Constitution.

Before the 1980s, when Samsung focused on quantity-driven growth in manufacturing, intangible values like humanity, integrity, manners, and etiquette were not regarded as significant factors for competitiveness. Employees simply had to do their own work, giving little consideration to what others were doing. Creativity and imagination were not that important; the employees just had to follow the instructions in the manual.

However, this focus on the concrete would not serve Samsung well in its new ambition to be a quality-driven corporation that combined manufacturing and services. High-value-added businesses require flexibility and creative thinking rather than mechanical repetition and precision. Workers have to understand the whole work process and cooperate with their coworkers rather than carrying out isolated tasks. In this context, the values in the Samsung

Constitution, as Samsung's "highest law of the land," were critical factors that would allow the company's employees to use their talents to the fullest.

Though some executives and employees initially regarded the New Management initiative as a simple campaign for quality improvement, the Samsung Constitution showed just how committed Samsung was to fundamental change. The Samsung Constitution decreed that no one could thrive in the organization without respecting and practicing its values and objectives.

Generational Shift

As Chairman Lee had already observed in his announcement of the Second Foundation, introducing a quality-driven management system at Samsung was going to be an uphill battle. Managers who had spent their entire careers devoted to pursuing quantitative growth posed a seemingly intractable barrier to quality-driven management.

In early September 1993, less than 100 days after the New Management initiative was unveiled, Chairman Lee learned that his plan was not being carried out properly. Lee then called a meeting in which he deplored the lack of progress to Samsung's senior executives (including then-CEO Kang Jin-Ku of Samsung Electronics). As a result, Samsung's "Measures for the New Management Initiative" emerged. This report called for realignment of the secretariat; the introduction of qualitative measurements in performance evaluations of CEOs and executives, and groupwide training for the successful execution of the New Management initiative.

Chairman Lee replaced Lee Su-Bin, the executive director of the group's secretariat, with Hyun Myung-Kwan, the CEO of Samsung Construction. Hyun was not someone who had been hired through Samsung's conventional open competitive recruitment procedures. This marked an unprecedented personnel move for Samsung at the time. The executive director of the secretariat had always been someone who had joined Samsung as an entry-level employee through its standard open recruitment procedures.

Hyun's appointment as executive director of the secretariat served as advance notice of a generational shift in Samsung's management and a firm demonstration of Chairman Lee's determination to push for fundamental change. On October 23, 1993, the secretariat was downsized and restructured, and younger executives with an international mindset were promoted to executive directorships. The secretariat would become Samsung's "control tower" for the New Management initiative, ensuring that all of the chairman's thoughts and plans were put into practice.

The New Management initiative also functioned as the driver of Samsung's annual year-end personnel reshuffling. In contrast with the past, Samsung's 1993 reshuffling gave strong preference to managers with technological backgrounds rather than those with administrative expertise. Change spread throughout the organization as younger, more globally oriented managers were promoted to top positions over those who had spearheaded Samsung's initial expansion, but were still wedded to quantity-driven management.

In short, Chairman Lee restocked his management ranks with those who would give priority to quality. He selected younger managers with flexible thinking and a sound understanding of future business needs and placed them in key posts, enabling them to serve as leaders of quality-driven management.

Dissemination of the New Management Initiative

Chairman Lee unleashed a barrage of methods, including lectures that he provided himself, classes, books, and internal broadcasts by the Samsung Broadcasting Center, to disseminate the New Management initiative throughout Samsung. Every executive and employee of Samsung Group had been trained in the basic concepts by the end of 1993, and refresher training was provided repeatedly.

From 1993 to 1997, Samsung published six books on the New Management initiative, and about 500,000 copies were distributed to employees. These included translations into more than 10 languages, including English, Japanese, Chinese, and Malay. After the employees had read the books, Samsung asked them to discuss the books in one-hour sessions every morning.

Shock Therapy

Chairman Lee did not hesitate to use more drastic techniques to gain his people's attention. When changes in top management and his own lectures were not enough to convey the message that fundamental change was required, Lee introduced new measures like the "7 to 4 working system," the "line stop," and the "grace period" for reporting nonperforming assets. More famously, Lee even publicly burned Samsung mobile phones that he found to be unsatisfactory.

The 7 to 4 Working System   A few weeks after the New Management initiative was introduced, Samsung's work schedule became one of the first examples of the company's commitment to quality over quantity. The workday for office workers changed from the previous schedule, where employees had routinely stayed for 10 to 12 hours, to a 7 a.m. to 4 p.m. schedule. Under this new regime, employees were expected to do the same amount of work in less time. Lee's underlying aim was to encourage executives and employees to abandon redundant and inefficient practices and raise their productivity, while allowing them to boost their competitiveness by using their increased free time for self-development. At the same time, employees could enjoy an enhanced quality of life, providing a win-win situation for both the company and its workers.

At first, many employees struggled to adjust and were tempted to slip back into their previous practices and work longer hours. To combat these habits, the secretariat formed a task force to enforce the new schedule and prevent employees from lingering after closing time. Samsung's new working schedule thus functioned as a signal of how profoundly Samsung under the New Management initiative was embracing change.

Line Stop   Chairman Lee described product defects as a "cancer" and declared war on defective goods. He believed, moreover, that Samsung's product quality was more the result of the employees' way of thinking than of the company's technology. He thus exhorted his employees to abandon their belief that "the longer production lines operate without stopping, the better they are." Lee ordered assembly line workers to stop operations completely whenever they found any defective products, and resume operations only after the problem had been fixed perfectly. Such willingness to interrupt production would have been unimaginable under the previous quantity-driven management system.

Line stop was also implemented in Samsung's nonmanufacturing businesses, including its insurance lines and theme park. Here, line stop was renamed "curtain stop," referring to a curtain interrupting a performance. Stores and branches that were found guilty of providing poor customer service were shuttered and not reopened until the problem was completely resolved.

Grace Period for Reporting Nonperforming Assets   In early July of 1993, Chairman Lee set a time period for voluntary reporting of business failures and troubled assets. People who reported failures would not be punished, but those who knowingly concealed failures thereafter would be subject to severe discipline. Chairman Lee was determined to expose hidden deficiencies, such as unsold inventory and bad debt, in order to prevent employees from pursuing the quantitative growth that could conceal such problems. Lee thus allowed all Samsung affiliates to start anew by disclosing their most troubled assets and adopting measures to improve or eliminate them. These measures also helped Samsung promote transparent accounting by using previous cases of bad accounting as case studies for employees.

Public Burning Ceremony for Defective Products   In 1995, Samsung distributed 2,000 cordless telephones to its employees as gifts for the Lunar New Year. Some employees, however, complained about the poor quality of calls made on these phones. When Chairman Lee found out about this, he was furious, stating, "Is the quality of our phones still so low? Aren't you afraid of what our customers might think? How can you take their money and sell them defective phones?" Lee then ordered that all of Samsung's phones be recalled from the marketplace and destroyed in front of his factory workers. As a result, more than 100,000 Samsung cordless telephones were collected. Production lines were stopped and product development was suspended until a solution to the defect was found.

On March 9, 1995, 2,000 workers at Samsung's factory in Gumi, sporting headbands that said "Ensure Quality!," gathered in the factory courtyard along with senior managers and executives. A banner declaring "Quality Is My Character and Pride" fluttered nearby. At the center of the gathering were cordless telephones, car phones, and fax machines valued at 15 billion won (about US$20 million). Employees then smashed the phones and set them on fire. Samsung had demonstrated, in the most spectacular way possible, that its commitment to quality would brook no compromises.

The 1997 Asian Currency Crisis and the New Management Initiative

Samsung was hit hard by the Asian currency crisis in the late 1990s. The company had to go through massive restructuring of its business portfolios. However, the crisis also gave Samsung an important momentum to accelerate fundamental reforms that Chairman Lee had proposed under his New Management initiative.

The Time for New Management Arrives

Although vigorous efforts had been made to put it into practice, the New Management initiative did not fully come into its own until 1997, the year of the Asian currency crisis. This was in part because of Samsung's strong performance in 1994, when it became the first Korean company to surpass 1 trillion won (about US$1.25 billion) in profits thanks to booming demand for memory chips. Samsung's performance lulled employees into believing that stellar growth was still possible even if they were clinging to the previous quantity-driven management.

Second, employees had not yet directly experienced the crisis that Chairman Lee had predicted, and they did not realize the need for change. Though they superficially accepted the New Management initiative and acted as if they did in front of others, they did not truly embrace and had not truly internalized its principles.

Third, the drastic shift to quality-driven management had caused considerable internal resistance, and employees tended to interpret it in ways that were favorable to themselves. They thus regarded New Management as a way to spend money, rather than a way to make money. Concepts like "macro-management," which emphasized strategy-oriented management styles and the autonomy of affiliates, instead of micromanagement, employee welfare, customer satisfaction, and corporate citizenship, were eagerly embraced. However, core business elements like revenue, profit, productivity, and competitiveness were largely neglected.

The arrival of genuine financial difficulties, however, rapidly made such resistance moot. The first signs of trouble began when Samsung's memory chip business began to slow in mid-1995, undermining the whole group's financial base. Samsung's thin-film-transistor liquid-crystal display (TFT-LCD) module business, in which it had made massive investments since 1994, was also coming under intense pricing pressure from Japanese rivals. In mobile phones, Samsung was having to catch up with Motorola even in its home market.

Against this backdrop, in February 1996, Chairman Lee directed Samsung's semiconductor division managers to prepare an emergency plan for a potential worst-case scenario. The semiconductor division, although slowing, had been in the black for the previous two years, bolstering complacency about Samsung's prospects. Nonetheless, Samsung's semiconductor employees spent the next two months simulating emergency situations and drafting restructuring plans—including the downsizing of Samsung's work-force—in accordance with the chairman's instructions. In April, Chairman Lee pointed to sharp fluctuations in the memory chip industry cycle and told his electronics executives to prepare for a severe downturn. The focus, he said, should be on streamlining operations and strengthening fundamentals. Later, Samsung strove to carry out the "right changes" by avoiding complacency about its successful memory chip business, reducing management bubbles, improving competitiveness, and upholding basic principles.

Later in 1996, after a meeting of Samsung CEOs in San Diego, Samsung introduced its "Expenditure 330 Campaign" to cut costs by 30 percent within three years, along with a partial downsizing of staff and business restructuring. Samsung was thus able to maintain a certain level of liquidity and to establish a strong risk management system.

When 1997 arrived, Samsung declared it the "Year of Sound Management" to emphasize its commitment to further restructuring. All management practices became subject to reform, creating a new sense of urgency among employees.

Restructuring Through the New Management Initiative

Samsung's preparations were proven wise only a few months later when the Asian currency crisis erupted. For years, Asia's booming economies had attracted large inflows of capital that had fed speculative asset bubbles. In 1997, however, this changed overnight when a foreign exchange crisis arose in Thailand. By the end of the year, the effects of the currency crisis were being felt throughout the region's economy. In Korea, the crisis led to massive instability, as the country's large and heavily indebted companies found themselves suddenly unable to service their debt. Many of Korea's largest firms failed, and those that remained had to undergo painful restructuring—including massive layoffs.

The Asian currency crisis presented a massive challenge for Samsung, which lost 500 billion won (about US$360 million) in 1998 alone. At the same time, the crisis also gave Samsung an opportunity to pursue fundamental reforms. With the crisis that Chairman Lee had predicted close at hand, Samsung's employees realized the urgent need for the New Management initiative in a way that they had never done before.

When the crisis erupted, Samsung's heavy industry and chemical businesses began running massive losses. Many of Samsung's overseas operations were also burdened with excess inventory and nonperforming loans.

As the Asian currency crisis made Samsung's weaker business lines increasingly untenable, the company was able to commence massive restructuring, "as fast as possible, as drastic as necessary, and with nothing and no one off limits." The secretariat was dismantled at the government's behest, and the Corporate Restructuring Office was created instead. This new group headquarters drafted an emergency plan to upgrade the competitiveness of Samsung's affiliates by 30 percent. Managers were given broader responsibility and autonomy, and performance evaluations and compensation were upgraded to international standards.

Businesses that were in the red or only barely profitable were dumped, reducing the number of Samsung's affiliates from 59 to 40 by the end of 1998. Less viable affiliates and divisions like construction machinery and forklifts were sold. Even profitable assets were not spared if they were found to add little long-term value. Samsung's semiconductor plant in Bucheon, which generated 100 billion won (about US$72 million) in profits annually, was sold so that Samsung could concentrate on higher-value-added products like large-scale integrated circuits (LSI) and application-specific integrated circuits (ASICs).

In the meantime, Samsung's affiliates strove to follow the government's guideline of lowering their debt-to-equity ratios to below 200 percent. They raised equity capital through new offerings, sold off unnecessary assets, and reduced debt. They also improved their cost structure to maximize profits. As a result, Samsung Group's average debt ratio had been reduced to 166 percent by the end of 1999.

Personnel restructuring was carried out in parallel. With the goal of shrinking the workforce by 30 percent, Samsung spun off its noncore businesses in an effort to reform its high-cost, low-efficiency structure. By the end of 1999, Samsung's workforce had shrunk from 163,000 to 113,000 (Table 2.4).

Restructuring Results

Organizational Restructuring

- *Noncore businesses sold.* The power device division was sold to Fairchild, the defense industry division to Thomson-CSF, the construction machinery division to Volvo, forklifts to Clark, retail to Tesco, HP Korea to HP, and so on.
- *Mergers.* Units in the aerospace, power generation facilities, and ship engines divisions were merged with their respective competitors and Samsung became minority shareholders of the new entities.
- *Withdrawal from unprofitable businesses.* Samsung withdrew from satellites, machine tools, Rollei cameras, and self-assembly bathtubs.

Table 2.4   *Personnel and Debt Reductions*

		End of 1997	End of 1999
Workforce (Persons)		163,000	113,000
Balance Sheet Improvement	Total debt (trillion won)	47.7	25.7
	Debt ratio (%)	366	166
	Interaffiliate loan guarantees (trillion won)	2.3	0
	Invested foreign capital ($100 million)	27.4	
	Asset sales and capital increases (trillion won)	14 (5.4 in asset sales, 8.6 in capital increases)	

- *Spin-offs.* Samsung spun off 231 firms employing 15,000 people, including audio systems and camcorder manufacturing, clothing factories, and retailers.
- *Divestitures.* Samsung divested 28 companies, including JoongAngIlbo, Bokwang, Hanil Cable, IPC, Daehan Fine Chemicals, Hantok Chemicals, and Daegyeong Building.

Former Samsung Securities CEO Hwang Young-Key explained Samsung's efforts to introduce change during this time:

> The New Management initiative was the secret to Samsung's ability to successfully overcome the currency crisis. The principles of the New Management initiative, including creativity, a spirit of challenge, R&D, globalization, and customer focus, all complemented each other, and Samsung's managers and core people worked hard to put them into practice. Samsung solved many of its problems through the quality-driven focus introduced by the New Management initiative, and this contributed to its rebounding from the crisis even stronger.

Even as it withdrew from unsuccessful areas, Samsung did not hesitate to invest in areas that it deemed strategic. The company continued to pour huge sums into electronics, finance, trade, and services to become a world-class firm in those areas. At the same time, the criteria for investment, particularly in nonstrategic businesses, switched to crisis mode so that Samsung could recover its investments as quickly as possible. Chairman Lee proclaimed that suffering losses was like a crime for society, motivating his employees to help Samsung recover from the crisis. Thanks to these decisions, Samsung returned to profitability in 1999, with a firm agenda to pursue a quality-driven transformation. The conditions for realizing the New Management initiative were finally in place.

Characteristics of Samsung's Transformation

By the start of the twenty-first century, the Samsung Group had reinvented itself. The transformation, which was slow to gain momentum, finally accelerated as a result of the pressures created by the 1997 currency crisis. Many companies of all sizes around the world can point to dramatic internal changes that allowed them to achieve growth on an unprecedented new scale. Samsung's metamorphosis, however, has three uncommon characteristics.

First, Samsung's New Management initiative represented a total commitment to transforming Samsung into a world-class corporation through a complete overhaul of management styles. New Management demanded a complete restructuring of Samsung's corporate culture and operations, and employees were expected to alter not only their methods of work, but also their way of thinking and their way of living. Thus, the New Management initiative required significantly more time and effort than other, more incremental efforts at other companies.

Second, changes were instituted in anticipation of difficult business conditions. The New Management initiative was undertaken specifically to prepare for a crisis. Postcrisis innovations tend to be passive, whereas precrisis innovations are proactive and have more lasting effects. With its transformation already in motion under the New Management initiative, Samsung was better prepared to handle setbacks like the slump in the memory chip market in the mid-1990s and the 1997 currency crisis later on. New Management thus continues to be a source of inspiration for Samsung employees to this day.

Third, the main agent of change in the New Management initiative was the founder's son, rather than a professional manager. In Western countries, descendants who inherit a family business tend to maintain the management style that the founder practiced. In most cases, innovation, if it occurs, is superficial rather than structural, to protect and preserve ownership. In contrast, Chairman Lee was willing to call for a Second Foundation and to take responsibility for all the risks involved. This attitude was disconcerting to Samsung's employees at the outset, but as time went by, it came to be widely understood as a strong commitment by Samsung to embracing innovation.

PART TWO

EVOLUTION OF THE SAMSUNG WAY

M anagement thinkers have devised a variety of models to account for corporate success. Raymond E. Miles and Charles C. Snow have pointed to strategy and structure as key factors. They contend that the best companies develop a strong "external fit" by creating a strategy that suits the market, and a strong "internal fit" by maintaining an organization that executes that strategy effectively.[1] To this, Lawrence G. Hrebiniak and William F. Joyce added incentive systems that encourage departments and individuals to act in a way that fulfills the demands of the strategy and structure.[2] Jay R. Galbraith has further added organizational processes and people,[3] claiming that a successful organization needs both processes that integrate divisions and departments horizontally, and people with the competence to carry out the strategies, structures, and processes.

The authors examined Samsung's management system based on these models and identified leadership and governance, strategies, human resource management, management control, and values and culture as key elements in Samsung-style management. Chapter 3 analyzes the role of Chairman Lee Kun-Hee and Samsung's Corporate Strategy Office, and the division of labor between Chairman Lee and the professional managers. Chapter 4 deals with the changes in Samsung's management system after the New Management initiative, as well as its current management system.

As mentioned previously, when Lee Kun-Hee became chairman, Samsung was already Korea's leading business group. However, even though it was the country's largest and most successful business group, Samsung was in many respects still a profoundly local business that reflected the business practices prevailing in Korea at the time. Leadership was patriarchal, with the owner-manager intervening at all levels of decision making. Corporate strategy consisted of the same type of unrelated diversification and vertical integration pursued by other Korean firms. In terms of human resource management, Samsung sought out and fostered a homogeneous and largely domestic workforce, with heavy reliance on the internal labor market, and rewarded its workers based on seniority. In terms of management control, Samsung gave priority to a micromanaging and perfectionist style in which executive managers intervened in minute details, as well as a hierarchical structure of downward communication from the owner-manager and the secretariat. In terms of values and culture, Samsung trumpeted "efficiency" and emphasized its status as Korea's leading business group.

Lee Kun-Hee introduced a new vision of Samsung as a world-class firm, and he claimed that this would not be realized if Samsung simply continued to use its existing management system. To fully realize the goals of the New Management initiative, and to deal with the 1997 Asian currency crisis, Samsung needed to decisively depart from the past and build a completely new management system, as shown in the accompanying figure.

Samsung's Evolution Under New Management

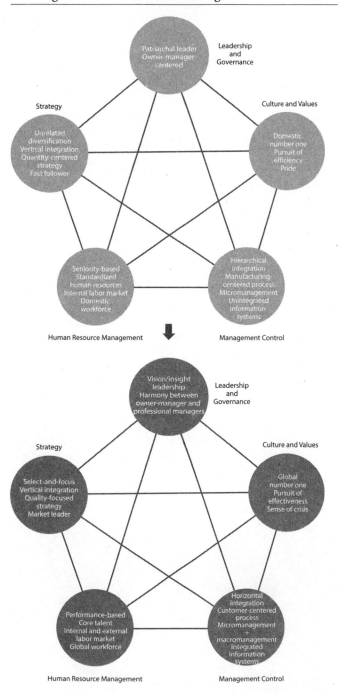

CHAPTER 3

LEADERSHIP AND GOVERNANCE

3

The Core of the Samsung Way

Chairman Lee's Visionary Leadership

One of the major factors leading to Samsung's success has been the strong leadership shown by its owner-manager, who set out the company's vision and values and nurtured management systems that were unique to Samsung. In fact, Western media like *Bloomberg Businessweek*, *Fortune*, and *Time* have all pointed to the critical role that Chairman Lee Kun-Hee played in making Samsung a world-class corporation. Chairman Lee brought Samsung global acclaim by developing a vision of the company based on talent and technology. He did this by relentlessly pressing Samsung to be the world's best, maintaining a constant sense of crisis, preemptively seizing business opportunities, nurturing core talent, prioritizing technology, and focusing on intangible assets.

Chairman Lee's contribution to Samsung's success is visible in many areas. He developed a vision of Samsung as a leading global enterprise that guides the company to this day, and he drummed up a continuous but healthy sense of crisis that stimulated Samsung's employees to achieve ever more ambitious goals. His insights took Samsung in new directions, including a commitment to building intangible assets, setting technology standards based on massive R&D investment, and strengthening the company's design capability and brand value. As an executive, Chairman Lee sometimes made strategic decisions himself. As the head of Samsung Group, he served as the focal point for integrating and coordinating Samsung's affiliates.

A Biography of the Chairman

Lee Kun-Hee was born in South Gyeongsang Province, Korea, in 1942, the third son of Samsung founder Lee Byung-Chull. He was raised by his grandmother, and amid the turmoil of the Korean War, he had to attend five different elementary schools. As a fifth grader, in accordance with his father's instructions, he left the Pusan National University Elementary School for Japan to learn from the example of advanced countries. After completing his first year of middle school in Japan, he returned to Korea and enrolled at the Middle School of Seoul National University.

Lee then went on to study at Seoul National University High School, Waseda University School of Commerce in Tokyo, and George Washington University in Washington, DC, where he received an MBA degree. He was a wrestler during high school, an experience that later led him to the presidency of the Korean Amateur Wrestling Federation.

Returning from the United States in 1966, Lee entered Tongyang Broadcasting Company (TBC), beginning his training as an executive of Samsung Group. He served as a director of JoongAng Ilbo and TBC, and as vice-chairman of Samsung C&T. JoongAng Ilbo was an affiliate company of Samsung Group that published a daily newspaper, while Samsung C&T was a general trading company at that time. In February 1979, he was promoted to vice-chairman of Samsung Group and began accompanying his father on visits to business sites.

After his father died in November 1987, Lee was installed as the chairman of Samsung Group. In 1996, he was appointed as a member of the International Olympic Committee (IOC) in recognition of his contribution to sports activities at home and abroad.

Since he assumed the chairmanship, Lee's role at Samsung has evolved as Samsung's environment and status have changed. At first, Lee took on many tasks himself, but as Samsung grew, he gradually shifted his role to that of a coordinator for groupwide cooperation and a visionary who set goals for Samsung as a whole. This delegation of authority was possible because the management system that he established had greatly improved Samsung's internal skills and competence, allowing routine decisions to be made by the professional managers.

Among Chairman Lee's diverse contributions, the most important have been his role as Samsung's visionary based on the creation of a continuous sense of crisis, and his presentation of strategic directions for Samsung based on his unusual grasp of business and upcoming trends. The authors have called these "vision leadership" and "insight leadership."

Vision Leadership

Chairman Lee practiced vision leadership. Considering Samsung's scale and its diverse portfolio of businesses, it naturally was impossible for him to be involved in the detailed decisions of affiliate companies. Therefore, Chairman Lee assigned himself the task of motivating and inspiring his employees, and instilling a sense of crisis that ensured that Samsung would always embrace change.

Far-Reaching Vision

Continuously projecting a far-reaching vision has been Chairman Lee's most important role in Samsung's transformation since the early 1990s (see Figure 3.1). He was the first chairman of a Korean major conglomerate to present a lofty vision and challenging goals, such as being a "world-class company" and earning a "trillion won in profits,"[1] and he has continuously stressed that "it is hard to survive without being the global number one or the only one."

Chairman Lee called for global leadership in nearly every area of Samsung's electronics operations, including semiconductors, mobile phones, TVs, notebook PCs, and printers. Newly launched business lines were no exception; they were given the task of becoming number one in the world regardless of the competitive landscape. This was the case when Samsung entered the mobile phone market, taking on and ultimately surpassing entrenched leaders like Motorola, Nokia, and Apple.

To achieve global leadership, Samsung's workforce adopted rapid-offense tactics to shorten the time needed to reach the top. This included aggressive

Figure 3.1   How Chairman Lee's Vision Shapes Samsung's Style

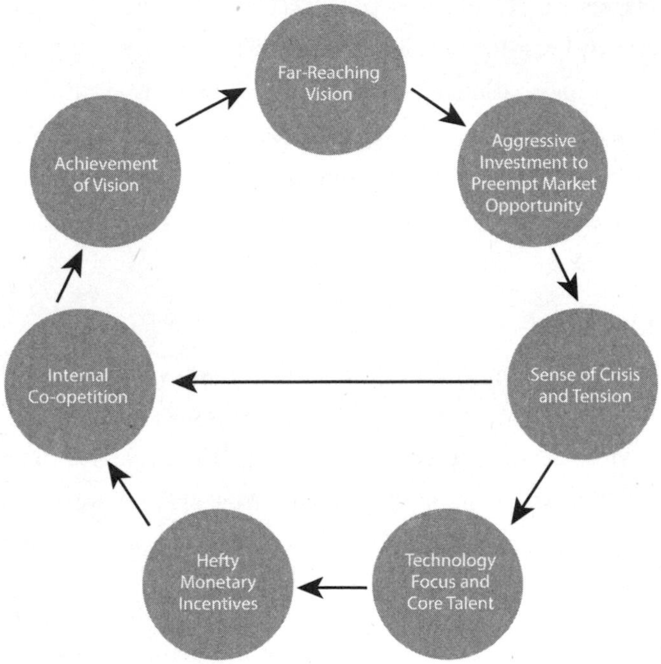

spending to preemptively seize opportunities; instilling a sense of crisis and tension in the workforce, a focus on technologies and core talent, generous incentives to top recruits and exceptional performers, and internal "co-opetition."

To achieve Chairman Lee's far-reaching vision, Samsung made massive investments to preemptively seize business opportunities. Catching up to the front-runners could not be simply a matter of following in their footsteps. Swift, audacious investments were needed. To grab the top spot in the semiconductor business, for example, Samsung committed prodigious amounts of money to build facilities even when the chip industry was in the doldrums. Likewise, to take the lead in liquid-crystal displays and active-matrix organic light-emitting diodes (AMOLEDs), Samsung invested heavily not only in next-generation models, but in next-next-generation models.

The scale of these investments instantly created tension and a crisislike atmosphere. The operating rates of the new facilities had to be increased, or else the entire investment would be in jeopardy. This would be difficult to achieve, however, simply by improving on available methods. Moreover, Samsung lacked the technologies, talent, and production capabilities to throttle up the start-up phase immediately.

Fast-track assembly of key talent thus became imperative. This, however, raised another issue: not enough of Samsung's personnel had the necessary experience and capabilities, and Samsung did not have the time to cultivate these skills internally. Consequently, Samsung went on an external hiring spree, and to persuade top-flight engineers and other personnel to join Samsung rather than go to one of its established rivals, lavish compensation packages were needed. In some cases, the starting pay of recruits exceeded the salary of Samsung CEOs. Furthermore, Samsung was compelled to pay hefty performance bonuses to encourage and reward maximum effort and to retain talent. The bonuses amounted to as much as half of an employee's annual salary, depending on the performance of affiliates or divisions.

Internal co-opetition, or a combination of cooperation and competition, was another offshoot of the tension and the sense of crisis. Fulfilling the chairman's vision meant that everyone had to pull in the same direction. Collaboration among Samsung's business units and divisions was vital in maintaining a fast pace. Samsung's flat-screen TV business provides an example of this close cooperation. It began in 2004, and within a few years it had the largest share in the global market. On the other hand, affiliates and divisions competed, trying to outperform one another in order to get greater chances of promotion and monetary incentives. This internal competition is as fierce as the competition in the marketplace.

Finally, Chairman Lee continuously raised the bar higher. Once his vision of Samsung's becoming a top-class company was realized to some extent, he pointed his workforce toward world-class heights. When that vision was achieved and Samsung was at the pinnacle in various business areas, the chairman said, "Find new businesses, since all of our businesses could disappear in 10 years." That directive has triggered another wave of outsized investments.

A Healthy Sense of Crisis

A sense of crisis never completely disappears at Samsung. In the early years of his tenure, Chairman Lee repeatedly stressed that without a genuinely held passion for innovation, Samsung could never become the world's number one. Failure to innovate not only would impair Samsung's progress, but would threaten the very survival of Samsung.

Chairman Lee has incessantly promoted a sense of crisis at Samsung, saying things like, "We are finished if we do not embrace change," and "Do not get comfortable with current success." When the media reported that Samsung had achieved record profits, Chairman Lee said, "My back is clammy with sweat whenever I think of how Samsung will make a living in five or ten years," and, "All of Samsung's number one products will disappear in five or ten years."

Similarly, in 2006, when Samsung Group again posted record profits, Chairman Lee told his CEOs, "Do not boast about today's success. Always try to grasp changes and trends with a sense of crisis." In his New Year's message of January 2007, Lee said, "Samsung has long chased after global front-runners but is now in a position of being chased itself. We have a tough journey ahead, since we have to explore new roads before others do, getting away from the easy road of following leaders." Lee asked his employees to fuse creativity, innovation, and a sense of challenge.

Insight Leadership

Inside Samsung, Chairman Lee's management style is often referred to as "topical management," since his role is to suggest the critical topics of Samsung's business for the next five to ten years. The authors feel that an even better description of Lee's management style is "insight leadership," because acute insight is needed to grasp business conditions and trends in advance.

Lee's insight leadership, rather than providing detailed strategies and tactics, focuses on establishing a vision and setting directions for investment. To this end, Lee has asked Samsung to invest heavily in intangible assets, preemptive setting of technological standards, and world-class design, branding, and human capital. Lee's insight leadership has allowed Samsung to turn itself from an anonymous original equipment manufacturer to a world-class brand for state-of-the-art, premium-priced products.

Soft Competitiveness and Core Talent

Chairman Lee has claimed that it will be impossible for Samsung to become and remain a world-class company without improving its intangible ("soft") competitiveness, in addition to its tangible ("hard") competitiveness. "Soft" here refers to intangible elements like emotion, knowledge, culture, and creativity. To this end, Samsung has greatly increased its investment in R&D, design, and branding.

Chairman Lee has strongly encouraged technology development, saying, "In an era of technology hegemony, Samsung will remain a second- or third-tier player subject to the whim of industry leaders if it does not have its own independent technologies." Samsung thus had to use technology to transform itself into a world-class company. As a result, Samsung's investments in R&D grew massively. Samsung Advanced Institute of Technology, which develops technologies for the future, has been cultivating R&D talent, while maintaining its budget regardless of Samsung's current management situation. Thanks to these efforts, Samsung ranks as the world's number two in the number of patents registered in the United States.

To ramp up Samsung's design capabilities, Chairman Lee declared 1996 to be Samsung's "Year of Design Innovation." Lee regarded design as an integral part of Samsung's intangible competitiveness, and believed that Samsung could not be a world-class business if it did not have its own innovative designs. Samsung thus established unique design philosophies and guidelines, while building and enhancing its infrastructure and systems for design innovation. As a result, Samsung increasingly recruited top designers and made massive investments in pursuing high-end design.

Samsung Electronics, for example, integrated its design innovation activities, establishing a Design Committee in 2000 and a Design Management Center in 2001 under the direct control of its CEO. With these efforts, Samsung Electronics soon won the prestigious International Design Excellence Awards (IDEA) and the International Forum (iF) design awards, allowing it to become number one in the electronics product category and to establish a premium image among consumers.

Along with design, Chairman Lee turned his attention to Samsung's brand power. In May 1996, Lee asked for a strategy to raise Samsung's brand status to world-class levels, and by the second half of 1997, such plans were in effect. Samsung Electronics, for example, had established a global marketing organization and adopted advanced marketing techniques. Samsung had also consolidated its message and image making around the world. Overseas branches and business units that had used separate advertising agencies were all placed under one advertising company. Samsung also committed billions of dollars to make Samsung an Olympic sponsor, a position that had long been dominated by the top global companies.

"It was something that I couldn't even imagine as a professional manager, since it cost a huge amount of money. However, it became possible thanks to the chairman's firm resolution," recalled Yun Jong-Yong, former vice-chairman of Samsung Electronics. Samsung continued to become an advertising partner for the Summer and Winter Olympics and the Asian Games. Such efforts were instrumental in propelling Samsung to eighth place in Interbrand's 2013 brand value index.

Chairman Lee's primary focus, however, was on the acquisition of talent. He asked his executives to "recruit geniuses who can receive higher salaries than CEOs" and "explore and nurture talent based on future insight."

Chairman Lee's focus on talent was to prove farsighted. Today, Samsung's talent management systems, like its regional specialist program and its recruitment of foreign talent, are among the main sources of its competitiveness. The regional specialist program, started on Chairman Lee's orders in 1991, now numbers some 5,000 people in 80 countries. Regional specialists have played a pivotal role in the rapid growth of Samsung's overseas business operations since the 2000s.

Some of Lee's hiring directives met initial resistance. In particular, the heads of Samsung's business units complained of communication problems with foreign personnel and of being forced to redo their work. Eventually, however, Lee's instructions to recruit more foreign employees have borne results, and foreigners are playing a critical role in globalizing Samsung's management systems and growing its businesses worldwide.

Decisive Strategic Decision Making

Chairman Lee rarely participates in day-to-day decision making. However, when an important decision on broad strategic matters needs to be made, he will step forward as owner-manager to determine Samsung's direction.

One of the keys to Samsung's success has been its ability to pinpoint ventures with huge earnings potential, then invest decisively in them. Samsung's professional managers identified the high potential return in memory chips, flat-panel monitors (thin-film-transistor liquid-crystal displays, or TFT-LCDs), and mobile phones, the mainstay of Samsung's business today, while the owner-manager made the resolute decision to invest in them.

Despite being a latecomer that lacked technologies and incurring prolonged, massive deficits, Samsung remained steadfast in pursuing its investments, thanks to Chairman Lee's support as an owner-manager. For example, in the second half of 1997, when the TFT-LCD industry was skidding, Samsung realized that Japanese firms were hesitating to invest in next-generation production lines to produce larger substrates. Upon seeing this, Chairman Lee approved massive capital investments, and Samsung leaped ahead to set the standard and become the market leader.

Chairman Lee also participates in some of Samsung's most critical decisions. When Samsung developed a 4M dynamic random access memory (DRAM), a dispute arose over whether to choose the stack design or the trench design, which had been adopted by the front-runner, IBM. The chairman selected the stack design. He explained, "The more complex a problem is, the more simplified it should be. When building a home, it is easier and more extensible to start from the ground rather than digging into it. The same applies to this circuit." Thereafter, Japanese semiconductor firms Toshiba and NEC, which had previously adopted trench designs, faced major problems, while Samsung gained ground.

Another example involved a proposal by Toshiba to jointly develop next-generation NAND flash in 2001. At the time, Toshiba had a source technology patent in NAND flash and was far ahead of Samsung Electronics in market share. Samsung's managers were divided on the disadvantages and advantages of the alliance. Chairman Lee persuaded them to decline the overture, saying, "To become number one, we should go for independent development, even if there is some risk." In one year, Samsung Electronics developed state-of-the-art technology in flash memory faster than Toshiba, becoming the most profitable company in this area.

The chairman's resolution also paid off when Samsung restructured during the 1997 Asian currency crisis. As the crisis weighed on the group's future, Chairman Lee decided to sell Samsung's Bucheon semiconductor factory to Fairchild Semiconductor of the United States. The factory was a legacy asset that had been established using the chairman's private funds, and thus Chairman Lee was emotionally attached to it. Nevertheless, as the only profitable factory making large-scale integration devices, it was a very attractive asset to potential buyers. The sale exhibited Chairman Lee's strong determination to restructure Samsung and thus helped Samsung restructure more rapidly in other areas and emerge from the crisis even stronger.

Harmony Between the Owner-Manager and the Professional Managers

One of the most striking features of Samsung's governance is the harmony the company has achieved between the owner-manager and the professional managers. This type of shared management often exposes various weaknesses. At Samsung, however, the strengths of the owner-manager (entrepreneurial decision making from a long-term perspective) and the strengths of the professional executives (professional management capabilities) are realized simultaneously. Chairman Lee's long-term vision for Samsung Group meshes with the detailed strategic decisions of professional managers to fully realize ambitious goals. At the same time, the chairman can assess his managers' performance and prevent them from falling into moral hazard while they provide insights that complement the owner-manager's decision making.

Changes in Leadership and Governance

Samsung's leadership and governance structure underwent drastic changes when Chairman Lee succeeded his father in 1987 (see Figure 3.2). In governance, the most significant change was the shift from an owner-manager-centered structure to joint management and a division of labor between the owner-manager and the professional managers. As the founder of Samsung, the elder Lee had intervened, even in minor decisions, through the group secretariat (today called the Corporate Strategy Office). In contrast, Chairman Lee Kun-Hee largely perceives his role as developing a broad vision and strategic direction for Samsung, and delegating other decisions to the CEOs of Samsung affiliates through the Corporate Strategy Office.

Today, the purpose of the Corporate Strategy Office is to create synergy among affiliates and build dynamic capabilities on a group level. If conflicts of interest arise between affiliates, the Corporate Strategy Office intervenes as the mediator. Professional managers of affiliates act autonomously to realize the vision presented by the owner-manager.

In the early days of his tenure, Chairman Lee explained that he would manage the group differently from the way his father had managed it.

> The former chairman tightly held 80 percent of the managerial rights and delegated 10 percent each to the secretariat and the professional managers of affiliates. From now on, I will change this so that the chairman and the secretariat exercise 60 percent, and the professional managers exercise 40 percent.

Figure 3.2   *Changes in Samsung's Leadership and Governance Structure*

	Before New Management		After New Management
Governance Structure	Ownership Management	Corporate Strategy Office's Coordination Function Triangular Governance Structure	Ownership + Professional Management
Owner-Manager	Patriarchal Leader	Far-Reaching Vision Group Management Guidelines	Vision-Presenting Leader
Professional Manager	Manager, Executor	Development of Professional Managers Hefty Monetary Incentives	Strategist

In defining his role, Chairman Lee has said, "I see my role as setting a broad strategic direction for the future, while delegating ordinary decision making to managers at each affiliate who have professional capabilities. I think the role of the chairman is to support them in managing according to their conviction on the basis of their responsibility and authority."

The role of Samsung's professional managers also changed extensively. During Lee Byung-Chull's tenure, managers saw their role as limited to being executors of the founder's orders and administrators who had been given the task of running affiliates with a minimum of problems. After Chairman Lee took over, Samsung's CEOs were given the autonomy to map out their own strategies after the chairman set Samsung's overarching vision.

Figure 3.3 illustrates Samsung's governance triangle, which plays a key role in Samsung's governance. The three points are Chairman Lee, the Corporate Strategy Office, and the professional managers of affiliated companies. Chairman Lee presents a far-reaching vision and strategic direction, while

Figure 3.3   *Samsung's Triangular Governance Structure*

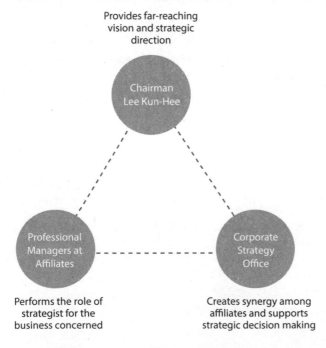

the Corporate Strategy Office supports the management's strategic decisions to ensure optimization on a group level and promote internal co-opetition among affiliates to create group-level synergy. The professional managers of affiliated companies lead their respective businesses on the basis of autonomy.

Ownership Structure

As of December 2013, Samsung Group had 75 domestic affiliates. Each Samsung affiliate is a legally independent unit, with 17 of them being publicly traded and the remainder unlisted. Samsung Group's legal structure differs significantly from that of U.S. conglomerates, which are made up of either legally subordinate and dependent business divisions or legally independent units whose equity is nonetheless wholly owned by a holding company. A significant amount of the equity of listed affiliates of Samsung is held by outside shareholders, in addition to that held by the Lee family or other affiliates, and the external shareholders of each affiliate vary. Each affiliate has its own board and outside directors, as stipulated under Korean law.

Samsung's ownership structure is characterized by the owner family's possession of core affiliates, core affiliates' equity investments in other affiliates, and complex cross-equity investments among affiliates. For example, as of December 31, 2013, Chairman Lee's family had a 46.04 percent stake in nonlisted Samsung Everland. Everland holds 19.34 percent of Samsung Life Insurance's shares, and Samsung Life Insurance holds 7.53 percent of Samsung Electronics. Samsung Electronics has positions in 24 affiliates, including a 20.4 percent stake in Samsung SDI, a 23.7 percent stake in Samsung Electro Mechanics, and a 17.6 percent stake in Samsung Heavy Industries. Samsung Life Insurance has stakes in 18 affiliates, while Samsung SDS has stakes in 11 affiliates. The older affiliates have stakes in several other affiliates. Chairman Lee's family holds a 20.76 percent stake in Samsung Life Insurance and a 4.69 percent stake in Samsung Electronics without having any stake in a substantial number of other affiliates.

For Samsung Electronics, the flagship of the group, Chairman Lee's family held a 4.69 percent stake as of late 2013, while Samsung Life Insurance,

Samsung C&T, and Samsung Fire & Marine Insurance had 7.5 percent, 4.1 percent, and 1.3 percent, respectively. The combined share of the Lee family and Samsung affiliates stood at 17.7 percent, while foreign shareholders held about 50 percent.

Since the share of equity held by the Lee family and affiliated companies is low, it is important that Samsung retain shareholders' confidence. In other words, the stock market acts as a protection against agency problems for the owner-manager. In addition, government bodies like the Fair Trade Commission and the Financial Supervisory Service and civil organizations like the People's Solidarity for Participatory Democracy and the Citizens' Coalition for Economic Justice monitor Samsung closely, making it difficult for the owner to act against the interests of minority shareholders.

Corporate Strategy Office

The organization that plays the largest role in Samsung's overall governance is the Corporate Strategy Office. It is often referred to as the group's "control tower."

The Corporate Strategy Office is a unique organization that pursues an optimum balance among the interests of shareholders, the owner-manager, and the professional managers. From the shareholders' perspective, the Corporate Strategy Office acts as a supervisor for the professional managers who are in charge of Samsung's various affiliates. From the owner-manager's perspective, the Corporate Strategy Office acts to maximize Samsung Group's overall profits. From the professional managers' perspective, the Corporate Strategy Office helps each affiliate maximize its profits and strengthen its competitiveness.

As Samsung's main body for the pursuit of optimization on the group level, the Corporate Strategy Office acts to promote co-opetition among affiliates to build synergy among them. To this end, the Corporate Strategy Office provides objective analysis and advice on the strategies of each affiliate, while supporting them in their efforts to improve their corporate value. It also serves as the group's knowledge hub to explore and spread best practices within the group, and promotes improvement in management efficiency. Its knowledge hub functions include personnel guidelines, public relations, management consulting, and legal services.

Leadership by Professional Managers

Considering the increased responsibilities and autonomy given to Samsung's executives since Chairman Lee took the reins, the type of managers required differs markedly from those sought when his father was leading the group. As a result, Samsung has had to readjust its human resource system.

Recruiting and Nurturing

Most of Samsung's CEOs are promoted from within. Samsung differs from other Korean firms in its emphasis on its executives' job accomplishments, rather than their prestigious academic credentials. As a result, the percentage of top university graduates among Samsung CEOs is lower than that at other large Korean conglomerates, and little emphasis is placed on prestigious degrees. Samsung's more limited direct managerial role for the family and founder also provides a greater opportunity for employees to rise to the highest levels. Competition for internal promotion is intense.

Since the New Management initiative, Samsung has also pursued executive talent from outside. Candidates with experience at prominent foreign companies are especially well regarded. They are recruited and mentored as future CEO candidates who can globalize the group's management system and lead change in the organization. For example, Choi Chi-Hun, CEO of Samsung C&T Corporation, spent 19 years working at GE before he was recruited by Samsung in 2007. After he joined Samsung, he went through an initiation process for outsiders who enter at senior levels, spending seven months as an advisor to Yun Jong-Yong, the former CEO of Samsung Electronics.

Opportunity and Incentives

Even if capable people are appointed as managers, they cannot contribute to corporate performance if they are not given the opportunity to exercise their capabilities, or if they lack the motivation to improve their performance.

Chairman Lee asked the managers of Samsung's affiliates "to work autonomously and avoid unnecessary reporting." Even when Samsung was undergoing drastic restructuring during the Asian currency crisis, he delegated most of the work to the professional managers, based on his belief that it would enable them to manage their companies better over the long-term. This spurred Samsung's managers to consider what would happen five or ten years later, rather than clinging to short-term results.

Control of the Agency Problem

Samsung has reduced agency problems for its managers. Under the professional management system in the United States, the CEO can also serve as chairman of the board and influence the selection of board members. This makes it difficult to prevent CEOs from pursuing their own interests instead of the company's. Issues of moral hazard have thus become a major issue for U.S. firms run by professional managers.

At Samsung, the Management Consulting Team at the Corporate Strategy Office and the HR teams at each affiliated company continuously assess the management capabilities and business ethics of Samsung's professional managers. Managers at Samsung thus have less leeway to make unreasonable and arbitrary decisions.

THE EVOLUTION OF SAMSUNG'S MANAGEMENT SYSTEM

4

This chapter looks at the components of Samsung's management system, including strategy, human resource management, management control, and culture and values, and discusses the internal fit between them.

Strategy: Shift from Quantity to Quality

The future belongs to those who explore and challenge earlier than others. In an environment that never stops changing, we need the insight to grasp opportunity fast, and the wisdom to turn a crisis into an opportunity. With strategic thinking and a preemptive and challenging mind, we can strengthen competitiveness by using our limited resources more efficiently.

—*Chairman Lee Kun-Hee*

The New Management initiative led to drastic changes in Samsung's strategy (see Figure 4.1). First, Samsung stopped being a "fast follower" and started to become a market leader by being the first to develop products and by developing products that were better than its rivals'. Second, Samsung shifted from pursuing unrelated diversification to upgrading its portfolio of existing businesses. The company thus pursued restructuring through a select-and-focus strategy and strengthened the core competencies of its organization through internal co-opetition.

To implement these new strategies effectively, Samsung decided that its competitive advantage going forward should be quality. Samsung's renewal

Figure 4.1   *Changes in Samsung's Strategy*

	Before New Management		After New Management
Strategic Orientation	Quantity-Focused	Customer-Oriented, Value Innovation, Strengthening of Soft Competitiveness	Quality-Focused
Competitive Strategy	Fast Follower	Gap Widening, Innovative Products/ Technologies, Digital Convergence	Market Leader
Corporate Strategy	Flying Geese Strategy	Select-and-Focus, Vertical Integration, Convergence	Upgrading of Business Portfolios

was embodied in its New Management vision of "becoming a world-class company through increased quality."

Quality-Focused Strategy

The core concept of Samsung's quality-focused management can be summarized as "improve the quality of people to improve the quality of management to improve the quality of products and services." "Quality of people" and "quality of management" are closely related to the other factors of Samsung's management system explained later in this chapter, while "quality of products and services" is directly related to Samsung's strategic orientation.

Since the introduction of the New Management initiative, Samsung has pursued its quality-focused strategy by aiming to provide the "world's best products" that can "stand with any others in the world," as well as "products and services with the world's best quality."

In its drive to the top, Samsung pushed each affiliate and division to produce at least one market-leading product. Samsung also pushed for increased soft capabilities based on intangible assets (in technology, design, and branding), customer-focused "market-driven change," and value innovation that creates new markets by developing new products that move beyond existing products and services.

In-house manufacturing has been central to Samsung's competitiveness, and it has continued to be so as Samsung pursues improved product quality. This contrasts with global giants like Apple that regard manufacturing as a low-value-added function that should be outsourced. Although Samsung also uses outsourcing, it still produces most products through its own vertically integrated production lines and continues to make substantial capital expenditures for factories and other manufacturing facilities.

Samsung's decades of manufacturing experience have resulted in a wealth of expertise in line sharing, flexible mass production, and "Lego-style" product development and production. With these methods, Samsung enhanced its manufacturing efficiency, improved its cost advantage, strengthened its mass customization capabilities, and enhanced its capabilities in developing leading innovative products and technologies, all of which became the basis for the competitive advantage that Samsung has today.

Such advantages enabled Samsung Electronics to produce a wider variety of smartphones, including the Galaxy S and Galaxy Note, within a short period of time, and then market them at attractive prices. Consequently, Samsung rapidly caught up with Apple, which relies on original equipment manufacturer (OEM) suppliers like Foxconn.

In the twenty-first century, the era of instant information sharing and digitization, the sources of competitiveness are very different from those of the industrial era in the twentieth century. In smartphones, for instance, the competitive advantage has moved from hardware and telecommunication functions to software and content. Accordingly, even in manufacturing, intangible factors like design have become more important. In this context, Chairman Lee has greatly stressed "soft power" and intangible competitiveness. From the moment when he declared the New Management initiative, Lee emphasized that "competitiveness in the twenty-first century stems from soft areas like R&D and design." Since 2006, Chairman Lee has identified "creative management" as a new management theme for Samsung, asking his employees to maximize the intangible capabilities required in the twenty-first century.

Market Leader Strategy

At the beginning of the twenty-first century, Samsung phased out its fast-follower strategy of imitating leading companies. This strategy had made Samsung a global player in TVs, semiconductors, thin-film-transistor liquid-crystal displays (TFT-LCDs), and mobile phones. In the new millennium, however, Samsung committed itself to being a market leader for the following two reasons.

First, a global knowledge-based economy had emerged. This meant that there was an increasingly "winner-takes-all" economy, where the companies that produce innovative products and set industry standards are the ones that sustain high profits over the long term. Second, although Samsung had initially succeeded in its fast-follower strategy, its revenue base was not sturdy and did not provide stable cash flow.

To become a market leader, Samsung deployed two overarching strategies. First, it worked to widen the gap with its rivals through the development of advanced technology and preemptive investment in the manufacturing facilities. If followers started to produce similar products, Samsung could lower its prices to depress their profits. Samsung employed this strategy mainly in areas requiring massive facility investments. It sought to maintain its competitive advantage by making it less feasible for competitors to match the size of its capital expenditures.

Samsung learned this strategy in its initial competition with Japanese firms in memory chips and TFT-LCDs, with Samsung Electronics applying this strategy to great effect. The global financial crisis in 2008 gave the company an opportunity to further widen the gap, as Samsung Electronics accelerated its internal efficiency and speed, while streamlining its organizations into efficient, decentralized ones.

The second strategy, which has become increasingly important, was to lead the market by releasing innovative new products first. This will be expanded upon in Chapter 7. Suffice it to say that Chairman Lee continuously stressed preparation for five to ten years into the future, highlighting the importance of technological leadership through state-of-the-art technologies and core talent. In 2000, Chairman Lee declared that the company would focus on "digital management," based on the belief that Samsung could achieve digital superiority and thus jump ahead of its Japanese rivals, who had led during the analog electronics era.

As part of this process, Chairman Lee enacted policies that required one innovative product from each company and each division. The goal was to motivate each affiliate or division to develop the world's first products in its main business lines. As a result, Samsung unveiled state-of-the-art fusion memory chips, phase-change random access memories (PRAMs), LED TVs, and organic light-emitting diode (OLED) panels, while attaining leadership in setting standards in the Moving Picture Experts Group (MPEG), wireless broadband (WiBro), International Mobile Telecommunications (IMT-2000), and high-efficiency video coding (HEVC).

Samsung also pursued a digital convergence strategy among its business divisions (see Figure 4.2). *Digital convergence* refers to the integration and processing of voice, text, and images—the three elements of information transmission. Samsung was able to fully leverage its unique suite of products, which consisted of memory chips, system large-scale integration (LSI), display panels, mobile phones, computers, and home electronics, to create new converged products and businesses that set it apart from its more specialized competitors. Since it achieved success with its first convergence product, the groundbreaking Samsung DVD Combo (a combination of a DVD player and a VCR), Samsung Electronics has continued to explore the possibilities of other hybrid products. Samsung's most recent convergence product is the Galaxy Camera, released in 2012, which added telecommunications functions to cameras.

To make its products into de facto industry standards, Samsung has built broad strategic alliances and friendly cooperative relations with other businesses and organizations, including suppliers of core components, competitors, and large-scale customers. A leading example of such cooperative

Figure 4.2   *Development of Digital Convergence*

Digitization	Device Convergence	Network Convergence	Ubiquitous
1960–1990s 1960s: Computers 1970s: Telecom 1980s: Audio 1990s: Video	Early 2000s Convergence Networking	Late 2000s Telecom + Broadcasting Service Convergence	2010s The Internet of Things and Networking

efforts is the Mobile Solution Forum, led by Samsung Electronics' semi-conductor division, and the Tizen Consortium for the development of its next-generation smartphone operating system.

Upgrading of Business Portfolios

CEOs should pay more attention to strategic issues like what business the group should pursue in the future. Efforts must be made to leverage the power of the entire group and to strengthen and foster businesses as future growth engines. We must continue to improve the competitiveness of our existing business with high growth potential, and foster new tech-intensive, future-oriented business by aggressively transferring or eliminating low-value-added areas.

—Chairman Lee Kun-Hee

Under the New Management initiative, Samsung shifted its focus from indiscriminate diversification to an emphasis on implementing a select-and-focus strategy and strengthening its core competencies through portfolio restructuring and internal competition for acquiring group-level resources. Previously, Samsung had followed the "flying geese strategy," in which the success of an affiliate would spill over to other affiliates, with the newly successful affiliates, in turn, guiding others. The sequence of Samsung's flagship companies thus proceeded from sugar manufacturing to general trading, and then on to home electronics and semiconductors. Each of these flagship companies grew on the coattails of its predecessors before assembling its own capabilities, capital, talent, and major resources. Previously successful business lines provided a stable stream of financial resources, allowing new affiliates to overcome their initial difficulties and secure the ability to survive on their own. The semiconductor business that Samsung began in the 1980s exemplifies this process.

Under the New Management initiative, Samsung departed from the flying geese strategy by spinning off or consolidating its noncore businesses. Further restructuring occurred during the 1997 Asian currency crisis with the removal of nonviable affiliates and divisions like Samsung Motor, while sparing no effort in supporting its high-performing core business lines. Samsung rigorously applied a "self-supporting, self-viable" criterion to its affiliates, meaning that any business that incurred losses for three straight years (excluding new businesses) was liquidated. Samsung continues to assess the viability of its businesses every year and constantly engages in restructuring.

Thanks to its continuous restructuring, Samsung Electronics has evolved from a department store–like supplier of numerous electronics products into a confederation of specialized companies, with high competitiveness in core segments like memory chips, mobile phones, LCDs, and digital media.

Samsung Electronics has continued to upgrade its portfolio on the division level as well. The semiconductor division, for example, has shifted from its memory chip–centered focus and now successfully competes in system semiconductors, including mobile application processors (APs). Samsung's semiconductor division also upgraded its memory chip business through the development of fusion memory solutions. The company's TV division was far ahead of Sony's in scrapping cathode-ray tube (CRT) TV business, which then accounted for 27 percent of its sales, to focus on digital flat-panel TVs.

Such efforts were not limited to Samsung Electronics, but took place at other affiliates as well. Samsung SDI transformed itself from a manufacturer of CRTs for analog video devices into a digital imaging parts maker engaged in the development and manufacturing of rechargeable batteries and plasma-display-panels (PDPs). Samsung Heavy Industries stopped taking low-value-added orders for bulk carriers and oil tankers and shifted toward high-tech plants and high-value-added drillships; liquefied natural gas floating production, storage, and offloading (LNG-FPSO) vessels; and icebreaking tankers. Samsung Fine Chemicals evolved from a fertilizer producer to a high-value-added fine chemical maker.

Vertical integration has likewise become a major competitive advantage under the New Management initiative. For example, the core parts of the Galaxy S5 smartphone, including memory chips, displays, and camera modules, are all made within Samsung Group. Vertical integration helps Samsung strengthen the competitiveness of its business ecosystem. Although the materials for active-matrix organic light-emitting diode (AMOLED) display screens for mobile phones are procured from outside companies, for example, Samsung SDI is also developing, producing, and supplying the same materials. In this way, not only can Samsung Electronics accelerate the development of new products, but it can reinforce the competitiveness of its overall ecosystem by transferring operational capabilities developed through internal production to subcontractors.

Samsung's bold investment decisions on future businesses seek out areas with growth and profit potential. Samsung has four classifications for its businesses. The first group is "seed businesses"; these are businesses that are expected to bear fruit within five or ten years and require immediate investment in technology, capital, and personnel. The second group consists of "seedling businesses," which can become flagship companies. They require efforts to preempt the market by promptly securing technologies and developing competitive products. The third group is "fruit trees," current growth drivers in an area where competitiveness needs to be upgraded. The fourth group is "old trees," which need to be resolutely removed. Samsung's future depends on the seed and seedling groups, and it is these areas that receive the largest investments.

When selecting new business areas, Samsung sticks to the select-and-focus principle. Assessments are based on the chances that Samsung can secure core competencies and achieve world-class competitiveness. After the businesses are selected, Samsung concentrates its resources on them. In 2010, for instance, Samsung identified five businesses that it will intensively foster at a group level: light-emitting diodes(LEDs), rechargeable batteries for automobiles, solar cells, medical equipment, and biosimilars. About 23 trillion won (about US$21 billion) will be spent in these areas before 2020.

Human Resource Management: Pursuit of High-Quality Employees

"People first" has been one of Samsung's three bedrock philosophies since its foundation. Although the details of Samsung's human resource policies have changed over time, the high priority that the company places on personnel has remained the same. This section explains the changes in Samsung's HR policies under Chairman Lee.

Changes in the Structure of Samsung's Workforce

Since the accession of Chairman Lee, Samsung's workforce has changed substantially. The percentage of Samsung Electronics' employees that is engaged in low-value-added work has dropped, while the percentage of highly educated personnel and experts has increased. The manufacturing workforce declined from 35 percent of the total workforce in 1988 to 21 percent in 2013, while the R&D workforce of Samsung Electronics soared more than 10 times, growing from 6,000 to 80,000 as of September 2013.

The share of experts in R&D, marketing, software, and design as a percentage of total Samsung employees has jumped 5-fold, while the number of professional executives has ballooned 15-fold. Although academic background is far from the only factor in Samsung's hiring, university graduates have become the majority. In particular, the number of employees with a master's degree has increased more than 14 times, while the number of employees with a PhD has multiplied dramatically, from 120 in 1987, when Chairman Lee was inaugurated, to 7,600 as of 2013, a 63-fold increase. The higher quality of employees has naturally led to a significant rise in productivity. Sales per person have increased 9-fold, while the number of employees working in Korea has doubled, from 110,000 in 1987 to 225,000 as of 2013.

Samsung's hiring of experienced employees from external labor markets has also increased, especially for highly specialized talent. Korean employees with extensive foreign experience and knowledge have also increased in number, including those who were educated abroad before joining Samsung, those who earned a foreign MBA as part of Samsung's employee training, and those who were sent overseas to become regional specialists. In addition, local employees hired by Samsung's overseas research institutes and design centers, foreign experts working in Korea, and foreign experts trained through local management nurturing programs have all also increased significantly.

Emphasis on Core Talent

Core talent refers to people who can move their industry to the global top three or top five. Recruiting only one person with such S-level talent is laudable enough. They are hard to attract, so even CEOs fail to recruit them despite asking them in person. It takes two to three years just to find S-level talent and another one to two years to bring them in. They may or may not come to Samsung even if a CEO visits them ten times and makes assurances about their families' convenience. We need to revamp our methods of securing talent, and CEOs should focus on this matter for more than half of their working hours. Our survival depends on this and if we fail, we cannot be a world-class company.

—Chairman Lee Kun-Hee

Before the New Management initiative, Samsung's approach to HR focused on motivating all of its employees (see Figure 4.3). Samsung focused on hiring people with standardized skills, inculcating loyalty by providing in-house job training and education, and then reaping the benefits of their hard work. However, as it entered the semiconductor business in 1983, Samsung increasingly focused on recruiting Korean engineers and managers from Intel, IBM,

Figure 4.3   *Changes in Samsung's Human Resource Management*

	Before New Management		After New Management
Core Human Resources	Standardized Human Resources	CEO's Involvement in Core Talent Recruiting Flexible Compensation System Customized Support for Core Talent	Core Talent
Employment Methods	Securing People Within the Company	Year-Round Recruitment Favorable Treatment of Experienced Outside Talent	Combined with Outside Talent
Characteristics of Human Resources	Domestic Human Resources	Regional Specialists Expanded Recruitment of Global Talent Development of Local Managers	Combined with Global Talent
Compensation and Promotion	Seniority-Based System	Fast-Track Promotion Incentive for Performance	Performance-Based System

and Bell Labs, even offering these employees higher salaries than its CEOs. When this strategy proved successful, Lee Kun-Hee ordered his other business units to follow suit and hire highly talented and experienced personnel. Securing a steady stream of gifted people thus became more and more crucial in Samsung's pursuit of the status of number one in the world.

Samsung classifies core talent into S, A, and H levels. S-level employees are those who can take on responsibility for a business division, who can lead industry standards, and who can handle the presidency of an affiliate. A-level employees are those who have at least five years' work experience in a rival company, either domestically or overseas, and whose career or performance has been recognized in the market. H-level employees lack experience and have not displayed proven abilities yet. However, they have high growth potential for senior and mid-level management positions. Chairman Lee's focus on developing, recruiting, and maintaining core talent has made these tasks the main priorities of Samsung's CEOs and HR executives. Since 2002, the CEOs of affiliates that have attracted core talent are given higher evaluation scores, and each affiliate must regularly report its performance in recruiting and retaining core talent.

Samsung provides customized support for its core talent. It has made compensation more flexible to ensure that such talent will not be put off by rigid compensation formulas, while providing generous incentives to encourage top performance and giving the best performers rapid promotions. Samsung also has various support policies, including transferring the new specialist's contact person at Samsung to the same division to ease the transition for the newcomer. Samsung can go as far as creating wholly new organizations and job titles for genius-level talent.

Expanded Recruitment from Outside

After the introduction of its open competitive recruitment system in 1957, Samsung focused on nurturing employees internally. The company hired a large number of new high school and university graduates every year after graduation, and new recruits competed against one another to climb the corporate ladder. Most of the CEOs of affiliates entered Samsung through the open system.

As mentioned earlier, Samsung's HR policy changed in the 1980s when the company entered the semiconductor industry. In an industry with high technological uncertainty and a rapid pace of change, Samsung had to look for people who had skills and knowledge that the existing employees did not have. The company realized that bringing in outside talent was critical to executing its market leader strategy. Most of the outside talent was hired for marketing, design, management, and R&D. As a point of comparison, Samsung Electronics hired 661 people in 1993; all of them were new graduates of high schools or universities. By 2012, 30 percent of the company's new hires had experience working at other companies.

Globalization of the Workforce

Before Chairman Lee's tenure, Samsung employed few Korean employees who had extensive knowledge of foreign markets, and even fewer foreign experts. This had to change if Samsung was to become a world-class company and a technology leader. A two-track approach was adopted: producing regional specialists from the Korean labor pool and hiring more foreign talent.

Regional Specialists

Regional specialists are the core of Samsung's globalization efforts. These are people who have been trained with an international perspective and who understand the situation in overseas markets. More than 5,000 regional specialists were trained between 1991 and 2013. Samsung employees with at least three years' experience working at the company (up to the manager level) can be assigned to various countries to train freely for one year. Candidates for these positions are chosen based on their language ability, their flexibility, and their acceptance of cultural diversity. Samsung bears the entire cost of their training, including paying their salary, their education costs, and their living expenses.

The costs of training a single regional specialist vary by country and time, but in most cases they exceed 100 million won (almost US$100,000). When the program was first introduced, executives initially opposed it, fearing the loss of their most capable workers and objecting to the high costs. Chairman Lee, however, insisted on the program, and it has continued to this day.

Regional specialists have gone on to lead Samsung's global expansion. At Samsung Electronics, about 60 percent of those trained as regional specialists work in foreign countries or are engaged in duties related to foreign business. While the overseas employees at Samsung's rivals mostly rely on English because of their lack of fluency in the local language, their counterparts at Samsung are fluent in local languages and understand the local situation. This allows them to harness the human networks they built during their regional specialist training. Samsung's regional specialists thus serve as human infrastructure that distributes Samsung's products across the world.

Samsung Electronics selects about 150 regional specialists each year. After their destination countries are determined, they train for 12 weeks at the Samsung Human Resources Development Center. Most of the training involves the language and culture of their destination country. After training, they are sent to their assigned country; their family members are not permitted to accompany them, in order to encourage them to absorb the language and culture of their destination country more rapidly. Upon arrival, trainees do not perform regular duties, but instead create their own self-development programs to learn the local language and culture, along with the characteristics and business practices of their local market. Normally, they spend the first six months traveling around their host country to meet residents and further study the language and culture. The next six months are devoted to a work-related project of their choosing. Samsung provides each trainee with a laptop and a digital camera, and has them upload useful information and knowledge about their host country to Samsung's intranet knowledge management portal, "Samsung Single."

Regional specialists have collected massive amounts of data on every region of the world and these have been available on Samsung's internal website since 2000. This has allowed all employees to tap into information on foreign markets and enhance the accuracy and speed of their work.

Regional specialists have contributed significantly to changing Samsung's way of working. Graduates of the program have gone on to work at Samsung's headquarters, business divisions, and overseas offices, and have found new ways of working by combining Samsung's conventional practices with local methods or adjusting conventional practices to suit local situations. By doing so, Samsung tests alternative management practices around the world and seeks out the best ones.

U.S. and Japanese managers who have visited Samsung have noted the impact of Samsung's regional specialists and their role as a source of Samsung Electronics' competitiveness. However, the system's high short-term costs and the long period of time needed to bring about results appear to have dissuaded other companies from adopting similar practices. Professional managers, who may have a relatively short tenure, may not see the system bear any fruit before they leave. Accordingly, the regional specialist system is a prime example of how long-term investment by the owner-manager ultimately becomes a source of lasting competitiveness.

Foreign Experts

Beginning 30 years ago when Samsung first employed a Japanese advisor, Samsung's employment of foreign experts has helped it secure technologies rapidly and allowed it to surpass its competitors.

The present cornerstone of Samsung's foreign talent deployment is the Global Strategy Group (GSG), established in 1997. This organization recruits foreigners who have either graduated from one of the world's leading business schools or earned a PhD. The main duties of this group are to perform research on overseas markets and to provide advice on entry into those markets. Occasionally, they will participate in benchmarking of overseas case studies. These foreign talents work at the GSG for two years and then move to business divisions.

Samsung had hired non-Koreans before the GSG was established, but Korean managers often had difficulty in harnessing their abilities because of the language barrier, while non-Korean employees often had difficulty relating to their Korean colleagues. A great deal of foreign talent left, prompting Chairman Lee to create an internal organization for foreigners only. The organization was originally named the Corporate Strategy Group, but to avoid confusion with Samsung's headquarters organization (the Corporate Strategy Office), it was renamed the Global Strategy Group in 2011.

In its early stages, executives strongly recommended abolishing the program, citing its high turnover rate and costs and its meager results. However, as with the regional specialist program, Chairman Lee maintained his convictions, saying that if the turnover rate was high, the executives should simply hire more people. Besides supplying an international perspective, the group has helped enhance Samsung's global branding. In 1997, few students paid attention when Samsung recruiters visited top American business schools. Today, recruiters talk to an auditorium full of potential job applicants.

Flagship Samsung Electronics has especially relied on the GSG, and has asked that group members be sent over after only one year, rather than two. As more employees arrive from the GSG to work at Samsung Electronics, Korean employees also benefit from working with them and learning foreign work styles and ways of thinking, as well as Western management styles.

In addition, Samsung has greatly increased the number of foreign employees working in Korea, with most of them working in the R&D and engineering divisions. Samsung Electronics employs about 1,200 foreign employees from 55 countries. In its early stages, Samsung Electronics employed a large number of Japanese engineers, and they still accounted for a large share of Samsung's foreign employees in 2013. However, many researchers from Russia, India, and China, which have an abundance of educated workers, but where salaries are low, are also recruited and placed in R&D in Korea. To attract talented people in those countries, Samsung selects the top 5 percent of the students at leading engineering schools in these countries and pays their tuition unconditionally.

Since some employees may want to stay in their home country, Samsung has also set up overseas R&D and design centers to tap these people's talent and local knowledge. As of 2013, Samsung Electronics alone employs more than 20,000 researchers at 27 institutes in 12 countries, including Japan, the United Kingdom, India, Russia, and the United States. Foreign experts who do move to Korea are given special support to help them adapt. For example, Samsung's Global Help Desk operates on a 24-hour basis, and Samsung's cafeterias provide special meals for foreign workers, including vegetarian and halal meals, for employees with dietary restrictions.

Performance-Based Compensation and Promotion

Under the New Management initiative, Samsung revamped its evaluation and compensation system to boost morale and secure talent. To this end, Samsung provides short-term incentives through performance-focused evaluations, bonuses, and fast-track promotions. Samsung also prepared a foundation for recruiting core talent by providing special compensation packages. To address the disadvantages of individual-level performance-based compensation, Samsung introduced collective productivity incentives and profit sharing, which encouraged all employees to cooperate to maximize results. The intention behind these changes was to maximize cooperation among affiliates, divisions, and employees while simultaneously encouraging them to compete to catch up with the industry incumbents.

Performance-Based Policy

Before the New Management initiative, highly profitable affiliates at Samsung were entitled to higher year-end bonuses, but aside from that, there was no official compensation system that was linked to the performance evaluations of affiliates or divisions. After the New Management initiative, however, Samsung changed its compensation system to stimulate both competition and cooperation. Today, performance evaluation is done at all levels—affiliates, divisions, teams, and individuals. Both absolute evaluation, which looks at the achievement of goals, and relative evaluation, which compares employees and divisions with one another, are used. Evaluations have a significant impact on determining promotion, employee status, salaries, and bonuses, and they stimulate both strong competition and cooperation within the company.

Compensation Policy

Samsung has strict performance-based reward policies, leading to vast differences in compensation depending on evaluation results. The distinguishing characteristics of Samsung's reward system are its hefty compensation, exceptional rewards for performance and capabilities, and collective incentive.

Hefty Compensation   Samsung is well known for being the highest-paying Korean firm in its respective industries. The goal of this wage policy is to attract, retain, and motivate the best people. Not surprisingly, Samsung is often the first choice of fresh university graduates.

The salaries of Samsung's executives are also much higher than those of executives at other large Korean firms because of performance-based compensation in addition to a high base salary. Lower-level employees can benefit from Samsung's profit-sharing system, which provides incentives amounting to up to 50 percent of their annual salaries, as well as smaller productivity incentives.

Performance- and Competency-Based Incentives   Samsung provides exceptional bonuses based on competency and performance. Special incentives are provided to core talent in order to recruit, retain, and motivate Samsung's most important managers and workers. These incentives are provided to attract employees who must be recruited if the company is to successfully pursue a particular business, or to retain employees whose resignation would cause significant difficulties for the company. They are provided to those employees who are recognized as core employees when they are hired, and to employees who have achieved top evaluation results for several years in a row. Naturally, these incentives are coveted, and employees work hard to either maintain their status as core talent or to attain that status.

In 1998, Samsung introduced an annual salary system across the board, under which salaries for the next year are determined based on a yearly individual competency and performance evaluation. As a result, differences among employees in annual salary alone can be as much as 50 percent, even if the employees are of the same rank. Thanks to the annual salary and core talent incentives, compensation packages are no longer a barrier to attracting talent.

Collective Incentives   Samsung also provides two kinds of rewards based on collective performance: productivity incentives (PI) and profit-sharing (PS) bonuses. A PI is a collective incentive that is based on an evaluation of affiliates, divisions, and teams. The maximum amount an employee may receive annually under PI is 300 percent of his or her monthly base pay. Evaluation criteria for an affiliate include economic value added (EVA) to the company, the affiliate's stock price to earnings ratio, and success in recruiting and retaining core talent. For a division, financial evaluations, including EVA and asset turnover, account for 60 to 70 percent of the score, with the remainder being based on the success of the division's core strategies. For smaller departments and teams, evaluation criteria vary depending on the duties of the unit being evaluated. Evaluations are performed every six months and are based on absolute performance scales that compare actual performance with goals.

PS was introduced in 2000. The basis for it was the EVA created by affiliates. However, for Samsung Electronics, PS is provided to employees based on the EVA created by their business division. About 20 percent of the EVA created by an affiliate or division funds the PS payment, which can be a maximum of 50 percent of an individual's annual base salary

Samsung benchmarked Hewlett-Packard (HP) when it introduced this system. However, compared to HP, which offers a maximum of 20 percent of an employee's annual salary, Samsung awards a much higher percentage of 50 percent. In the case of Samsung Electronics, PS was based entirely on the performance of particular divisions at first. This was later revised when complaints arose at divisions with lower performance, and by 2006 the system was changed to 11 percent of annual salary for all employees of Samsung Electronics; this was increased to 20 percent in 2009.

Promotion Policy

The climb to executive status at Samsung requires a lengthy verification process. A slew of factors are involved, including work performance, work ethic, management skills, and relationships with others. Even critical issues in potential executives' private lives are investigated.

Strong performance-based incentives can unintentionally spur collective selfishness within individual affiliates, divisions, and teams. To discourage this, and to promote interaffiliate and interdivisional cooperation, Samsung uses qualitative factors in its evaluations of the CEOs and executives of affiliates. Any conduct that is intended to produce gain for a particular affiliate or division at the expense of the company as a whole or of Samsung Group is treated negatively in the evaluation.

Under the New Management initiative, Samsung expanded its fast-track promotion policy, which puts exceptional employees on a fast track to higher ranks by skipping intermediate ranks. Under this system, for example, a senior manager whose performance is exceptional can be promoted to vice-president, reducing time between promotions and ensuring that Samsung can harness his or her abilities to the utmost. The time required to reach higher ranks has also continuously shrunk. In the past, for example, employees had to work at least three years in a position and receive at least three sequential A-grade performance ratings to be entitled to a promotion, but this criterion has been abolished. Fast-track promotions are now a stable part of Samsung's HR system.

At present, Samsung uses an entirely performance-based promotion policy. For an employee to be promoted, both the individual's and the department's performance have to be good, and those who work at high-performing affiliates and divisions are given more opportunities for promotion. Executive managers of affiliates or divisions with lackluster performance are often replaced by better performers from high-performing units. Moral evaluations are also very important. Employees who are found to have engaged in questionable conduct or whose behavior is not in accord with Samsung's vision and core values are not considered for promotion, regardless of their performance.

Finally, Samsung scrupulously avoids awarding promotion based on arbitrary factors that are unrelated to performance, competency, and ethics. Such factors include regional, school, or blood ties; these factors are always excluded from consideration, as they undermine morale and the competitiveness of the whole company.

Management Control: Micro and Macro Tracks

This section discusses Samsung's core management processes, including the simultaneous pursuit of micromanagement and macromanagement, and management by numbers. It also covers the role of Samsung's information technology (IT) infrastructure in supporting Samsung's management processes.

Micro- and Macromanagement

Before the New Management initiative, Samsung's approach to management focused on meticulous attention to minor details and incremental improvements in operational efficiency. However, applying this approach uniformly for everyone from CEOs to entry-level employees can result in the company's losing business opportunities and a loss of autonomy, creativity, and a spirit of challenge for employees. Thus, under the New Management initiative, Chairman Lee shifted Samsung's focus from micromanagement to macromanagement, and from improving operational efficiency to fulfilling ambitious strategies (see Figure 4.4).

Nevertheless, the introduction of the New Management initiative did not mean that Samsung abandoned its attention to detail. On the contrary, meticulous attention to detail became a crucial part of Samsung's drive to improve quality in its products and services. The New Management initiative introduced a division of labor between executives, who focused on strategy and macromanagement, and middle managers and on-site workers, who

Figure 4.4　*Changes in Samsung's Management Control*

	Before New Management		After New Management
Management Control Style	Micromanagement	Executives: Macromanagement Middle Managers: Micromanagement	Combined with Macromanagement
Core Process	Manufacturing Efficiency–Centered	Operations of Global Operations Center for Customers	Customer-Centered
Information System	Unintegrated Information System	Global ERP and Global SCM	Globally Integrated Information System

focused on micromanagement. Samsung thus succeeded in combining the meticulous attention to detail of Japanese management with the strategic thinking of U.S. management.

Management by Numbers

Professional managers at Samsung have said that Chairman Lee seemingly relies on intuition in making business decisions, but in reality his decisions are based on detailed numbers and data. Likewise, Samsung's founding principle of "pursuit of rationality" has always required that decisions be based on quantifiable data, rather than intuition or vague goals. Decisions at Samsung are made through rigorous discussions between the Corporate Strategy Office and the affiliates, based on detailed numbers and with the alternatives fully considered.

Samsung Electronics' production, sales, and operation plans exemplify the impact of its management by numbers. Immense investments have been made in identifying and aggregating the data needed to set production and sales targets. By investing heavily in global enterprise resource planning (G-ERP), and global supply chain management (G-SCM), Samsung Electronics has developed the ability to identify inventory, sales at major retailers, production capacity at plants, and financial and administrative accounting data in near real time, allowing the company to adjust its global production and sales plans every week. The company's Japanese rivals did not invest in such information systems and can perform operational planning only on a monthly basis. Samsung Electronics' operational decision making is thus more precise and more adaptable to changes in market demand, and the company can identify and correct issues more quickly and frequently. Further details on Samsung's resource planning will be provided later in the discussion of the Global Operations Center in the "Process Integration Through SCM" section.

Another example of Samsung's management by numbers is its policy deployment to employees. This involves setting clear goals and specific methods to achieve those goals, and then evaluating the degree to which those goals have been achieved. Simply telling employees to "increase customer satisfaction," for example, provides a vague and nonmeasurable goal. Instead, Samsung strives to identify the factors underlying customer satisfaction. If the underlying factors in a particular business are low price, high quality, and early delivery, a measure of customer satisfaction is developed based on those factors. In addition, Samsung looks to improve other factors that affect quality by setting very specific goals like "below 1 percent absence rate" and "below 5 percent facility failure rate." Consequently, field managers are motivated to pursue measurable goals while HR managers can better evaluate work performance.

Samsung also employs the Six Sigma quality control process, which is intended to achieve defect rates of less than 3 to 4 per 100,000 products or services. Introduced in 1986 in the United States, Six Sigma was first adopted by Samsung SDI in 1996 and spread throughout the Samsung Group. Samsung Electronics embraced Six Sigma in October 1999 to produce "the best and most affordable products the most rapidly." The goal was to eradicate waste in the manufacturing process. Samsung Electronics thus established a "Six Sigma Academy" to train employees and build up a team of quality specialists, and reviewed the entire production process from beginning to end to shorten its length. As a result, productivity more than doubled.

Samsung Electronics' implementation of Six Sigma has two notable characteristics. One is the company's efforts to minimize defects by pursuing Six Sigma jointly with partners, while the other is its measurement of the financial contribution of each Six Sigma project. The latter tactic in particular allowed Samsung to ensure that its implementation of Six Sigma was more than a formality, as the results were audited by the finance departments. Six Sigma had its greatest impact in quantifying all of Samsung's manufacturing processes, rather than in the end products themselves. As a result, Six Sigma provided a foundation for management by numbers at Samsung.

Core Management Control Processes

Samsung's management control involves five core processes: new product development; parts procurement; manufacturing; logistics; and marketing, sales, and service. These processes were revamped to simplify operations, increase work speed, and build customer-focused business operations.

New Product Development

The defining characteristic of Samsung Electronics' product development is the close cooperation between all stages of the process, from product planning to R&D, design, production, and procurement. Samsung affiliates that produce core parts, parts suppliers, and large customers like Best Buy, AT&T, and Verizon also participate in this process. The starting point for product development at Samsung Electronics is customer need. Samsung develops the initial product plans with the single goal of creating value for its customers, removing any functions that do not contribute to customer value. Only then does it develop the parts that are used in its products. This process has helped Samsung reduce the time from planning to production, allowing it to secure greater cost competitiveness versus its competitors while fully reflecting customer needs.

Parts Procurement

Samsung Electronics' parts procurement is characterized by just-in-time delivery that keeps inventory to a minimum, achieved through close cooperation and the sharing of information with suppliers via its own online portal. To this end, Samsung Electronics has built joint complexes with both other electronics affiliates and suppliers to increase speed and reduce delivery costs. It has built a purchasing information system connected to its SCM system that provides suppliers with forecasts for products (including descriptions and quantities) and production schedules three months in advance, ensuring the timely delivery of materials and a decreased need for parts inventory.

Simultaneously, Samsung Electronics runs a three-day review that finalizes and confirms production plans three days before parts hit the assembly lines. Although suppliers are informed of tentative production plans 20 weeks ahead of time, the review system confirms parts orders, allowing suppliers to act as needed in a particular time frame. Suppliers can, on occasion, deliver parts jointly.

Samsung Electronics procures core parts like semiconductors, displays, and camera modules from within Samsung Group, and it also sets targets for internal procurement of parts and materials that were not originally produced within the group. This policy is intended to raise productivity and lower costs by leveraging Samsung's own capabilities and transferring the relevant know-how to partners, improving the competitiveness of the entire value chain.

Manufacturing

Samsung Electronics' manufacturing efficiency is a major source of its product competitiveness. The starting point of Samsung's manufacturing capabilities is Samsung's SCM system and the Global Operations Center (GOC) at each business division. Since sales and production plans are developed on a 20-week rolling basis, plans are made 20 weeks in advance, and adjustments are made weekly. Every Tuesday afternoon, the GOC sets or revises production plans for each plant, confirming the type and quantity of products to be produced by each worker at each production line and plant three days in advance (see Figure 4.5). This system is strictly followed, as changes in production plans after the three-day lead inevitably cause confusion among partners and undermine efficiency in the entire value chain.

In principle, plants are required to meet the sales offices' demands when it comes to the types and quantities of products made. However, because it is too complex to decide what 36 plants across the world can produce and what 63 sales offices can sell, Samsung's production sites are required to meet the demands of the sales offices no matter what they are. More important, Samsung's underlying philosophy is to strictly follow the needs of the market and of customers. After six months of applying this philosophy, Samsung Electronics was able to supply 98 percent of the sales offices' requests, while the sales offices made efforts to forecast sales more accurately.

Samsung's production motto is "by the book," meaning that it produces the allotted number of products in the allotted time, and then ships them on the same day. This proved to be an easy goal to meet at the outset, as employees were eager to work overtime to meet production targets. However, since overtime allowances raised labor costs, Samsung set the reduction of overtime

Figure 4.5   Samsung's Three-Day Finalization System

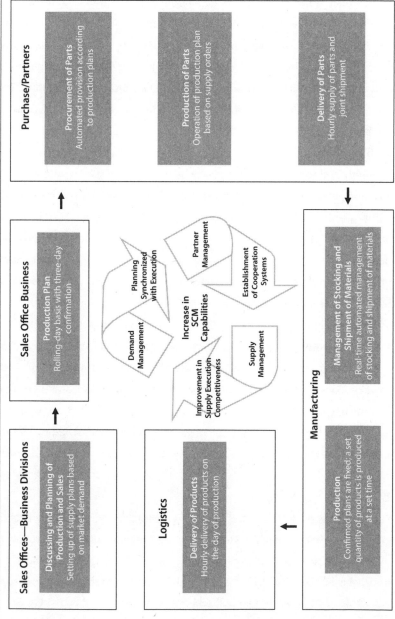

as an evaluation criterion the following year. By doing so, Samsung was able to increase its ability to produce the targeted quantity within the allotted time.

Another defining characteristic of Samsung Electronics' production is its ability to quickly adjust output to meet changing demand for an item. To this end, Samsung has decreased its dependence on traditional fixtures of mass production like the conveyor belt and introduced new production systems like flexible manufacturing that enable the company to produce numerous types of products on a single line, "Lego-style" production (referring to the modular disassembly and reassembly of production lines), and "cell production," where one worker does all the assembly and quality inspection for a finished product.

Samsung used one-person cell production to particularly strong effect in mobile phones. This process, in which a single worker performs the entire assembly and testing of a smartphone, is used by companies with exceptionally competent workers. Each worker is given a quota based on his or her abilities, and the types of products that the worker is assigned can be changed hourly. Parts are supplied by robots located in the production process as needed to meet the production schedules of workers. Samsung's integrated production system ensures that parts are supplied and classified based on the individual production schedule of each worker via an automated process, leading to higher productivity and fewer defects compared to competitors who use assembly contractors that rely more on manual labor.[1]

Samsung also uses a block cell production system, in which four to eight workers collectively assemble and test a smartphone. Most of the employees in Samsung's Vietnam plant work under this system, as they are semiskilled as a result of high turnover rates. Samsung has also outsourced production to independent manufacturers who used the conveyer belt production system.

Logistics

Samsung Electronics' logistics system is characterized by a high degree of global integration. The GOC acts as the command center, deciding on production for each product at each plant, and stock for the sales offices on an hourly basis. Likewise, delivery schedules for parts and materials from suppliers are decided for each hour. All schedules are confirmed by the GOC.

Logistics at Samsung Electronics involves two kinds of shipments: the delivery of products from Samsung's plants to sales offices and major clients, and the delivery of parts and materials from suppliers to Samsung's plants. Deliveries from Samsung are managed by logistics departments in 10 regional headquarters for the United States, Latin America, Europe, Africa, the Middle East, Southwest Asia, Southeast Asia, China, and Japan, as well as Korea. Each headquarters selects a primary logistics firm to handle the majority of its products and distributes the remainder of the work to a number of other firms. DHL, for example, is Samsung's main logistics firm in the United States. Samsung Electronics chooses the most competitive logistics company for each shipping route and encourages its logistics providers to compete with one another for its global shipments, while lowering costs through unified global contracts.

For delivery of parts and materials, Samsung has asked its primary suppliers to deliver on an hourly production schedule basis, rather than on a daily basis, thus reducing inventory costs. Since Samsung does not receive large quantities of parts from each supplier, the suppliers are free to select a logistics company. Recently, however, Samsung has experimented with integrated oversight of deliveries from its major suppliers.

Marketing, Sales, and Service

Samsung's marketing, sales, and service function is characterized by close cooperation with core clients, advertising firms, and retailers, and marketing activities that are tailored to different clients. Samsung Electronics helps its major clients to develop their own product competitiveness by developing new products in conjunction with Samsung. For example, while Apple is generally unwilling to modify its products to meet the needs of telecommunications providers, Samsung freely modifies the specs of its phones or develops new ones to meet the demands of telecommunications carriers. In advertising, in the past, Samsung Electronics has used up to 55 overseas agencies simultaneously. However, these days, Samsung Electronics uses only one global advertising agency so that it can deliver unified images to customers all over the world. Samsung has asked the agency to be involved from the development stage onward. Likewise, in distribution, Samsung cooperates closely with electronics retailers like Best Buy from the product development stage onward. Samsung has also introduced a customer relationship management (CRM) system that permits smooth information exchange and tailored sales activities for each major purchaser.

Recently, Samsung's SCM organizations have offered consulting on the improvement of processes for core customers, thus promoting the prosperity of both Samsung and its clients and binding those clients closer to Samsung.

Process Integration Through SCM

Samsung carries out the integrated management of the foregoing five processes through its SCM system. Although it is possible that Samsung could handle its processes more rapidly if it approached them separately, it would not be able to optimize them on a companywide scale if it did so. By integrating product development, procurement, manufacturing, logistics, and marketing, sales, and service, Samsung Electronics has been able to rapidly develop and sell products that its customers want, reduce the time required to move from planning to commercialization, and minimize parts and finished goods inventory.

SCM decisions are made weekly based on sales, production, and product development data. For sales, Samsung makes weekly sales forecasts for a 20-week period for each region and product, and confirms the sales plans for the immediate week ahead using its sales capacity index. For production, Samsung determines a production capacity index for each plant for 20 weeks. In product development, Samsung assembles data on new product development schedules and product properties.

The GOC integrates all the relevant data and produces various indexes that apply to the supply chain. These include "return to forecast," which assesses whether production has satisfied the demands of sales; "shipment release approval," which assesses when products from R&D will be delivered to production; and "return to sales," which determines when new products will be handed over to the sales organization (see Figure 4.6).

The GOC determines the type and quantity of products to be made at each plant, taking into account the inventory and sales forecasts at each sales

Figure 4.6   *Samsung Electronics' Conceptual Diagram for SCM*

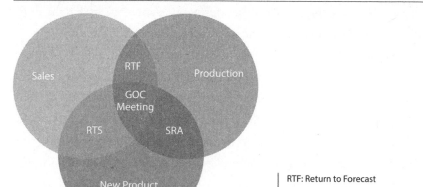

RTF: Return to Forecast
RTS: Return to Sales
SRA: Shipment Release Approval

organization worldwide and the production capacity at each production organization worldwide. It also determines such things as whether a particular
region's inventory can be transferred to another region, and what and how
many products from a particular plant should be sent to a particular sales
organization at a particular time. Since the GOC meets every Tuesday afternoon, it can coordinate and integrate Samsung's business processes for each
division in nearly real time on a global scale.

GOC meetings are held through videoconferencing, and are attended by
the people who are in charge of various businesses worldwide under the supervision of their chief operating officer (COO). Anyone who is affiliated with a
participating department can participate. This allows younger employees to
learn how management makes decisions and how to resolve conflicts among
the various players. SCM and the GOC are a major source of Samsung's competitiveness, and Samsung places a high priority on both.

IT Infrastructure

Under the New Management initiative, Samsung put special effort into
improving the accuracy and speed of its information networks. Previously,
each affiliate or division used separate information systems, hampering the

rapid sharing of information and slowing down operations. Samsung thus began building a single groupwide information system, including the introduction of ERP at all affiliates and an SCM system at some affiliates.

Samsung Electronics in particular established a world-class SCM system that greatly contributed to its competitiveness. Between 1994 and 2001, it invested about 700 billion won to build its new information system, including SCM and ERP and since then has spent approximately 400 billion won (about US$360 million in 2013) a year for maintenance. Samsung's integrated IT infrastructure has enabled all the players in its value chain to rapidly share accurate information on production, sales, inventory, credit, and logistics worldwide in nearly real time. As a result, headquarters can provide critical information to employees overseas within 24 hours, and overseas offices can provide information on sales and performance in terms of profit and loss as they occur. Samsung can also easily determine consolidated companywide sales and income.

Figure 4.7 provides an overview of Samsung Electronics' information systems. Samsung Electronics has established information systems for each of its five core business processes, which it integrates using SCM and ERP.

Figure 4.7 Samsung Electronics' Information System

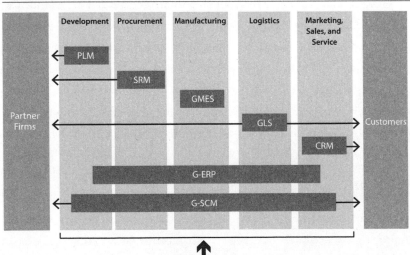

The master data system is the heart of Samsung's information system. This system assigns a serial number to every product, component, factory, sales office, supplier, customer, facility, and account title at Samsung, enabling easier searching and identification of items. Since it introduced the system, Samsung Electronics has reduced its base reference data and number of codes from 900,000 to less than 200,000. It has also invested in updating its constantly changing operations data, including information on products and procured parts.

For product development, Samsung Electronics uses a product life-cycle management (PLM) system (Chapter 7 provides a detailed explanation of PLM). For procurement, Samsung uses a supplier relationship management (SRM) system to facilitate cooperation with partner firms. SRM enables batch processing of parts procurement, product delivery, billing, and payments. It also provides data and recommendations on the price and quality of components to the PLM system; this information can be used for new products, allowing advance forecasts of production costs and product quality.

For manufacturing, Samsung Electronics uses a global manufacturing execution system (GMES) that calculates each factory's supply capacity index on a weekly basis and provides the results to the SCM system. After the GOC sets the production schedule for each plant, production line, and worker, Samsung's material requirement planning (MRP) system forecasts the demand for parts and informs suppliers. Workloads and schedules for each manufacturing process are then assessed.

For logistics, Samsung Electronics uses a global logistics system (GLS) to share the forecasted demand data with logistics firms and increase the speed of deliveries. Logistics firms can collect data on deliveries in all stages of the process, including those from suppliers to Samsung's plants, from Samsung's plants to sales offices, and from sales offices to customers, allowing them to devise better shipping plans that will allow them to deliver parts at the right time, and to deliver finished products to the customer the day they are produced. GLS reduces Samsung's inventory of parts and products and its time to market for products.

For marketing, sales, and service, Samsung Electronics uses a CRM system. This system connects Samsung's sales offices with major purchasers (for example, telecommunications carriers), allowing them to acquire accurate information on Samsung's products and to place orders that are in line with demand forecasts. Samsung Electronics integrates data on each customer from the CRM system and deploys individually tailored marketing strategies.

With the exception of the PLM system, all of Samsung's information systems serve as a link between parts suppliers, plants, production lines, sales offices, and customers. Samsung Electronics' SCM system then connects all of these core processes and functions as a complete information system for all the links in the value chain, including product development, manufacturing, quality assurance, logistics, marketing, sales, and after-sales service. All participants, including suppliers, affiliates, subsidiaries, overseas offices, branches, and dealerships, are interlinked. Anyone who accesses this system for decision making can gain information in nearly real time. Employees at headquarters, for example, can easily determine how many products are being sold at a particular U.S. retailer, how much inventory that retailer maintains, and when the inventory will be depleted. Since establishing the global SCM system at all of its domestic and overseas offices in 2002, Samsung Electronics has used the SCM system to make decisions regarding production, sales, and logistics at the weekly GOC meeting.

If SCM is a system that supports the decision-making process, ERP supports the execution of those decisions. Samsung established its ERP system as a single data processing system for both the logistics (purchasing, production, and sales) and the financial (accounting, financing, administration, and investment) functions. ERP helps reduce inventories and shortens delivery lead time.

In January 2003, Samsung established its worldwide trade network (WTN), which integrates business processes for its production and sales offices around the world. This system uses the Internet to merge the individual ERP systems of Samsung's various organizations, allowing affiliate organizations of Samsung to automate their transactions and share core management information in real time. The WTN has drastically shortened the lead time between orders and production, and dramatically improved the accuracy of orders. Simultaneously, the standardization of systems across organizations that the WTN has introduced has helped to reduce errors and waste, while allowing a rapid and accurate understanding of interorganizational transactions between overseas offices and improved transparency. In 2008, Samsung went further, establishing a global ERP system that covers finance, logistics, and inventory data for all of its overseas offices. As a result, a consolidated financial statement, which once required a week to complete, can be prepared in only two days.

Culture and Values: Pursuit of Excellence Based on a Sense of Crisis

Samsung's culture and values refer to the presiding culture that forms the basis of Samsung's management and the values that Samsung pursues. "Culture" reflects the state of Samsung today, and "values" reflect Samsung's aspirations for the future.

Core Values

To be a premier world-class company, Samsung asks its employees to internalize its trinity of values, to develop creative culture, and to maintain "Single Samsung" spirit. Since these core values are not fully embraced by its employees, those values are not Samsung's dominant cultural values yet.

Samsung's Trinity of Values

In its early days, Samsung created a strong corporate culture based on open competitive recruitment of new employees, continuous employee training, internal sourcing of human resources, and cultivation of a uniform workforce. The company prioritized and enforced its core values in its recruitment, evaluation, compensation, promotion, and dismissal decisions. Since the New Management initiative, Samsung has pursued a more flexible HR policy that includes active recruitment of women and foreigners. Nonetheless, Samsung did not change its policies concerning the creation of a strong corporate culture to govern its huge organization.

As Samsung's vision evolved, its business concepts changed accordingly. By 1973, Samsung had adopted "contribution to the nation," "people first," and "pursuit of rationality" as its management philosophy. In 1984, after gathering opinions from executives and holding an executive-level seminar, Samsung declared that "creativity," "integrity," "excellence," "perfectionism," and "co-prosperity" were its core values.

However, these too were modified on the fifth anniversary of Samsung Group's Second Foundation in 1993. As Samsung set its sights on becoming a world-class company, the company's new management philosophy became equally ambitious: to "devote its human resources and technology to create superior products and services, thereby contributing to a better global society." For employees, Samsung's guiding spirit became "be with the customer," "challenge the world," and "create the future."

Samsung's core values evolved once more in 2005 to meet increasing challenges from within and outside the group. Externally, Samsung needed a culture that could respond to drastically increasing global competition, practice social responsibility in a manner befitting Samsung's global status, and provide the ethical and environmentally friendly management that the international community wanted. Internally, Samsung needed to maintain cohesion despite an influx of new employees, both at home and overseas; rapid growth in the number of experienced employees recruited from outside; and an increased level of management autonomy. To meet these challenges, Samsung introduced the "Samsung Trinity of Values" to harmonize and fulfill its management philosophy, core values, and management principles (see Figure 4.8).

The overriding management philosophy in this system continued the values proclaimed in 1993 that defined the company's raison d'être and its future path. The philosophy also incorporated Samsung's "pursuit of excellence" and its focus on human resources and technology.

Samsung's core values, as announced in March 2005, were "people," "excellence," "change," "integrity," and "co-prosperity" (see Table 4.1). People and excellence, of course, were values that were already deeply rooted in Samsung's organizational culture. These two values had long played a critical role in Samsung's growth, and they would continue to guide the future of the com-

Figure 4.8   Samsung's Trinity of Values

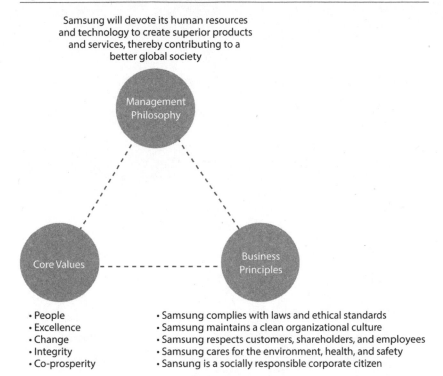

Samsung will devote its human resources
and technology to create superior products
and services, thereby contributing to a
better global society

Management Philosophy

Core Values

Business Principles

- People
- Excellence
- Change
- Integrity
- Co-prosperity

- Samsung complies with laws and ethical standards
- Samsung maintains a clean organizational culture
- Samsung respects customers, shareholders, and employees
- Samsung cares for the environment, health, and safety
- Sansung is a socially responsible corporate citizen

pany. Since the accession of Chairman Lee, Samsung has made the continuous embrace of change one of its core values, a move that has recently been further underscored by Samsung's calls for creative management. Integrity and co-prosperity were added to Samsung's core values to boost the company's social legitimacy in response to the changing external environment.

Samsung believes that it can become a respected world-class company by fulfilling its social responsibility in accordance with its increased global status while meeting the needs of its external stakeholders. Samsung has set forth core items that were to be followed by all employees as its management principles. The company has 5 overarching principles, 15 detailed principles, and 42 conduct rules that its employees are expected to follow. The first two overarching principles involve Samsung's commitment to complying with laws and ethical standards, while the other three principles focus on serving the interests of stakeholders, promoting social development, and contributing

Table 4.1 Samsung's Core Values

People	A company is its people. Samsung is dedicated to giving its people a wealth of opportunities to reach their full potential.	Excellence		Everything at Samsung is driven by an unyielding passion for excellence and an unfaltering commitment to developing the best products and services on the market.
Change	In today's fast-paced global economy, change is constant and innovation is critical to a company's survival. As it has done since its foundation, Samsung sets its sights on the future, anticipating market needs and demands to steer the company toward long-term success.	Integrity		Operating in an ethical way is the foundation of Samsung's business. Everything that Samsung does is guided by a moral compass that ensures fairness, respect for all stakeholders, and complete transparency.
Co-prosperity	A business cannot be successful unless it creates prosperity and opportunity for others. Samsung is dedicated to being a socially and environmentally responsible corporate citizen in every community where it operates around the globe.			

to the realization of justice. These principles serve as standards that can help employees when they encounter ambiguous situations.

As with the New Management initiative, Samsung widely disseminated its new value system throughout the group. First, it had each affiliate and overseas office declare the new values as standards, and it established a Management Principles Steering Committee and an Office for Culture and Values at each affiliate, with the new Culture and Values Team at Samsung Human Resources Development Center acting as an overseer. Samsung also published and distributed books on its core values and management principles in Korean, English, Chinese, Japanese, and Spanish. At the same time, Samsung designated and trained 191 employees to train other employees on its core values. By the end of 2006, some 35,000 employees had participated in training at the group level, while individual affiliates had provided training to some 70,000 employees. Overseas offices were also included in the training. By August 2006, Samsung had opened its Samsung Values portal site to facilitate further understanding of the company's value system worldwide. The portal site provides information on Samsung Group's history, current status, management philosophy, and value system to Samsung's employees in five languages.

Creative Organizational Culture

In the 2000s, Chairman Lee began advocating creative management at Samsung and campaigned to shift Samsung's culture from "well-managed Samsung" to "creative Samsung." His most significant effort was directed at building a creative organizational culture, which he regarded as a prerequisite if employees were to be creative and to come up with ideas that would lead to the realization of creative management.

To this end, Samsung reduced restrictions on employees and allowed greater individual autonomy through, among other things, a casual dress code and flexible work schedules. Another measure was the Great Work Place program, which was first introduced at Samsung Electronics' semiconductor division in 1998 and was later adopted at Samsung Fire & Marine Insurance in 2002, with successful case studies being shared throughout Samsung Group. Each affiliate also established its own core cultural values in line with

Samsung's overall strategy for market leadership and creative management. Samsung Electronics' semiconductor division, for example, chose "pioneer," "innovator," and "team player" as its cultural keywords in 2005. Samsung Life chose "customer focus," "people first," "professionalism," "challenge," and "communication" as its corporate values. Samsung C&T declared "creation," "challenge," "love," and "trust" to be its cultural values.

Since the 2008 financial crisis, Samsung has accelerated its efforts to develop a creative organizational culture. In October 2008, Samsung Electronics expanded its casual dress code to all of its work sites. The dress code would henceforth be "business casual" instead of formal suits, and employees could dress as they wished so long as they did not offend others. This allowed employees greater leeway to express their individuality and to think differently from others.

In April 2009, Samsung introduced flexible working schedules by allowing employees to arrive at the office at any time between 6 a.m. and 1 p.m. It also introduced "cyclical vacation days," which let employees take turns enjoying three-day weekends, as well as announcing the company's holiday schedule in advance so that employees could make vacation plans more easily. While such measures do not directly promote employees' creativity, Samsung's management's shift from controlling the work process to allowing employees to autonomously determine the method and process of work while focusing on the results has allowed employees to express more creativity.

Samsung's effort to achieve a creative organizational culture is also evident in its push for greater diversity in its workforce. The company has expanded its recruitment of women and increased its efforts to make a better workplace for them. It has also recruited more foreigners to work at its domestic and overseas business sites. In this way, Samsung has moved away from a uniform management style and has embraced diversity while adopting a more flexible management style.

"Single Samsung" Spirit

Although they work at different affiliates, all Samsung employees recognize that they are part of Samsung Group. All Samsung affiliates use the same corporate logo and brand, and follow the same group-level business philosophy. Training courses for new employees are also carried out at the group level, and employees of different Samsung affiliates are trained together in Samsung's philosophy, values, beliefs, and standards to become members of Samsung Group. Moreover, there have been cases where an executive from one affiliate has become the CEO of another affiliate. Samsung's employees can thus feel a sense of belonging both to their particular company and to Samsung Group as a whole.

The idea of a "Single Samsung" spirit was already well established among employees before the introduction of the New Management initiative. Despite being legally independent, Samsung's affiliates still operated as if they were a single company. Financial and human resources moved freely between affiliates, and interaffiliate financing and debt payment guarantees meant that all Samsung companies shared a common destiny. Financial problems at one affiliate, for example, meant that other Samsung affiliates would suffer. In recruiting, Samsung scouted employees at the group level, allocating them to specific affiliates only after the hiring process was finished. This, along with a common HR management system that was applied groupwide, encouraged employees to identify with Samsung as a whole, rather than with their specific affiliate.

The sense of a "Single Samsung" faced significant challenges during the introduction of the New Management initiative and the outbreak of the 1997 Asian currency crisis. After those events, each Samsung affiliate conducted its own hiring, and the compensation gap among affiliates widened as strong performance-based compensation was introduced. At the same time, moving between different affiliates became more difficult, and fewer transfers occurred. This resulted in a significant decline in the "Single Samsung" spirit among employees, spurring management to strengthen Samsung's collective identity by encouraging voluntary cooperation between affiliates and pursuing intragroup synergy.

Dominant Cultural Values

Since Samsung's foundation, its management has focused on a strong corporate culture. The core foundations of the company's corporate culture before the New Management initiative were "pursuit of excellence," "pursuit of rationality," and "people first." After the New Management initiative, these were revised to fit with Samsung's vision of becoming a world-class company through qualitative growth. The company realized that it was impossible for it to grow into a world-class company with only its existing cultural values. Accordingly, it shifted the object of its pursuit of excellence from domestically focused, quantity-driven excellence to globally focused, quality-driven excellence. Likewise, the central element of "pursuit of rationality" was shifted from "efficiency" to "effectiveness," while the "people first" policy was shifted from securing and fostering standardized human resources to securing and fostering core talent.

Pursuit of Excellence

The most important value that Samsung Group holds is the "pursuit of excellence based on a sense of crisis." Samsung's path to global status has been based on its belief that it will fail if it does not embrace change, does not seek to become number one in its industry, and does not unleash its creativity.

Samsung's pursuit of excellence began at its foundation, and this is reflected in the names of some of its affiliates, like Cheil Industries and Cheil Worldwide. These include the word *cheil*, which means "number one" in Korean, reflecting Samsung's belief that it had to be number one in all its business lines. In 1984, Samsung officially included "excellence" in its core values, and since then has made continuous efforts to achieve this. Also, Samsung's philosophy of "devoting our human resources and technology to create superior products and services, thereby contributing to a better global society," also includes the word *superior*, further reinforcing Samsung's commitment to excellence.

Samsung's pursuit of excellence begins with setting being "number one" as the goal. To reach this goal, first Samsung's people must be number one, and then Samsung's performance must be number one.[2] While in the past, Samsung's policy of being number one meant being number one in domestic market share in all its businesses, today Samsung is committed to being number one in the world in quality, in line with the principles of the New Management initiative (see Figure 4.9).

Figure 4.9   *Changes in Samsung's Corporate Culture*

	Before New Management		After New Management
Pursuit of Excellence	Within the Domestic Market in Quantity	Provide the Best Products and Services Faster than Others	In the Global Market in Quality
Pursuit of Rationality	Pursuit of Efficiency	Seize Opportunities Preemptively and Pursue Corporate Value	Pursuit of Effectiveness
People First Policy	Emphasis on Standardized Human Resources	Emphasize Competence and Performance	Emphasis on Core Talent

Before the New Management initiative, Samsung's pursuit of excellence was driven by quantitative growth aimed at expanding market share by providing the lowest prices. Even in businesses that it entered as a latecomer, Samsung was able to secure a leading position by mobilizing vast amounts of resources and making bold investments. Samsung has a repeated history of coming from behind to win the race, beating Miwon in the market for artificial seasoning, LG Electronics in the market for home appliances, and Motorola in the domestic mobile phone market.

If Samsung's business lines or products are not number one or the only one in their industry, they will not survive. In the past, companies could survive in second place by imitating advanced products. Today, however, it is almost impossible to survive in the market in second place.

—Chairman Lee Kun-Hee

When Samsung adopted "becoming a world-class company" as its goal, it shifted the focus of its pursuit of excellence to "providing the best products and services first" based on quality-driven management. Chairman Lee Kun-Hee's "world's best" philosophy, that Samsung must be either number one or the only one, has been the basic motto guiding Samsung since Lee's accession. Samsung's new pursuit of excellence has found expression in numerous projects and campaigns, including the "one product, one company" campaign encouraging each affiliate to produce at least one world-class product, the "world's best" campaign to spur Samsung to produce the world's best products, and the "wow project," aimed at producing products that could astonish consumers around the world. At the same time, Samsung Electronics continued its custom of holding regular internal exhibitions of advanced products in the industry, allowing employees to directly compare Samsung's products with those of competitors and to seek out strategies to make Samsung's products better. Other initiatives that reflect Samsung's pursuit of excellence include its strategy to become number one in all its core markets and to produce at least one hit product in each business line.

Recently, Samsung has revised its vision of what it means to be number one, taking it beyond being first in market share and technology. Samsung now hopes to lead progress in the industry and to create new trends and culture. To this end, the company has continued to select and develop the best people, but is also making massive investments in marketing, design, and branding in addition to technology. Such efforts have furthered Samsung's efforts to be a world-class company.

Samsung's previous history of achieving market leadership in almost all of its business lines and becoming Korea's foremost business naturally instilled pride in its employees and allayed any sense of impending danger. However, starting with its entry into the semiconductor industry, a sense of crisis has become a pervasive part of Samsung's culture, and this feeling spread throughout the whole group when massive restructuring took place with the introduction of the New Management initiative and the arrival of the 1997 Asian currency crisis. After the New Management initiative, Samsung boldly shed its lowest-performing businesses and product lines, and its pursuit of excellence has tended to merge with the continuous sense of crisis advocated by Chairman Lee.

Pursuit of Rationality

"Rationality" was one of Samsung's three founding philosophies, and the company has pursued it more thoroughly than any other Korean conglomerate. Although rationality per se was not included in Samsung's new philosophy in 1993, it continues to underlie Samsung's management philosophy as a dominant cultural value.

Samsung's understanding of rationality underwent some modifications in the wake of the New Management initiative. Before the initiative, rationality found its expression in cost savings, yield improvements, and increased speed as the company carried out its fast-follower strategy. These indexes are primarily indicators of efficiency, or the ratio of Samsung's inputs to its outputs. After the New Management initiative, the company set a goal of developing innovative products ahead of its rivals, and to this end, goal achievement, or effectiveness, became the core target. Samsung therefore adopted numerous management strategies in which increasing effectiveness was the primary goal.

Today, pursuit of rationality at Samsung finds expression in a variety of ways. These include management based on the principles of a market economy, accountable management, management by numbers, systematic employee education and training, performance-based HR systems, and a clean organizational culture.

People First Policy

Samsung has emphasized the importance of human resources from the beginning with its "people first" policy. The company's business philosophy of "devoting our human resources and technology to create superior products and services, thereby contributing to a better global society" also clearly states that human resources are the main elements in the creation of products and services. Samsung thus regards human resources as the most important source of its competitiveness.

Samsung defines its people first policy as "respecting people, creating an environment where each individual can exhibit their ability to the fullest, and making the individual a driving force for social development."[3] Founder Lee Byung-Chull practiced Samsung's people first policy throughout his life. He said, "A company is its people," and "I spent 80 percent of my life looking for and training talent."

His successor, Lee Kun-Hee, has showed even greater enthusiasm for people. Lee has said, "If I have only one desire, it is a desire for people. I may be the person with the strongest desire for people in the world." He added, "Samsung has to be willing to change everything . . . its organizational culture, way of thinking, even its corporate structure if it helps people fully realize their abilities." Samsung's interest in people is more akin to an obsession than to mere enthusiasm.

In the past, Samsung defined the people that it sought to recruit as "talented workers who can fit in with Samsung's culture." People who had strong personalities and a penchant for independence were not considered, no matter how talented they were. Samsung's criteria for employment thus followed the criterion of "high-quality, standardized people." However, when Samsung realized that it could not become a world-class company with this policy, "core talent" and "genius-level talent" became the guiding criteria for its recruitment activities.

Alignment of Management System Components

Companies can achieve strong results when the components of their management system are well aligned. Samsung's unique management system was based on a strategic vision provided by Chairman Lee. Table 4.2 illustrates the changes in Samsung's management system after the New Management initiative.

Samsung's attainment of "fit" between the components of its management system can be assessed by focusing on the strategies it used to become a world-class company. As noted several times throughout this book, Samsung established a commitment to quality as the basis of its strategy, and used this to develop further strategies of market leadership and upgrading of the business portfolio. The company revised the components of management system to carry out these strategies.

Market Leader Strategy

In leadership and governance, Chairman Lee instilled a sense of crisis at Samsung by warning affiliates and business divisions that they would fail

Table 4.2 Samsung's Management Systems Before and After the New Management Initiative

Before the New Management Initiative	Management Factors	After the New Management Initiative
Governance: Owner management CEO (owner-manager): Patriarchal leadership Affiliate CEOs: Administrators and executors	Leadership and governance	Harmony between owner-manager and professional managers CEO (owner-manager): Vision presenter Affiliate CEOs: Strategists
Quantity-focused strategy Fast follower Flying geese strategy	Strategy	Quality-focused strategy Market leader Upgrade of the business portfolio based on a select-and-focus strategy
Standardized human resources Internal sourcing of human resources Domestic human resources Seniority-based compensation and promotion	Human resource management	Core talent Internal sourcing of human resources combined with external sourcing of human resources Domestic human resources combined with global human resources Performance-based compensation and promotion
Micromanagement Management by numbers Manufacturing efficiency–centered process Unintegrated information system	Management control	Micromanagement combined with macromanagement Sophisticated management by numbers Customer-centered process Globally integrated information system
Pursuit of excellence (within the domestic market) Pursuit of efficiency Emphasis on standardized human resources	Culture and values	Pursuit of excellence (in the global market) Pursuit of effectiveness Emphasis on core talent

unless they made the world's number one products and achieved market leadership on a global level. Lee provided further emphasis on this in executing Samsung's strategy by taking on risk and making the large-scale entrepreneurial investment decisions required to be a market leader. The Corporate Strategy Office has supported this approach by helping affiliates make decisions and encouraging mutual cooperation among them.

Samsung's organizational culture is based on its becoming number one (pursuit of excellence) through a quality-focused approach that is driven by a sense of crisis and a people first policy that is centered on core talent. Samsung tries to create an optimal environment in which these people can display their ability to the fullest, supporting its pursuit of market leadership.

In human resource management, Samsung practices strategies like securing core talent, opening the internal labor market, globalization of human resources, market-based annual salaries, incentives for core talent, and hefty collective profit sharing. Compensation and promotions are based on individual performance, while collective profit sharing is based on the performance of affiliates and divisions. Samsung also aggressively recruits people with the skills and knowledge that it needs regardless of nationality, and invests in them to develop their capabilities.

In terms of management control, Samsung pursues market leadership by building cooperative relationships with core suppliers and large customers, promoting horizontal integration between divisions, and providing an integrated information infrastructure that connects all the participants in Samsung's value chain.

Upgrading of the Business Portfolio

In order to achieve its vision of becoming a world-class company, Samsung abandoned its previous policy of unrelated diversification and replaced it with a strategy of upgrading its business portfolio through a select-and-focus policy. This involved a shift from quantity-driven practices to a focus on quality and profitability. Samsung's top managers were thus ordered to give priority to the firm's corporate performance rather than personal empire building, and to use profitability as the primary standard for determining whether to launch a new business or make an investment decision. The support of Chairman Lee and his continuous advocacy for a corporate transformation at Samsung, along with responsible and accountable professional managers at each affiliate, enabled the execution of this strategy.

HR management provided further support for the select-and-focus policy through the application of strong performance-based compensation and promotion, on the one hand, and collective incentives, on the other. Profitability-based performance evaluations and corresponding compensation and promotion helped to discourage indiscriminate business expansion while encouraging investment in promising and profitable businesses. Hefty collective incentives also encouraged affiliates and divisions to target profitable business lines and concentrate on them, and to divest unprofitable business lines.

Groupwide Dissemination of the Management System

Although Samsung had established a vision of becoming a world-class company in the New Management initiative, not all Samsung affiliates had achieved a level of global competitiveness. In fact, except for the DRAM business, few Samsung affiliates had reached a global level of competitiveness. After the New Management initiative, however, Samsung's mobile phone, TFT-LCD, and TV business lines achieved strong success in the global market, and today Samsung's electronics-related affiliates are globally competitive. Global competitiveness, however, remains a work in progress for many of Samsung's other affiliates.

As mentioned earlier, the elements of Samsung's management system have found a strong fit in the electronics industry, but the fit between some of Samsung's other businesses and the elements of the company's management system (see Table 4.3) is less secure. Therefore, it is still premature to say that Samsung's strategy of market leadership and upgrading its business portfolio through a select-and-focus policy has completely achieved its goals. These strategies date only to the introduction of the New Management initiative in 1993 and were not completely embraced until 1997, during the Asian currency

Table 4.3   *Fit Between Samsung's Strategy and Management Elements*

Leadership and governance	Owner-manager + professional managers (coordinating function from the Corporate Strategy Office, triangular governance structure) Vision management from the owner-manager: presentation of a far-reaching vision and future strategic directions Professional managers as strategists: sophisticated system of recruiting, developing, delegating, compensating, and monitoring CEOs		
Strategy	Quality-focused strategy	Market leader	Upgrading of the business portfolio
HR management	Core talent Opening of the internal job market	Core talent Globalization of the workforce Performance-based compensation and promotion Hefty collective incentives	Performance-based compensation and promotion Hefty collective incentives
Management control	Macromanagement Integrated information infrastructure	Customer-centered process Cooperation with business partners	Customer-centered process Integrated information infrastructure
Culture and values	Global pursuit of excellence, pursuit of effectiveness, emphasis on core talent, "Single Samsung" spirit		

crisis. While Samsung's pursuit of market leadership has led to outstanding results in the electronics industry, the company has yet to develop source technologies that will create either a new industry or innovative, "goose that lays the golden eggs" products. Although Samsung's electronics-related affiliates, and particularly Samsung Electronics, have strengthened their business structures by jettisoning uncompetitive product categories and businesses, Samsung as a whole still retains the structure of a typical conglomerate.

Samsung thus needs to expand its success to other affiliates based on its experience at Samsung Electronics. At the same time, despite its success in designing strategies and management systems for becoming a world-class business, the company still urgently needs to embrace further change if it is to achieve its vision. The last chapter of this book will touch upon these issues and discuss the future challenges that Samsung will face.

PART THREE

HOW DID SAMSUNG SUCCEED?

This section analyzes Samsung's core competencies as key success factors for the company. After the 1990s, a company's "core competencies," or its unique and inimitable competitive resources and capabilities, became an important strategic concept. Companies that have developed core competencies can create a sustainable competitive advantage over the long-term.

Various conditions must be satisfied to turn a resource or capability into a core competency. First, the resource or capability must fit in with the main factors for success in a particular industry. Samsung refers to this as the "concept" or "nature" of a business.[1] For example, semiconductors and cosmetics each have a different concept of the business and consequently require different core competencies. Furthermore, a particular resource or capability must be relatively superior to those maintained by competitors if it is to increase a company's value. Second, the resource or capability in question must be inimitable. Capabilities that are quickly and easily imitated by rivals cannot create a sustainable competitive advantage. Likewise, resources must be rare if they are to be a core competency. Finally, resources that constitute a core competency cannot be things that can be purchased on the open market, but must be resources that have been accumulated and developed within a company over a long period of time.[2]

As a result of in-depth analysis of interviews and data, after the New Management initiative, Samsung was found to have created three types of core competencies in its electronics business. These core competencies are speed, synergy through convergence, and evolutionary innovation. "Speed" refers to Samsung's ability to make decisions and carry them out faster than its competitors and to reduce the time from product development to market launch. "Synergy through convergence" refers to Samsung's ability to create additional value by seamlessly linking its knowledge, information, and technology resources through cooperation both within the company and throughout the group. "Evolutionary innovation" refers to the company's ability to develop new products or technologies through new methods within existing technological paths or product domains.

Samsung Electronics' top managers have defined these three capabilities as Samsung's key success factors that cannot be easily imitated by rivals. In interviews conducted in 2013, they had these observations:

Speed and technology are at the heart of Samsung's semiconductor business. More recently, service has grown in importance, and we have to be able to provide total solutions to our customers. Samsung Electronics' semiconductor division has successfully built strong core competencies in speed, technology innovation, and the ability to provide total solutions.

—Kwon Oh-Hyun, Vice-Chairman and CEO
of Samsung Electronics and Head of Device Solutions

Samsung Electronics' mobile division's strategic strength lies in creating synergy through co-opetition with the world's best supplier of memory, application processors, display panels, and batteries, while pursuing continuous innovation. Samsung wants to be number one, and once it determines what direction it needs to go in, it can execute faster than anyone.

—Shin Jong-Kyun, President and CEO of Samsung Electronics and
Head of IT and Mobile Communications

Samsung Electronics' TV division was able to succeed because of speed and innovation. Another success factor was its ability to organically cooperate with the semiconductor and display divisions within the company.

—Lee Sun-Woo, Executive Vice-President of Samsung Electronics and
Head of Samsung Electronics Europe Headquarters

Samsung's success and competitive edge come from consistent technological innovation based on consumer needs and bold and rapid decision making and execution based on prescient forecasting of the market. Creating synergy and accelerating development speed through cooperation with affiliate firms is a critical part of Samsung's process of innovation.

—Kim Chang-Yeong, Executive Vice-President of Samsung Electronics
and President of the DMC R&D Center

Chapters 5, 6, and 7 discuss Samsung's three types of core competencies (see the following illustration) in detail and how they manifest themselves in Samsung's business.

Samsung's Three Types of Core Competencies

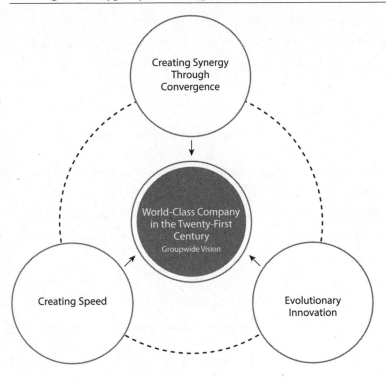

CHAPTER 5

SAMSUNG'S FIRST SUCCESS FACTOR

5

Competency in Creation of Speed

The core competency of Samsung Electronics' semiconductor business is speed and the desire to be number one.

—*Woo Nam-Sung, President of Samsung Electronics*

and Head of System LSI Business

The most important factor in the success of Samsung Electronics' smartphone business is speed. Just as "mass x speed² = energy" is a basic law of physics, using the same resources twice as fast increases our competitiveness four times.

—*Hong Won-Pyo, President of Samsung Electronics*

and Head of the Media Solution Center

Speed Matters in the Twenty-First Century

After the 1990s, dramatic advancements in semiconductor and digital technology made communications tools like the Internet, mobile phones, and social networks ubiquitous worldwide. This digital revolution is no less profound than previous social transformations like the Agricultural Revolution and the Industrial Revolution. In the twenty-first century, digital information can flow everywhere almost instantaneously, and it accumulates in massive reservoirs of "big data." In this respect, Bill Gates was prescient when he said that the digital economy of the twenty-first century would be an "age of speed."[1]

In the digital economy, the rapid development and expansion of communications networks are eroding the barriers of distance, time, and location,[2] making economies of scale based on size give way to "economies of speed" based on the velocity and flexibility of companies' responses to their markets and customers. In addition, as the Internet enables consumers to be better informed, the information asymmetry among consumers, manufacturers, and distributors has declined considerably. Consumers are increasingly able to identify and choose those companies that can deliver the best-quality products at the best prices at the right time.

More recently, the widespread adoption of smartphones, tablet computers, and social networking and cloud computing services is ushering in a "smart revolution" or "smart age." This smart revolution will transform individuals' lifestyles and companies' business models and will blur the lines between industries and between national economies. This global transformation will usher in an era of hypercompetition, with competitive advantage being created and lost ever more rapidly. In this era, only those companies that quickly seize opportunities and embrace change will survive.[3]

In the era of speed-based competition, fast decision making and execution are pivotal for corporate performance. This is particularly true in the information technology (IT) industry, where product life cycles are shrinking as the speed of technological change and innovation increases. Having the first-mover advantage is critical in this high-velocity industry. Competitiveness depends on rapid strategic decision making and execution, preemptive product development and technology innovation, and the setting of market and technical standards.

If the pace of product innovation can be accelerated, development time can be cut and resource use can be made more efficient. Ultimately, product quality will improve as participants' levels of learning and understanding of the products increases. Moreover, by developing and launching new products faster than their competitors do, companies can seize the first-mover advantage and all the benefits associated with it. Such benefits include the learning curve effect, preemptive access to inputs, economies of scale, improvement in brand awareness, and various network effects, leading to high profit margins.[4]

In an increasingly uncertain environment, companies with strong capabilities in creating speed can minimize their risks, as they can afford to wait to enter new markets or new businesses until there are fewer uncertainties. Simply put, in the new paradigm of the digital revolution where global hypercompetition, a changing environment, and growing uncertainty reign, time and speed serve as core competencies for business, as noted by George Stalk.[5]

Even as speed is becoming an increasingly important source of competitiveness, however, large companies are increasingly finding themselves lagging behind smaller firms in the speed of their decision making and execution. This is especially true for businesses with diversified business structures, where complex decision making and management processes can get in the way of speedy decision making and execution.

The New Management Initiative Brings Speed Management

Before the New Management initiative, Samsung was not seen as being a fast-moving company. Its penchant for meticulous analysis, micromanagement, and internal control and its preference for careful pursuit of business meant that it was never as fast as its competitors. With the New Management initiative, however, Chairman Lee placed particular emphasis on using speed and preemptively seizing opportunities as sources of sustainable competitive advantage for Samsung.

> Today, losses incurred from missed opportunities are much greater than direct losses incurred from commercial trade. Recurring losses are nothing compared to those incurred by missing an important opportunity. The bigger the company, the bigger the losses will be, while capturing opportunities represents genuine profits. Short of misusing company funds, we have to be ready to do whatever it takes. When we decide on something we have to do, we have to go all in to seize opportunities, or at the very least, minimize opportunity costs. If

we do not bring creative products and services to market faster than others, we will not survive. This is an era when timing is critical and speed is vital.

In 2000, Chairman Lee's New Year's message declared that "digital management" would lead the twenty-first century, and he stressed the importance of seizing new opportunities and rapidly embracing change.

> As the new millennium commences, I declare this year as the beginning of the age of digital management at Samsung. We will adopt digital technology in all aspects of management, from our business structure, to our leadership perspectives and systems, to our organizational culture. We will launch a second New Management and a second restructuring. Most of all, we need to anticipate changes ahead of others, and be the first to seize opportunities.

After the New Management initiative, Samsung was able to lead the semiconductor, liquid-crystal display (LCD) panel, mobile phone, and digital TV industries by leveraging its ability to make fast and bold decisions on investing in new products, then bring them to market faster than its rivals. Samsung's ability to pursue premium pricing for its products depended on these capabilities.

Strategic decision making and execution are two areas in which speed has become a major source of Samsung's competitiveness. Faster velocity in these two areas allowed Samsung to transform itself from a fast follower to a market leader. How was Samsung able to create speed and use it as a competitive advantage that could not be imitated by competitors? Figure 5.1 illustrates the structure of Samsung's speed creation capabilities.

How Did Samsung Increase Decision-Making Speed?

As the speed economy takes hold, rapid strategic decision making has become critical in seizing opportunities before others can do so. Delaying in the face of rapidly encroaching competitors can be as damaging to a company as making a bad strategic decision.

Figure 5.1   *Speed as a Competitive Advantage*

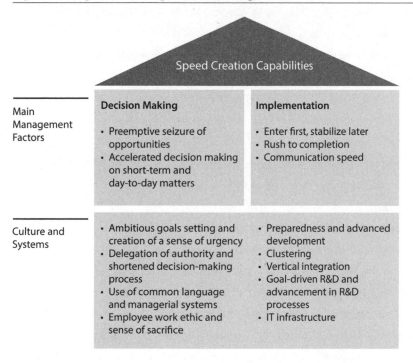

Speed Creation Capabilities

	Decision Making	Implementation
Main Management Factors	• Preemptive seizure of opportunities • Accelerated decision making on short-term and day-to-day matters	• Enter first, stabilize later • Rush to completion • Communication speed
Culture and Systems	• Ambitious goals setting and creation of a sense of urgency • Delegation of authority and shortened decision-making process • Use of common language and managerial systems • Employee work ethic and sense of sacrifice	• Preparedness and advanced development • Clustering • Vertical integration • Goal-driven R&D and advancement in R&D processes • IT infrastructure

Studies have shown that rapid decision making leads to higher performance than slower decision making. This is especially true in rapidly changing industries like IT.[6] This is because when an environment is changing rapidly, opportunities themselves are always changing, making it difficult for companies to catch up with the front-runners if they ever fall behind.

Investments to Preemptively Seize Opportunities

The importance of fast and bold decision making showed itself most clearly in Samsung's memory chip business. In the 1980s, Japanese chip makers dominated the market, but they soon found themselves rapidly losing ground to Samsung, which did not begin dynamic random access memory (DRAM) production until 1983. Tokyo University Professor Katsuya Okumura offered the following explanation:

Investments into chip making remained at the 10 billion to 20 billion yen level in the 1980s, when Japanese firms led the market for DRAM. At the time, business divisions at Japan's chip makers had the authority to make decisions on facilities investment, allowing Japanese firms to maintain competitiveness. Unfortunately for them, however, as required investments began to exceed the 100 billion yen mark, investment authority fell out of individual business divisions' hands. Japanese firms thus lost mobility in their investment decisions and continually fell behind in the timing of their investments. The Japanese method of decision making, which seeks consensus throughout the entire company, precluded the high speed needed for success in the semiconductor industry.[7]

Success in the semiconductor industry requires the rapid acquisition of advanced technologies as well as massive and aggressive investments. Even a few months of inaction can result in astronomical opportunity costs and long-term declines in competitiveness. Success in memory chips thus depends on speed, requiring even huge investments to be made boldly and rapidly. Moreover, demand for memory chips tends to fluctuate rapidly. This prevented Japanese chipmakers, with their tradition of achieving consensus before taking action, from making fast and decisive investment decisions when the industry was in a slump or when its prospects were uncertain. In contrast, Samsung was able to make bold decisions rapidly thanks to its owner-manager governance system, allowing it to surpass its Japanese rivals.

Studies show that CEOs who are willing to take on higher amounts of risk also make decisions faster. Owner-managers, in contrast to professional managers, can have a longer-term perspective and be willing to take on higher amounts of risk, allowing them to make bold decisions quickly.[8] At critical turning points and times of crisis in Samsung's history, Chairman Lee has been empowered to exercise leadership and make bold decisions fast. As a result, Samsung became number one in the global DRAM market only 10 years after entering the business.

Samsung's success in semiconductors was soon repeated in the LCD industry, which Samsung entered in the 1990s. Like the semiconductor business, LCD manufacturing is also capital- and technology-intensive, requiring massive investments in facilities and R&D. After struggling as a latecomer, Samsung reached a turning point in late 1997. Because of a prolonged slump in the thin-film-transistor LCD (TFT-LCD) market, Japanese companies that had been focused on producing 12.1-inch panels were reluctant to invest in next-generation panels. In contrast, Samsung invested aggressively in facilities to manufacture 13.3-inch and larger panels. Later, as the new size became the industry standard, Samsung was able to surpass Japanese producers and grab leadership of the market.

Samsung's success in digital TV, where it has been number one for years, was equally attributable to its ability to make rapid investment decisions and preemptively seize opportunities. Samsung was the first in the industry to move from analog to digital technologies. To gain an advantage in digital technologies, Samsung channeled huge investments to this area to secure the most advanced source technologies. The company spent 50 billion won over 10 years on product development that involved 600 researchers. As a result, Samsung developed 1,600 core technologies and had applied for patents on 1,500 of them by early 1998. In particular, Samsung developed the world's first digital TV in December 1997 and hosted the world's first product launch of a digital TV at the World Trade Center in New York in October of 1998. From that point on, Samsung was at least three to six months ahead of its competitors in all parts of the TV business, from development to production.

Samsung's ability to make massive investment decisions boldly and rapidly in an uncertain environment is the engine that powered its success in the semiconductor, LCD, and TV industries. According to Stefan Wally and J. Robert Baum, CEOs who enable rapid decision making typically combine keen intelligence and intuition with a high tolerance for risk.[9] Samsung's current success is due in no small part to the presence of these characteristics in Chairman Lee, whose investment decisions allowed Samsung to preemptively seize opportunities.

Alvin Toffler has said that companies need systems that can enable immediate decision making and action if they are to succeed in a speed-based economy.[10] Since the New Management initiative, Samsung's systems have fulfilled precisely this function. Samsung's ability to preemptively seize opportunities has depended on its ability to understand key emerging paradigms, to rapidly take action before others do so, and to accept a high degree of risk.

Preemptively seizing opportunities is a core factor in Samsung's management. Opportunity management at Samsung is classified into five stages (see Table 5.1), and these stages are well known not only among executives but among all employees.

Samsung has established four principles for its digital businesses: foresight, moving first, preemption, and seizing opportunities first. Samsung also provides all employees with training in practicing these principles in their daily work, relying on four keywords: "first, fast, on time, and frequent" (see Table 5.2). Samsung's emphasis on speed and seizing opportunities enabled it to break the vicious cycle of low quality, low prices, low brand equity, low sales, and low profitability to create a virtuous cycle of understanding customers, releasing products and services at the right time, seizing markets first, securing high-end distribution channels, increasing sales, raising brand value, and increasing profitability. This change helped Samsung sustain a continuous competitive advantage.

On-the-Spot Decision Making

Another pillar of Samsung's speed management is its policy of giving professional managers the authority to make decisions on short-term, routine mat-

Table 5.1 *Stages of Samsung's Opportunity Management*

Stage	Management Level	Concept
1	Lost opportunities	Permanent or temporary loss of opportunities
2	Recovery of lost opportunities	Whole or partial recovery of opportunities missed during the previous stage at the earliest possible time
3	Prevention of lost opportunities	Minimizing potential lost opportunities by changing business structure, institutions, and systems
4	Creation of opportunities	Assessing and forecasting the business environment to build a base for seizing opportunities
5	Seizing opportunities in advance	Turning opportunities to real business ahead of competitors to secure competitive advantages and maximize profits

Table 5.2   Keywords for Samsung's Speed Management

Keyword	Meaning	
First	Seizing opportunities first	Preemptively seizing opportunities in times of change
Fast	Shortening time to market	Shortening the time from R&D to sales to create future competitiveness
On time	Timing	Producing precise timing by differentiating big and small projects and reducing low-value-added tasks
Frequent	Flexible management	Assembling the relevant employees frequently to make decisions immediately

ters on the spot. Samsung greatly simplified its decision-making process after the New Management initiative so that the approval process took three steps or less, even for issues that required the CEO's approval. Less important issues could be approved orally or online. After the 1997 Asian currency crisis, for example, Samsung's reporting and meeting practices were drastically revised to delegate authority to employees via a digital corporate culture, paperless meetings, and electronic approval.

To overcome the global financial crisis of 2008 rapidly, Samsung Electronics integrated its six business divisions into Digital Media & Communications (DMC) for finished products and Device Solutions (DS) for components. Simultaneously, it downsized its administrative departments by transferring most of the administrative personnel at headquarters to the field. These restructuring measures enabled Samsung to make decisions completely on the spot, further strengthening its speed-focused management system.

How Did Samsung Increase Execution Speed?

Fast execution was as critical to Samsung's success as fast decision making. In terms of execution speed, Korea's "ppali ppali" spirit and Samsung's stretch goals, sense of crisis, passion among employees, and massive investments in IT infrastructure (such as global supply chain management [SCM]) worked effectively for the company. Korea is a very competitive society, and Koreans have always emphasized speed. One of the Korean words that is most noted by foreigners who work for Korean companies is "ppali ppali," which means "quickly, quickly." Samsung is even speedier than most other big corporations in Korea, as Chairman Lee and the company's top management have always set stretch goals. Such challenging goals, along with tight deadlines, ensured that employees both would be fully committed to their work, and would work together in teams, helping Samsung to quicken the pace.[11]

Samsung has a cultlike culture. Samsung people accept top-down goals without question. Samsung's employees were able to enhance speed because they shared the sense of crisis communicated by Chairman Lee, who has strong charisma—akin to a religious leader. The only way to achieve such ambitious goals was to maximize execution speed.

Chairman Lee continued to warn that Samsung will lose the competition in the fast-changing and hypercompetitive IT industry unless it innovates and changes constantly. The IT industry is ruled by the law of increasing returns and winner-takes-all economics.[12] First movers who gain significant market share early on can make it difficult for later entrants to compete. In this industry, it is thus desirable for a company to enter markets and build production lines first, then focus on stabilizing the business later. This method of rapidly entering and then leading markets has been Samsung's favored business strategy since it successfully entered the memory chip market.

After entering a new market, Samsung did not hesitate to rush construction and mobilize massive amounts of people and resources to catch up with competitors. If necessary, Samsung would have its employees work 7 days a week and operate assembly lines 24 hours a day. The passion of the employees, who share Samsung's corporate philosophy of constantly gearing up to be number one, led to the "Monday-Tuesday-Wednesday-Thursday-Friday-Friday-Friday" attitude.

Samsung's execution speed was also enabled by rapid communications. With a shared belief in a "Single Samsung" community and a shared identity as "Samsung people," the company was able to unify its management techniques throughout the group, helping to accelerate its pace of communications. Since 1996, Samsung accelerated its internal communication speed using the Six Sigma methodology, which required all employees to share common practices, language, and problem-solving skills. Communication was further bolstered through Samsung's globally integrated enterprise resource planning (ERP) and SCM systems, which enabled the company to obtain data in nearly real time.

Infrastructure and Systems to Raise Speed

Figure 5.2 describes Samsung's acceleration mechanism. The organizational culture consists of ambitious goal setting; creation of a sense of urgency; delegation of authority to field managers and a simplified decision-making process; employees' aspirations to become the world's number one; willingness to sacrifice and diligence; and use of common language and managerial systems based on Six Sigma. The management systems include preparedness and advanced development; speedy collaboration through clustering and vertical integration; goal-driven R&D and advancement in R&D processes; and innovations in IT processes based on global SCM and ERP systems.

Figure 5.2   Speed-Up Mechanism

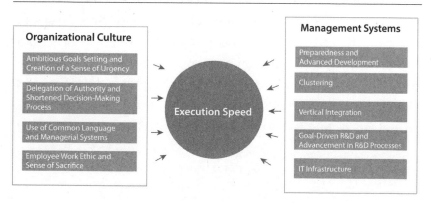

Preparedness and Advanced Development

In most cases, our starting line is different from that of competitors. We keep watching technology trends and developments in society. By doing so, we ready ourselves for any developments that will unfold in the future.

—*Kim Chang-Yeong, Executive Vice-President of Samsung Electronics*

and President of the DMC R&D Center

Chairman Lee stressed the importance of preparedness, saying, "We may slip into a crisis at any time if we are complacent about today's good performance. We need to prepare ourselves for five to ten years ahead." In line with this, he made hiring top-tier talent and securing technologies the top priorities in establishing mid- to long-term strategies and goals.

Chairman Lee's emphasis on preparedness compelled Samsung Advanced Institute of Technology and Samsung Electronics' Semiconductor R&D Center and DMC R&D Center to jointly draft and constantly update a 10-year road map to next-generation technologies. This readiness helped Samsung overcome difficulties later. For example, Samsung began full-scale research into core technologies for smartphones in 2006, which helped it ride out the sweeping effects of Apple's introduction of the iPhone 3G, which hit the market in 2008. In addition to this, Samsung Advanced Institute of Technology and the DMC R&D Center developed the mobile Digital Natural Image engine (mDNIe) technology optimized for smartphones, which was borrowed from Samsung's latest television models. By applying this to the Galaxy series smartphones from 2010, Samsung was able to maintain its technological lead, especially in display resolution.

Clustering

Samsung is speeding up its logistics processes by clustering the location of activities in its value chain. In addition to speeding the movement of physical goods, clustering also increases Samsung's ability to accelerate execution through problem solving and knowledge sharing. Samsung Electronics has located its division headquarters, major R&D, and production units in Suwon, Giheung, Hwaseong, and Cheonan, which are located within a radius of 30 kilometers. Most affiliate companies that supply materials and parts to Samsung Electronics also have their facilities in those areas.

Samsung has built 16 semiconductor fabrication plants in the adjoining cities of Giheung and Hwaseong, and has located its R&D facilities nearby.[13] The DS unit handling its semiconductor business also has its headquarters in Giheung. This clustering of headquarters functions, R&D, and production has enabled rapid and close-knit collaboration and communication between R&D and production units, significantly shortening both development time and the time required to establish mass production lines, stabilize processes, and raise yields.

Our competitors generally run their design and process architecture (PA)[14] functions in physically separate and distant locations. However, we have located these two functions close to each other. When we were developing our 1-megabyte DRAM chip, our design director would ask the PA division every morning, "What changes do you need?" The design team would then make the necessary changes within the day, with the PA team receiving improved mask sets three or four days later. In contrast, our competitors would take up to a week to get this process done.

—*Lee Won-Shik, former Executive Vice-President*
of Samsung Electronics

Raising yields is the goal of most semiconductor manufacturing. However, the sheer complexity of the process, which can entail some 400 to 700 steps, makes it critical that all the stages of production are seamlessly linked. This, in turn, makes interdepartmental cooperation imperative for rapid decision making and problem solving.

To this end, Samsung formed cross-functional task forces in which engineers and other professionals met on a daily basis to discuss issues and make necessary decisions on the spot. This would have been impossible if the R&D facilities and manufacturing plants had been in separate locations. Moreover, clustering plants made it easier for Samsung to transfer knowledge, information, and human resources from one plant that had already reached an efficient operational level to another, thereby enhancing yields.

Such "agglomeration economies" proved themselves again when Samsung Display concentrated its panel production lines in the city of Cheonan, which is located 50 kilometers from Suwon. Major parts and materials suppliers moved to the region, increasing the benefits that Samsung enjoyed in terms of rapid procurement.

In particular, to realize agglomeration economies in R&D, Samsung clustered all its related facilities in one area, an uncommon move for a multinational business. Research facilities for the Consumer Electronics (CE) and Information Technology and Mobile Communications (IM) divisions were all located in a single complex in Suwon. This made it easier to ensure face-to-face communications and collaboration, thereby accelerating the convergence of products and technologies as well as product development.

How has clustering become one of Samsung's core competencies? Samsung's competitors were less able to cluster their labs and plants because of geographical and budget constraints, or because of concerns about natural disasters (including earthquakes). Samsung's ability to cluster its facilities allows it to gain an advantage in speed relative to competitors that is difficult to replicate.[15]

Vertical Integration

Vertical integration, where internal business units or affiliates manufacture critical parts and materials, is another major factor that has contributed to Samsung's ability to create speed. An integrated local supply chain eliminates barriers like language, business culture, and way of thinking that arise when a company uses external suppliers. Thus, communication problems are minimized, resulting in time savings.

To prevent conflicts of interest, there is a strong wall between Samsung's consumer products division and its components division, ensuring that customer information is secure and confidential. Samsung's semiconductor division, for example, supplies its products not only to Samsung Electronics' mobile division, but also to competitors like Apple and Nokia. If confidential information from Samsung's semiconductor division were leaked to its mobile division, Apple and Nokia would end their relationship with the semiconductor division.

Accordingly, Samsung's parts divisions, including semiconductors, stress equal treatment of in-house users and external clients, ensuring that confidential information about parts customers is never leaked. Nonetheless, Samsung's common language and culture and the units' geographical proximity allow smoother communications and feedback between the divisions than with external clients.

By the mid-2000s, Japanese companies needed 10 months on average to plan and release camera-equipped mobile phones. Samsung, in contrast, could complete the process in only 5 months through interaffiliate collaboration, an approach that continues today. Samsung's pursuit of leadership in the TV industry also benefited from the clustering of Samsung Advanced Institute of Technology, the DMC R&D Center, the System LSI division, and the Visual Display division. By collaborating, these organizations completed the development of A1, a core system-on-chip (SoC) technology for digital TV, in 14 months, allowing Samsung to commence mass production of TVs only 6 months later. By assembling all of the company's know-how and expertise in a single place and making decisions quickly, Samsung was able to slash the time from development to commercialization from 36 months to 20 months.

Likewise, clustering led to strong returns in Samsung's display panel business. Samsung's LCD plant in Cheonan sharply reduced time and production costs by transporting unpackaged glass from Samsung Corning Precision Materials,[16] which is located near its production lines, through underground air .tables. Collaboration with the system semiconductor division in developing display driver integrated circuits helped cut development time in half compared to rivals.

Goal-Driven R&D

Parallel Development

To hasten the development of a new product or technology, Samsung often encourages internal competition, with different teams trying to develop the same product or technology. For example, a domestic team and a team from Samsung Semiconductor (SSI) in San Jose, California, competed to develop the first 1-megabyte DRAM chip, greatly increasing the development speed. In a race to find the best alternative to a traditional TV screen, Samsung SDI and Samsung Electronics competitively developed plasma display panels (PDP) and LCD panels, respectively.

Leapfrog R&D

We develop first-, second-, and third-generation technologies simultaneously through competition and cooperation. We do this because we do not know when or how our efforts to develop technologies will end in success.

—*Kim Hak-Sun, Executive Vice-President of Samsung Display and Head of the Display Research Center*

Leading companies are generally reluctant to transfer their technologies to latecomers such as Samsung. To catch up with industry leaders early on and lead in the technological development race, Samsung adopted a leapfrog R&D strategy, investing in next-generation, next-next-generation, and next-next-next-generation technologies simultaneously. By applying this strategy, Samsung managed to narrow the gap between it and the industry leaders through intense commitment of manpower and resources, and even put its technology two or three steps ahead of its rivals in some areas. When even this process of internal technology development proved too slow, Samsung began to rely on "Lego-style" R&D, boldly introducing technologies from outside—even at great cost—and merging these technologies with Samsung's own. Moreover, by recruiting experienced engineers and top-rated scientists by offering high salaries, Samsung was able to further accelerate its speed of technology acquisition, application, and development. More recently, as technology has grown more complex and the need for speed has grown, Samsung has increasingly recruited outside technologies through open innovation and strategic alliances.

Upgrading of the R&D Process

Most companies complete the development of products before they set up their production lines. In contrast, Samsung uses concurrent engineering to carry out various activities—including product development and the setting up of production lines—simultaneously. This allows the company to respond more rapidly and flexibly to changes in the technological environment. Since the 1990s, Nokia and other innovation-driven companies have scrambled to adopt this methodology.

Samsung's successful use of concurrent engineering is evident in its mobile phone development process. When it develops phones, Samsung mobilizes not only its R&D personnel, but also employees from marketing, product planning, design, production, and procurement to work together from the earliest stages of development. This has allowed the company to drastically reduce time to market. In contrast, sequential development requires much more time and makes it more difficult to reflect customer needs during product planning, development, and design. By involving the marketing department from the product planning stage, concurrent engineering allows the development of more customer-focused products. Furthermore, concurrent engineering facilitates collaboration among production, procurement, and R&D, allowing Samsung to preemptively address technical problems or specific issues in the product development process. The end result is that product designs are easier to manufacture, defect rates are lower, and the time needed to procure parts and commence mass production is reduced.

Concurrent engineering was used to great effect when Samsung caught up with its rivals in the DRAM business by engaging in product development and setting up production systems almost simultaneously. From the early stages of the process, Samsung's development and production units worked closely together, allowing the production units to begin installing assembly lines while development was still underway. Thanks to this collaboration, Samsung was able to reduce the time from development to mass production by one year compared to its rivals. At times, production lines were built even before the development stage was completed.

Kim Ki-Nam, president of the memory business at Samsung Electronics, who had previously led the Semiconductor R&D Center, said that Samsung was able to shorten the time needed for development thanks to close integration between development and production, which laid the groundwork for Samsung's securing competitiveness by building its production systems rapidly.

> Samsung Electronics tightly integrated development and production by closely involving engineers in all stages of the process, from design to mass production. By building a system where engineers could participate in every process, Samsung was able to facilitate better information sharing and rapidly resolve technical issues. This allowed Samsung to apply its production expertise in the development stage, helping it anticipate technical issues that might arise when mass production began. The biggest driver behind this close integration of development and production is the fact that Samsung Electronics is the only semiconductor manufacturer in the world with design and manufacturing facilities in the same place.

Process Innovation Through Advanced IT Infrastructure

As was explained in Chapter 4, deploying IT-based innovations throughout its processes, including the establishment of globally integrated ERP and

SCM systems, played an important role in making speed one of Samsung's core competencies. Studies have shown that managers who have access to real-time operations data can make good strategic decisions more quickly. Samsung's securing of real-time data through its advanced IT infrastructure has greatly contributed to its rapid decision making and execution.

In the wake of the 2008 global financial crisis, demand for durable goods declined sharply worldwide, and market volatility and uncertainty rose. Despite this, Samsung was able to use its world-class ERP and SCM systems to adjust production, sales, and inventory at the right time, with the result that it suffered significantly less impact from the crisis than rivals like Sony. As explained in Chapter 4, Samsung has built a Global Operations Center at its headquarters where managers can swiftly respond to changes in the environment based on accurate, real-time data from the ERP and SCM systems.

CHAPTER 6

SAMSUNG'S SECOND SUCCESS FACTOR

Synergy Through Convergence

6

When the Galaxy S4 was released in March 2013, *Bloomberg Businessweek* mused on the competitiveness of Samsung's smartphones.

Samsung's ability to produce displays, memory, processors, and other high-tech parts gives it a flexibility competitors can't touch. That flexibility enables it to produce much more diverse product line-ups than competitors can.[1]

—Bloomberg Businessweek

Insiders at Samsung have similar views about the unique factors powering Samsung's success. In fact, the majority of Samsung executives that the authors have interviewed over the last 10 years point to synergy resulting from interaffiliate cooperation as the key factor that differentiates Samsung from its competitors. President Shin Jong-Kyun, who oversees Samsung's IT products, including mobile phones, has said, "Samsung Electronics' mobile division's strategic strength lies in creating synergy through co-opetition with the world's best supplier of memory, application processors, display panels and batteries (that is, other Samsung Electronics affiliates), while pursuing continuous innovation."

Samsung's pursuit of synergy through convergence goes back to the reforms initiated by Chairman Lee under the New Management initiative. Lee held that the synergy that Samsung creates through its diversified business structure is its main source of competitive advantage.

Samsung Electronics is one of the few companies in the world that handles components, digital products, home electronics, and communications businesses under one roof. These divisions cooperate with and support each other.

—*Chairman Lee Kun-Hee in an interview with* Korea Economic Daily *in 2002*

The core of corporate competitiveness in the twenty-first century lies in convergence. Convergence merges infrastructure, facilities, functions, technologies, and software to create organic synergies that maximize Samsung's competitiveness and efficiency.

—*Lee Kun-Hee at a London Samsung meeting on June 30, 1993*

The Basis of Synergy Creation: Diversified Business Structure

To realize the benefits of convergence, Samsung pursues horizontal diversification and vertical integration, convergence of products and services, and regional clustering of major activities (see Figure 6.1).[2] By linking these three factors organically, Samsung can pursue synergy, making the whole of Samsung's business greater than the sum of its parts.

Conglomerates and Synergy Creation

Rosabeth Moss Kanter, a professor of business at Harvard Business School, has stated that a business group that fails to create synergy has no reason to exist.[3] Notwithstanding her assertion, many conglomerates in fact do not create synergy; even worse, they may create negative synergy.[4] During the 1997 Asian currency crisis, for example, more than 10 of Korea's largest business groups including Daewoo collapsed because they continued to support

Figure 6.1   *Synergy Creation Through Convergence*

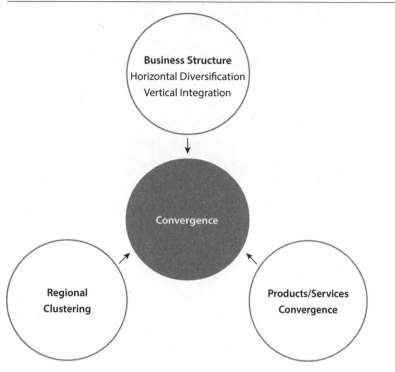

insolvent affiliates, instead of spinning them off or liquidating them. This support of businesses that were not viable then caused the conglomerates' main business lines to fail. Empirical studies have shown that unrelated diversification, in which a company expands laterally into an unrelated business, is likely to have a negative impact on performance.[5] Likewise, the resource-based view of the firm emphasizes the importance of dynamically optimizing a company's resources and capabilities in line with the characteristics of its industry, rather than the indiscriminate pursuit of diversification into fields whose relationship with the existing business is tenuous. Samsung, however, has repeatedly defied these predictions by successfully operating businesses in seemingly unrelated areas ranging from manufacturing to finance and services. Samsung has been able to do this by realizing synergy through the optimization of its businesses at a group level based on diversification, vertical integration, clustering, and groupwide cooperation.

Synergy in the Era of Convergence

As the Internet, communications networks, and other digital technologies continue to develop rapidly in the twenty-first century, industries, products, services, and businesses are tending to converge. Convergence is erasing the boundaries between industries, requiring new business models that can leverage such effects. Convergence has been particularly evident in the electronics industry, where it began appearing in the early 2000s in the form of multipurpose devices. By the late 2000s, "network convergence" among communications, broadcasting, and services had appeared, while the 2010s saw the rapid diffusion of smart devices, social networking services, and cloud computing. Along with convergence, a "ubiquitous era" is fast approaching, in which every product will come with its own internal computer that communicates with other products over networks (for example, the "Internet of Things").[6]

In this age of convergence and ubiquitous communications, Korean business groups are uniquely positioned to gain a competitive advantage against foreign rivals who focus on a single business. This is because such business groups, under the guidance of their headquarters organizations, share a common corporate culture and philosophy that allows them to handle internal communications smoothly and coordinate interests within their organizations. Samsung is the leading example of a successful business group for the new era.

Samsung has built a business structure that has a strong fit with the era of digital convergence—it produces everything from core technologies and parts to finished products in semiconductors, liquid-crystal displays (LCDs), and digital media, as well as home electronics and communications devices. Samsung's diverse business structure, along with its pursuit of vertical integration, realizes the benefits of synergy from the convergence of products with other products as well as the convergence of products with components. By leveraging convergence and network effects to provide solutions to customer needs rapidly, Samsung has ensured that it will be a leading business in this new era.[7] Samsung has the technologies and businesses needed for leadership of the digital convergence age, as well as speedy decision making and execution, effective management systems, and strong leadership from the owner-manager, allowing it to organically coordinate its diverse businesses for maximum effect.

Historical Background for Samsung's Business Group Structure

Like those of other Korean business groups, Samsung's business structure focusing on diversification, vertical integration, and clustering was a result of Korea's status as a developing country after the 1960s. The company's need to grow into a large business was particularly spurred by Korea's less developed markets for capital, finance, labor, and products, as well as its embryonic domestic market for parts and materials.[8] As Korea's economy increasingly coalesced around conglomerates, it became increasingly difficult to purchase parts, materials, and services from competing business groups, with the result that companies had to either import them from foreign companies or produce the needed items themselves. Therefore, Samsung formed a business group that produced parts, materials, and services internally, creating an internal market and allowing it to overcome the constraints posed by an underdeveloped external market.

In the past, moreover, Samsung was also able to create an internal capital market that procured funds from existing affiliates and used those funds to enter promising new businesses. Today, however, regulations have made it very difficult to enter new businesses by transferring funds between listed affiliates.

Like its business structure, Samsung's "people first" policy emerged as a means of coping with conditions in Korea at the time. These conditions included an underdeveloped labor market that suffered from a shortage of managers and engineers with strategic insight, management skills, and technical capabilities. Under this policy, Samsung aggressively fostered people internally and then assigned them to enter new businesses. By circulating its core human resources through different businesses in the group, Samsung effectively created an internal labor market. Furthermore, quality assurance and consumer protection institutions were not well developed in Korea at the time. This spurred Samsung to ensure that its brand symbolized trustworthy products of high quality by developing quality assurance and consumer protection systems that were consistent among affiliates. In this way, Samsung supplemented the underdeveloped external product market by developing internal markets within the group.

Samsung's successful entry into the semiconductor industry is a prime example of the functioning of Samsung Group's internal market mechanism. With the active support of existing Samsung affiliates, Samsung Electronics was able to secure world-class competitiveness in a short time.

If Samsung Group had not concentrated its human resources, technology, funds, and overseas marketing skills in semiconductors, it would not enjoy the tremendous success it has achieved today.

—*Rhee Pil-Gon, former Chairman of Samsung C&T Corporation*

Samsung's successful entry into the LCD industry is another example of the company's ability to achieve success through transfers of capital, technologies, and human resources, particularly from its electronics and semiconductor divisions. Of course, not all of Samsung's attempts have been successful, as can be seen from Samsung's failed venture into the automobile industry. Entering new businesses in this way has significant risks, as a failed entry can cause healthy affiliates that provide funds to the venture to themselves become insolvent, leading the entire group into bankruptcy or collapse.

Nevertheless, a well-designed synergy creation strategy supported by a coordination mechanism providing capable managers and management systems can give a conglomerate a competitive advantage over specialized businesses. GE and Samsung are leading examples. At Samsung Electronics, the experience, resources, and capabilities accumulated in the process of achieving success in one division are rapidly shared with other divisions. Thanks to this sharing, Samsung can pursue various businesses and products simultaneously, making them world-class in a short time. Samsung has thus developed a virtuous circle of technologies, human resources, funds, and information within its organization that connects and coordinates various products and businesses. In particular, Samsung's semiconductor division shared its DNA for success with other divisions, including display panels, TVs, mobile phones, and home electronics, allowing each in turn to achieve a global level of competitiveness. Samsung's diversified business structure also ensured that Samsung as a whole could easily weather a downturn in one product category, as another product category would probably be in a favorable position, allowing Samsung to expect stable revenues and income.

Convergence Synergy: How Was It Created?

How was Samsung able to leverage synergy through convergence in its diversified business structure by creating product convergence, regional clustering, and vertical integration of components? Management theorists have come up with various definitions of the types of synergy that can be created through corporate strategy, but two overall definitions prevail. One kind of synergy provides tangible and immediate benefits, such as entry into new markets through the transfer or linking of core competencies, increased sales through joint product development or joint marketing, and cost reduction through shared services. The other kind of synergy is more intangible, with benefits emerging over the long term based on shared knowledge, know-how, and branding. According to Michael Goold and Andrew Campbell, leading scholars on business synergy, the forms of synergy include shared tangible assets, shared know-how, a unified negotiation window, consolidated strategy, vertical integration, and joint creation of new business. The value achieved through these synergies can include increased sales, reduced costs, and shared knowledge and information.[9]

As Figure 6.2 indicates, Samsung's synergy begins with the owner-manager, who serves as an anchor for the group, and the spirit of "Single Samsung" as a cultural community. With this foundation, the Corporate Strategy Office can monitor and coordinate Samsung's affiliates. Various committees and conferences that have been established between affiliates and business divisions, and between business functions, allow the sharing of technology, information, knowledge, and branding, while conflicting interests and activities can be dealt with systematically. Samsung's unique clustering and knowledge management systems further stimulate and promote this process. Through cooperation and convergence, Samsung can leverage synergy that enhances its cost competitiveness, leading to higher sales, as well as its "soft competitiveness" based on its unique intangible assets, throughout the entire organization.

Synergy from Increased Sales

Samsung has achieved sustainable growth in the form of increased sales by consolidating the sources and capabilities of the group, including experience from successful businesses, core competencies, and human resources, to successfully enter new businesses or jointly develop and market new products.

Success in LCDs

The LCD business is a prime example of a situation in which Samsung leveraged the core competencies that it had built in existing related businesses to rapidly climb to the world's number one spot, achieving massive sales in the process. LCDs and memory chips are fundamentally similar and share the same business concept in that they both require large-scale facilities for production and demand a rigorous devotion to refining the production processes to increase yields. Having already secured a leading position in pro-

Figure 6.2   Samsung's Structure for Creating Synergy

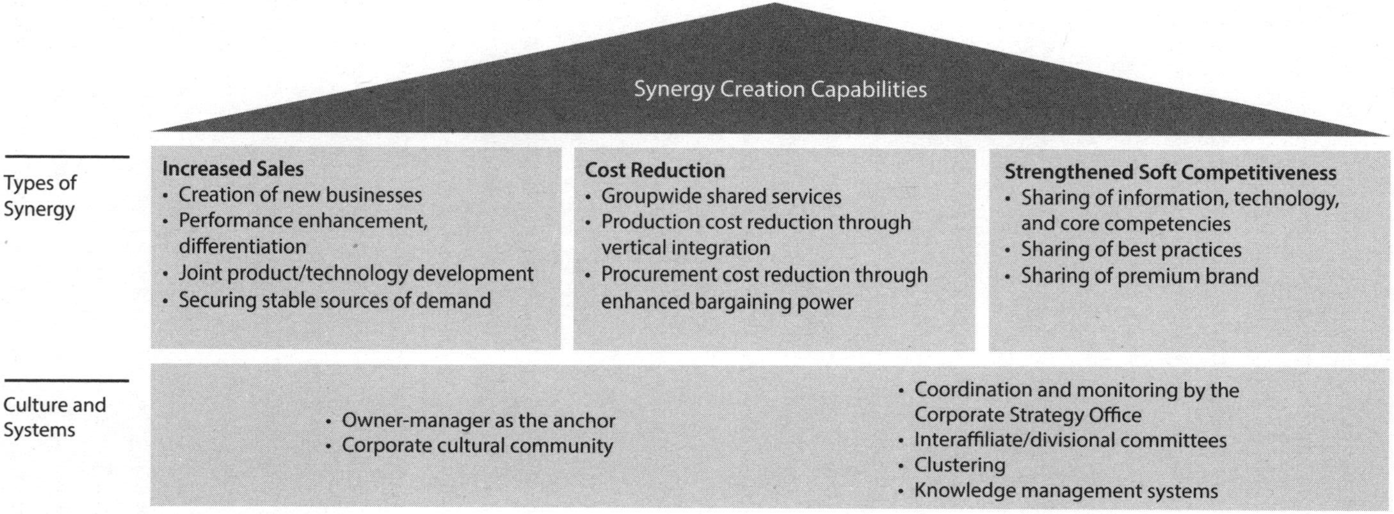

Synergy Creation Capabilities

Types of Synergy

Increased Sales
- Creation of new businesses
- Performance enhancement, differentiation
- Joint product/technology development
- Securing stable sources of demand

Cost Reduction
- Groupwide shared services
- Production cost reduction through vertical integration
- Procurement cost reduction through enhanced bargaining power

Strengthened Soft Competitiveness
- Sharing of information, technology, and core competencies
- Sharing of best practices
- Sharing of premium brand

Culture and Systems
- Owner-manager as the anchor
- Corporate cultural community
- Coordination and monitoring by the Corporate Strategy Office
- Interaffiliate/divisional committees
- Clustering
- Knowledge management systems

cess technology in memory chips in the early 1990s, Samsung transferred its technical expertise and skilled human resources from semiconductors to its LCD business to develop the necessary core competencies in a short period. Furthermore, since almost 90 percent of its customer base in the LCD and memory semiconductor businesses overlapped, Samsung was able to use a unified marketing network to provide customers with one-stop service, boosting its bargaining power with customers while simultaneously reducing marketing costs.

Success in Mobile Phones

The semiconductor sector has always played a central role in creating synergy for Samsung Electronics' product development. This is because semiconductors are a critical component of final products like mobile phones and TVs, and are likewise critical to creating product differentiation and competitiveness. In the early 2000s, semiconductors helped Samsung realize synergies for its mobile phone business: its semiconductor division designed and produced system semiconductors for mobile phone display control chips, and also audio chips that could produce 40 polyphonic ringtones. The system semiconductor operation also collaborated with the mobile division to jointly develop a modem chip. More recently, Samsung's semiconductor division has developed the world's most powerful mobile application processors for use in Samsung's smartphones. Samsung Display also contributed to this synergy when it became the first company in the world to develop and produce active-matrix organic light-emitting diode (AMOLED) display panels. Since there was only one supplier of panels at the time, the demand for panels vastly exceeded supply. Samsung Display was able to provide almost 90 percent of its output to Samsung's mobile division, allowing Samsung smartphones to secure a competitive advantage in image quality.

As shown in Figure 6.3, Samsung's mobile division, the world's top producer of mobile phones, provided Samsung's semiconductor division and Samsung Display with a stable source of demand. In addition, the semiconductor and Samsung Display could use the mobile division as a "test market" for their products, receiving speedy feedback and allowing them to make

Figure 6.3   *Synergy in the Mobile Phone, Semiconductor, and Display Panel Businesses*

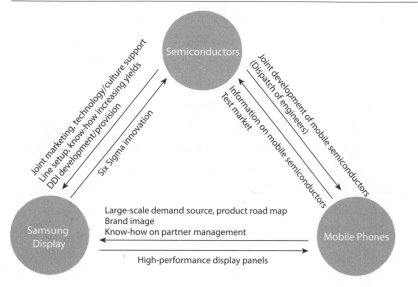

prompt fixes and upgrades to components. This, in turn, allowed Samsung's component divisions and companies to provide high-quality products to outside customers.

Success in TVs

As in the previously discussed cases, the convergence synergy that stemmed from cooperation between the components and finished product ("set") divisions played a conspicuous role in the success of Samsung's TV division. Samsung's 1995 Plus One TV, for example, was the first wide-screen cathode-ray tube (CRT) TV to be sold. During its development process, a task force of 55 researchers from Samsung's four electronics-related affiliates (Electronics, SDI, Electro-Mechanics, and Samsung Corning Precision Materials) met several times a month. As a result of their efforts, Samsung was able to develop and launch the Plus One successfully in only seven months. Similarly, Samsung Advanced Institute of Technology and Samsung's semiconductor division contributed greatly to the development and mass production of the

Digital Natural Image engine (DNIe) chip, a core part of Samsung's TV chipset that introduced groundbreaking improvements in digital TV image quality. Likewise, Samsung Electronics collaborated with Samsung Display to realize Samsung's "One Design" styling of ultraslim panels and frames, helping Samsung achieve product differentiation and cost competitiveness through unified component design, in addition to structural innovation.

This close cooperation between Samsung's component and set divisions has allowed it to achieve convergence synergy, which in turn has led to product performance differentiation and enhancement. As a result, Samsung has enjoyed increased sales and market share. Furthermore, as with Samsung's entry into the LCD and organic light-emitting diode (OLED) markets, the company was able to transfer the experience, core competencies, and human and other resources that it had accumulated elsewhere to successfully create a new business in digital TVs. At the same time, Samsung's vertical integration ensured both a stable supply of components and materials and a stable source of demand, allowing it to both offer its largest customers attractive terms and increase its bargaining power. For affiliates, the result was a win-win outcome for everyone involved.

Synergy from Cost Reduction

Samsung has achieved cost-reducing synergy by centralizing and consolidating shared services at a group level, increasing bargaining power through joint purchasing, and vertical integration. Samsung's Human Resources Development Center is a leading example of its ability to provide shared services within the group. The center acts as a single source for all of the company's executive and managerial education and training. This ensures greater expertise and effectiveness, as well as cost savings compared to running separate programs at each affiliate. Likewise, think tanks like Samsung Advanced Institute of Technology and Samsung Economic Research Institute provide shared technology and management services, respectively, for all of Samsung Group's affiliates.

Moreover, Samsung has established a degree of vertical integration that is unprecedented in the electronics industry by developing its materials, parts, and finished products divisions simultaneously. In the early 2000s, only 40 percent of the components and materials for Samsung's mobile phones were purchased internally. By 2013, the figure had reached 63 percent with the introduction of the Galaxy S4 smartphone, according to the bill of materials estimates that IHS made.[10] This vertical integration allows Samsung, as a company that produces finished products, to shorten development times and integrate designs while reducing costs.[11] Samsung's mobile division, for example, receives the majority of its main components from Samsung's semiconductor division, Samsung Electro-Mechanics, Samsung SDI, and Samsung Display. Samsung Display, in turn, procured core components like LCD boards from Samsung Corning Precision Materials.[12]

Synergy That Builds Soft Competitiveness

Synergy between Samsung's affiliates produces further benefits in the form of increased soft competitiveness based on the affiliates' unique intangible assets. Active sharing of information, knowledge, and core competencies, along with the dissemination of best practices throughout the entire group, has allowed Samsung to increase the strength of its intangible assets, contributing to a premium brand image that, in turn, benefits the entire group.

Sharing Information and Best Practices

A majority of the products that are now available in the electronics industry are produced somewhere within Samsung Group. This wide scope provides Samsung with unprecedented access to industrial and technological data about the electronics industry on a worldwide scale. Such data, moreover, are closely shared among affiliates, allowing each affiliate to gauge the potential for product and technology convergence more accurately, and then achieve that convergence. While this type of information sharing and joint product development is also feasible with outside partners through strategic partnerships and outsourcing, Samsung's common language, culture, and management systems give its affiliates an extra advantage in reducing transaction costs and saving time.

In addition, this type of sharing is not limited to information, but also includes core competencies like knowledge, expertise, and best practices, which are actively transferred throughout the group. As mentioned previously, Samsung achieved great success through this form of sharing when it transferred process technology and knowledge from its semiconductor division to its LCD division. Core talent from the successful semiconductor division has regularly moved on to lead other divisions within Samsung Electronics and other affiliates in the group. This has greatly invigorated the sharing and transfer of knowledge throughout Samsung.

In particular, the sharing of best practices is active and ongoing. A prime example of this is Samsung's groupwide sharing of Six Sigma methodology. With all employees sharing the language and concepts of Six Sigma, Samsung has bolstered the sense of community embodied in "Single Samsung" and improved its synergy management. This type of sharing has allowed Samsung to disseminate best practices from a single successful affiliate to all affiliates in the group, creating management synergy.

Brand Sharing

Samsung's affiliates also benefit from the synergy provided by sharing a single brand. In 2013, Samsung ranked eighth in Interbrand's rankings of global brand value. The company's high brand value and name recognition have paid dividends, helping to grow Samsung's market share in areas where it is a relative newcomer, such as digital cameras, laptop computers, printers, and home appliances. This growth is also attributable, in part, to Samsung's ability to create synergy through product differentiation and cost reduction via interaffiliate cooperation, as it did with the Galaxy Camera. At the same time, growth in these areas also owes a great deal to the halo effect of Samsung's powerful brand in mobile phones and TVs, creating synergy from a shared brand.

Moreover, in a global knowledge-based economy, the synergy achieved by sharing intangible assets like knowledge, information, best practices, and brand is gradually becoming more important than the synergy achieved by sales increases and cost reductions resulting from direct internal transactions. In addition, although achieving the latter kind of synergy became more complicated after the 1997 Asian currency crisis, when pressure from shareholders and the Korean government for corporate governance reforms made it difficult for companies to transfer or share tangible assets, the synergy achieved by sharing intangible assets within Samsung Group is still very much feasible, and thus is growing in importance as a further source of groupwide synergy.

Infrastructure and Systems for Synergy Creation

Samsung recognizes that synergy—created through the convergence of its major products and business lines—is its main core competency. As a result, the company has attempted to establish infrastructure and mechanisms that facilitate the creation of synergy (Figure 6.4). These include

- The owner-manager functions as the anchor for synergy creation.
- Samsung shares common values, culture, and language, enabling it to foster loyalty and solidarity among its people.
- The Corporate Strategy Office adjusts and monitors relationships between affiliates to create synergy.
- Various committees discuss and propose collaboration between divisions and affiliates.
- Regional clustering and the construction of knowledge management systems build a common knowledge community.

Figure 6.4   Samsung's Synergy Creation Mechanism

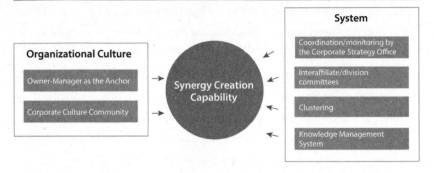

Governance Structure and Organizational Culture

The Owner-Manager as the Anchor for Synergy Creation

Samsung's owner-manager functions as both the sponsor and the anchor for the achievement of convergence synergy. Chairman Lee stressed synergy at the outset of the New Management initiative, and since then he has continued to emphasize convergence and synergy as key to Samsung's competitiveness. More recently, as creative management has grown in prominence, Lee has stressed the role of convergence synergy in successfully realizing creative management. In his 2007 New Year's address, for example, Lee stressed the importance of convergence for creativity by saying, "In contrast to the twentieth century, when production ruled, the current era requires convergent creativity that integrates soft capabilities like technological capabilities, marketing, design, and branding."

Corporate Culture Community

Samsung has created a close-knit culture by establishing a common set of values, as well as a common culture and language. This has enabled all Samsung employees, regardless of where they work, to have a strong sense of solidarity and belonging as members of the Samsung community. This groupwide community spirit, in turn, fosters cooperation and the creation of synergy among affiliates. Although each Samsung affiliate is an independent corporate entity, with its own board of directors, it also shares a common ideology and values with all the other affiliates.

This formation of a "Single Samsung" identity is in large part attributable to the shared education and training programs provided by the Samsung Human Resources Development Center, daily groupwide broadcasting from the Samsung Broadcasting Center, and "Single," Samsung's groupwide corporate intranet. Like Crotonville, GE's leadership development center, the Human Resources Development Center's programs for high-ranking executives and its shared education programs for different job ranks give Samsung's employees an opportunity to feel a sense of unity on a group scale. The center also allows the company to understand the current status and strengths of each affiliate, as well as providing the affiliates with a space where they can seek out common business opportunities. Samsung's groupwide education programs and meeting places allow Samsung employees to learn a common language, reducing communication costs and time and fostering greater unity.

Systems for Synergy Creation

Coordination and Monitoring by the Corporate Strategy Office

If a business group is to achieve synergy, it is critical that it has a headquarters organization that coordinates the relationships among its affiliates. Moreover, academic research in this area has confirmed that a business group must have a headquarters organization that acts as a control tower, and must tie the evaluations and compensation of the affiliates' executives to the performance of the entire group.

The core of Samsung's synergy management lies in the monitoring and coordination of Samsung affiliates that is done by the Corporate Strategy Office, which acts as a de facto headquarters for the group. The Corporate Strategy Office acts as an overseer for Samsung Group's business restructuring and for the sharing of Samsung's intangible assets. Rather than being an administrator, however, the Corporate Strategy Office acts as a "control tower," supervising groupwide strategy implementation, knowledge creation and sharing, and managerial support to affiliates.

The majority of the foreign business groups that practice synergy management maintain similar organizations. Disney's Synergy Group, for example, oversees and coordinates the sharing of information across the company's business lines and adjusts joint marketing and promotion plans.[13] For this kind of large-scale operation, a headquarters organization that coordinates interests between business units is essential.

In addition to the Corporate Strategy Office, Samsung has established other oversight organizations that coordinate the operations of affiliates and divisions. In 2004, for example, Samsung Electronics sought to invigorate its digital convergence and R&D synergy by coordinating technology development between affiliates and related divisions. To this end, it expanded and reorganized the role of Samsung Electronics' chief technology officer to include technology oversight. Although the technology oversight organization was disbanded when the organization had to be slimmed after the global financial crisis of 2008, the oversight function itself was preserved and transferred to Samsung Advanced Institute of Technology.

Groupwide Committees and Task Force Teams

Samsung consistently focuses on having "one direction" in its business plans. After the group's overall business plan has been set at the beginning of the year, each affiliate and business division determines its own business plan based on that of the group. In addition, in formal and informal committees and meetings at both the group and the affiliate levels, CEOs, executives, and experts in specific fields engage in detailed discussions and make decisions on how to create synergy.

Samsung holds regular weekly meetings of affiliates' CEOs to discuss cooperation among affiliates and future business directions. The results of these meetings are then acted upon under the leadership of each CEO. Likewise, executives of affiliate companies who are working on similar management functions meet regularly to coordinate activities across affiliates. A good example is the regular technology meeting for the chief technology officers of all the affiliates.

Task force teams and committees formed for specific objectives have also contributed greatly to synergy creation. Within Samsung Electronics, various committees have been formed to ensure that Samsung's strategy continues to have a single direction or to share know-how and coordinate interests among divisions, ensuring that activities are consistent across business lines. In addition, conferences for each operational function across the group are held regularly. One example of this kind of conference is Samsung's HR Conference, where HR staff from all over the world meet at the Samsung Human Resources Development Center to discuss the future of HR at Samsung.

Clustering

Regional clustering is another strategy that Samsung uses to pursue synergy among affiliates and divisions. Clustering refers to locating related companies, businesses, and departments in one site or within a certain region.[14] Through this strategy, Samsung has increased the efficiency of concurrent engineering, drastically cutting the time required to go from product development to mass production, while facilitating the transfer of knowledge and information and reducing logistics costs and time.

Samsung's strategy of clustering affiliates and business units' research institutes has facilitated the development of new converged technologies and products that have successfully achieved differentiation. In particular, Samsung's Suwon site has been transformed into a large-scale R&D cluster for Samsung's consumer products, including TVs and digital video devices, home electronics, mobile phones, and IT products. Previously, Samsung's research manpower in telecommunications and telecommunications-related semiconductors had been dispersed among Seoul, Suwon, Bundang, and Giheung. All of these research operations were brought together at the information communication research institute in Suwon in 2001, strengthening R&D synergy. In 2013, Samsung established the R5 building, the largest research institute in Korea, at its Suwon complex. R5, built to strengthen Samsung's research capabilities in smartphones, can accommodate 10,000 employees and brings all of Samsung's smartphone-related researchers together in a single build-

Figure 6.5   Regional Clustering Overseas

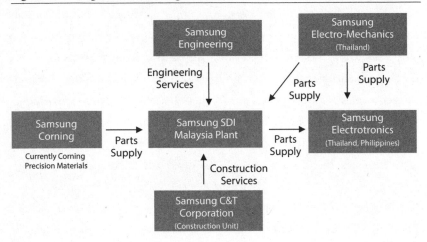

ing. For semiconductors and displays, Samsung has clustered its activities in Giheung. By clustering its research institutes into a one-stop system, Samsung has optimized synergy effects for an age in which speed is a requirement for competitiveness.

Samsung also pursues regional clustering in overseas markets. For example, the Seremban Industrial Complex in Malaysia is Samsung's first overseas industrial complex, developed jointly by Samsung SDI, Samsung Corning Precision Materials, and Samsung Electronics (see Figure 6.5).

Through such overseas entry strategies, Samsung can reduce logistics costs while leveraging synergy in employee training, recruitment, information sharing, and government relations. When Samsung's mobile business was in its early stages, for example, Samsung was able to use the sales, logistics networks, and data that it had already built in its overseas home electronics operations to attain synergy.

Knowledge Management System

More recently, with the rise of the knowledge-based economy and the increasing importance of intellectual property, Samsung has focused on creating synergy through smoother knowledge sharing among its affiliates and business units. The leading example of this is "Single," Samsung's groupwide intranet, which provides domestic and global information to all Samsung employees and serves as a platform for online community activities.

Since 2001, Samsung also has been holding a "Samsung Technology Exhibition" as a means of building an infrastructure that creates technology synergy between affiliates. The exhibition consists of a display of technologies developed by Samsung's affiliates and a technology forum in which the R&D workforce shares its important technological developments and discusses directions for future R&D. Moreover, the exhibition provides an opportunity for Samsung to assemble its entire R&D workforce in one place to create synergy by having R&D engineers from different affiliates exchange ideas on technology and build networks. Since 2004, Samsung has held the Samsung Tech Conference to promote the improvement of its technology workforce's capabilities through technological exchanges.

In sum, Samsung still maintains a diversified business structure, as before. However, the company has developed various mechanisms to facilitate convergence and synergy in line with the overall trends of the digital convergence era. By doing so, Samsung has created a strong competitive advantage for itself relative to most competitors, who are restricted to a single or several industries.

CHAPTER 7

SAMSUNG'S THIRD SUCCESS FACTOR

Evolutionary Innovation

7

The foundations for Samsung's success lie in continuous technological innovation to meet consumer needs. In TVs, Samsung successfully anticipated the shift from analog to digital by releasing the world's first commercially available digital TV. Samsung then leveraged collaboration between its semiconductor and display affiliates to release innovative products like the Bordeaux TV, light-emitting diode (LED) TVs, 3D TVs, and smart TVs, attaining the number one position worldwide. In smartphones, Samsung accurately predicted the direction of the market and allied with Google, the developer of the Android platform. This resulted in innovative products like the Galaxy S and Galaxy Note.

—Kim Chang-Yeong, Executive Vice-President of Samsung Electronics
and Head of DMC R&D Center

Becoming a global leader in an intensely competitive industry requires incessant development of new products and technologies. This makes Samsung's rise from a latecomer to a leader all the more remarkable. Samsung's ascent to number one in semiconductors, organic light-emitting diodes (OLEDs), smartphones, and digital TVs was powered by its nature as a "learning organization," one that is dedicated to the creation, sharing, and dissemination of knowledge. *Learning* and *innovation* are keywords in all aspects of Samsung's management, and Samsung pursues both on all fronts.

Early on, Samsung made a commitment to giving priority to technology. The company then realized this commitment through continuous long-term investments in R&D, scouting of "genius-level" engineers, and acquisition of advanced technologies—even at a massive cost. Samsung then combined the knowledge that it obtained from these external channels with the knowledge that it produced internally to raise its dynamic capabilities in innovation to world-class levels.

At the same time, soft capabilities have become increasingly important as the knowledge-based economy creates a revolution in information, knowledge, and content. Even in manufacturing, soft values like creativity, software, content, design, branding, tailored solutions, and other innovations have gained ground on traditional sources of competitiveness like economies of scale and hardware superiority. Recognizing this, Samsung has increased its efforts to strengthen its technological innovation capabilities. Confronted with the constant need to produce new innovations and pioneer new markets, Samsung has placed the highest priority on gaining technological competitiveness through continuous innovation.

To build these capabilities, Samsung's leaders focused on learning, change, and innovation. They established highly challenging goals that could be met only through innovation, instilling a sense of crisis and a spirit of challenge throughout the organization. Samsung also made massive R&D investments to strengthen its internal innovation capabilities. Some of these investments took the form of organizations that specialized in learning, such as the Samsung Human Resources Development Center, Samsung Advanced Institute of Technology, and Samsung Economic Research Institute. These learning-oriented bodies functioned as Samsung's main agents for promoting systemic and long-term knowledge creation. As a result, Samsung built a culture that was highly receptive to learning and innovation, while upgrading its systems and processes from a multidimensional perspective.

To obtain further knowledge, Samsung also benchmarked and established strategic alliances with leading companies. More recently, Samsung has built a global R&D system by promoting open innovation and founding research institutes overseas. Moreover, Samsung has long recognized that people are the source of the knowledge that makes it competitive, something that is embodied in its "people first" philosophy. By securing core talent and making aggressive investments in employee education and training, Samsung has strengthened its people's capabilities while sharing and disseminating knowledge throughout the organization.

The Current Status of Samsung's Evolutionary Innovation Capability

In this section, we first elaborated what we mean by the evolutionary innovation capability. And then, we analyzed Samsung's evolutionary innovation capability in its major business lines of semiconductors, display panels, modile phones, and digital video devices.

What Is Evolutionary Innovation Capability?

Samsung's innovation capabilities are the by-products of aggressive investments in internal innovation along with the active pursuit of external knowledge. These capabilities have been demonstrated primarily through the improvement of existing technologies and product domains. Business scholars commonly refer to this type of innovation as "incremental innovation," "exploitative innovation," "continuous innovation," or "sustaining innovation."[1]

This book, however, prefers the term *evolutionary innovation* to refer to Samsung's style of innovation. This is because Samsung's innovation has evolved along existing technological trajectories. Before it became a world-class company, for example, Samsung was a fast follower that relied on cost savings or adding new features to gain competitiveness. This represents incremental innovation.

After Samsung achieved number one status, however, it began to push the frontiers of technology and to create new product categories. Examples of the former are Samsung's introduction of the world's first 3D memory chip design and its introduction of curved-edge technology for LED TVs. Examples of the latter can be found in Samsung's creation of the "phablet" category of smartphones and its development of the world's first fusion memory and active-matrix OLED (AMOLED) displays.

Innovations of this type cannot be described by terms such as *continuous innovation* or *sustaining innovation*. At the same time, Samsung's present form of innovation cannot yet be described as *discontinuous innovation* or *creative innovation*—the kind that changes the world by providing an entirely new technology, product domain, or business model. *Evolutionary innovation* is thus the best way to describe Samsung's form of innovation.

Samsung recognizes that building up its creative innovation capabilities will be its primary task in the future, and it has been pursuing creative management since 2006. Innovation to create industry-leading technologies, products, and services is Samsung's first priority in the global knowledge-based economy. Samsung has thus committed itself to securing creative innovation capabilities that can change the direction of the industry and create entirely new business areas.

This book examines Samsung's evolutionary innovation capabilities and contrasts them with its creative innovation capabilities, an area where Samsung is less competitive. Samsung is a world-class firm in terms of its speed of innovation and the efficiency of its R&D (as measured by the number of patents) in improving on existing technologies and products. This evolutionary innovation has been a major factor powering Samsung's success, and constitutes one of the main sources of its competitive advantage.

Samsung's Current Position

Samsung has leveraged its evolutionary innovation capabilities to secure a top position in semiconductors, display panels, TVs, and smartphones. In semiconductors, Samsung developed charge trap flash in 2006 based on its experience in pioneering the "gigabyte dynamic random access memory (DRAM)" era in 2003. Samsung's new flash memory technology was viewed as the successor to NAND flash, the first form of nonvolatile memory, which was invented in 1971. Samsung was also first to apply a 3D structure to DRAM and flash memory, widening its market share lead. Furthermore, Samsung developed the world's first commercial phase-change random access memory (PRAM) product, ensuring that it remains the leader in the next generation of memory chips.

Evolutionary Innovation in Semiconductors

In recent years, the semiconductor industry has undergone a shift in focus from PCs to mobile devices, and then to mobile convergence, with multiple functions being combined in a single device. In response, Samsung has created a new market in fusion memory. In 2004, Samsung introduced the world's first fusion memory chip, the One NAND, which leveraged the high read speeds of NOR flash and the fast write speeds and high capacity of NAND flash. In 2006, it developed its second fusion memory product, the 512-megabyte One DRAM, which combined DRAM and static RAM (SRAM) into one DRAM chip for mobile devices. Samsung's groundbreaking fusion memory innovations have contributed greatly to the miniaturization of today's mobile and digital devices. Fusion memory was also a turning point for the memory chip industry, which had once been seen as peripheral to the central processing unit (CPU). Samsung was able to broaden demand for fusion memory chips to new markets in smartphones, full-high-definition (HD) TVs, interactive content TVs, digital cameras, and digital picture frames. By providing a "total memory solution," Samsung has transformed itself into the world's top total mobile solution provider.

More recently, Samsung has been pursuing evolutionary innovation in system chips, an area where it had been comparatively weak. Samsung's innovation is particularly notable in mobile application processors, the "brains" of today's smartphones. Samsung's systems semiconductor division recently adopted the world's first "big little architecture" and introduced the Exynos 5 Octa processor, a chip with eight cores that powers Samsung's Galaxy S4. As a result of its mobile applications processor innovation, Samsung grabbed the world's number one ranking in quad-core applications processors in 2012, with an overwhelming market share of 74.6 percent.[2]

Evolutionary Innovation in Display Panels

Samsung has also pursued evolutionary innovation in display panels. Samsung was the first manufacturer in the world to mass-produce OLED displays; it also pioneered AMOLED displays for mobile devices, gaining dominant global market share. In liquid-crystal display (LCD) panels, Samsung developed the world's first 3D panels using shutter glass technology, increasing its global market share in televisions. In 2004, Samsung Advanced Institute of Technology became the first organization in the world to successfully develop a 60-inch carbon nanotube field-emission display (CNT-FED). This technology is regarded as the next generation in display panels because of its greatly reduced power consumption, its thin size, and its vivid color.

Evolutionary Innovation in Telecommunications and Mobile Phones

Samsung's telecommunication technologies have also risen to world-class levels. Samsung developed the world's first wireless broadband (WiBro or mobile WiMAX) Internet service and supplied it to Sprint, one of the leading mobile communication providers in the United States. In 2006, Samsung became the first to develop and successfully demonstrate 4G technology. Samsung was also the first to release dual folder phones and MP3 phones, and the first to introduce thin-film-transistor LCD (TFT-LCD) screens on mobile phones. In smartphones and tablets, Samsung was first to market with pen computing solutions, and it pioneered the "phablet," a device with the features of both a smartphone and a tablet, with its successful Galaxy Note.

Evolutionary Innovation in Digital Video Devices

Samsung also leveraged its evolutionary innovation capabilities to increase its global share in digital video devices. After investing 50 billion won and dedicating 600 researchers to the project for more than a decade, Samsung released the world's first mass-produced digital TV in 1998. In the process, Samsung registered 1,500 patents. This marked a turning point for Samsung, as it surpassed Sony to become the reigning player in digital TVs. In 2000, Samsung developed the world's first combined VCR/DVD player. In 2006, it beat Japanese firms to market with its Blu-ray player, cementing its leadership in the next generation of digital media playback.

Samsung Electronics' TV division has advanced its evolutionary innovation capabilities in collaboration with its system semiconductor and display affiliates and releases new products every year—particularly in digital TVs.

Following the innovative Bordeaux TV in 2006, Samsung launched its Touch of Color (ToC) line of TVs in 2007, using double-injection technology. In 2009, Samsung released LED TVs, creating a new category in the market. Samsung's LED TV line arose out of the company's development of the industry's first curved-edge screens, providing consumers with an innovative ultra-slim (29.9 mm) high-definition screen.

Maintaining the momentum, Samsung Electronics, along with Samsung Display, launched the world's first shutter glass 3D TV in 2010. In 2011, Samsung once again created a new product category by developing smart TVs. In 2013, it further upgraded its smart TVs by equipping them with program recommendation functions, as well as a modular "Evolution TV" system that could upgrade the unit to the latest specifications.

Beginning in 2006, Samsung Electronics embarked on research for the High Efficiency Video Coding (HEVC) codec, a next-generation media encoding and playback technology. HEVC was approved as an international standard on January 25, 2013, and will be used in next-generation video services like ultra-high-definition (UHD) broadcasting, contributing greatly to the future development of TV.

A great deal of the credit for Samsung's innovation is due to the Samsung Advanced Institute of Technology. The institute, through close collaboration with other Samsung research institutes, has played a key role in the development of many of Samsung's core technologies, including charge trap flash (CTF), long-term evolution (LTE), OLED, image processing chips, and graphene chips.

How Were Samsung's Evolutionary Innovation Capabilities Formed?

Samsung's evolutionary innovation capabilities were built on both Samsung's own internal innovation and its ability to absorb knowledge from outside. When Samsung was still a fast follower, it relied on external knowledge derived from technology licensing, reverse engineering, strategic partnerships, and recruitment of experienced engineers, which allowed it to catch up with the leading companies rapidly. Simultaneously, Samsung strengthened its internal innovation capabilities through massive R&D investments and cooperation among affiliates, allowing it to absorb outside knowledge, improve on that knowledge, and achieve rapid and effective evolutionary innovation.

Since then, internal innovation has taken increasing precedence as Samsung has grown into a global leader. While the company continues to incorporate external knowledge through its overseas research institutes and its pursuit of open innovation, Samsung's internal capabilities now push the frontiers of technology and create new product categories. Figure 7.1 illustrates Samsung's evolutionary innovation capabilities.

Internal Innovation

To improve its internal innovation capability, Samsung has invested massive amounts in internal R&D. Additionally, the company changed its R&D strat-

Figure 7.1   *Structure of Samsung's Evolutionary Innovation Capabilities*

	Evolutionary Innovation Capabilities	
	Internal Innovation Capabilities	**Absorptive Capacity of External Knowledge**
Main Structural Factors	• Massive R&D investment • Upgrading of R&D and innovation approaches: Lego-style/leapfrog R&D, concurrent engineering, parallel development • Long-term technology road map	• Mix of internal and external technologies • Open innovation • Global R&D network • Securing overseas knowledge and talent
Culture and Systems	• Sense of crisis and stretch goals • Learning-oriented thinking and culture	• Systems to secure talent • Organizations specialized in learning • World-class manufacturing process technologies

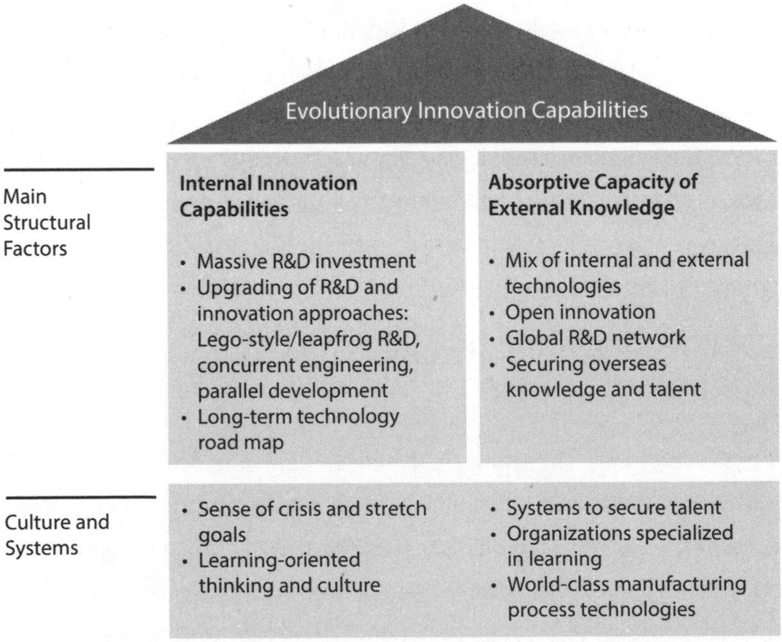

egy to emphasize R&D speed, efficiency, and technology leadership. In this section, we elaborate how Samsung has enhanced its evolutionary innovation capability internally.

Large-Scale Investment in R&D

In the twenty-first century, gaps in productivity will narrow. Competitiveness will be determined by soft capabilities or intangible assets like R&D and design.

—Chairman Lee Kun-Hee

Investment in R&D is crucial if companies are to secure and develop their technology and innovation capabilities. However, such investment is time-consuming and costly, and has very uncertain returns. According to agency theory, moreover, such investments are likely to result in a divergence of interests between the major shareholder (that is, the owner-manager) and the hired leaders (that is, the professional managers). Owner-managers typically pursue long-term profits, and will thus be more enthusiastic about R&D investment than professional managers, whose compensation is based on their short-term performance.[3]

After Chairman Lee launched Samsung's Second Foundation, Samsung shifted from process-oriented management to technology-oriented management. Samsung's regard for technology can be seen in the high percentage of science and engineering graduates among its CEOs—including Yun Jong-Yong, Lee Yoon-Woo, Kwon Oh-Hyun, Yoon Boo-Keun, Shin Jong-Kyun, Hwang Chang-Gyu, and Lee Ki-Tae. The company's focus on technology has given its technology departments a strong say in setting the company's direction. Moreover, achieving technological superiority and securing core technologies has become Samsung's first priority in any reviews of business feasibility.

Samsung has fully committed itself to investing in R&D, a practice it continued even as it restructured in the wake of the 1997 Asian currency crisis. As shown in Figure 7.2, Samsung Electronics invested 14.8 trillion won

Figure 7.2   Samsung Electronics' R&D Investment and Number of PhD Holders in R&D

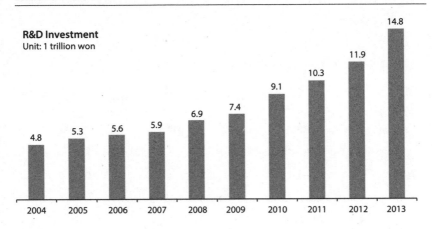

R&D Investment
Unit: 1 trillion won

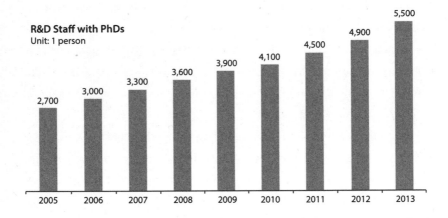

R&D Staff with PhDs
Unit: 1 person

(US$13.5 billion) in R&D in 2013, or 6.5 percent of total revenue. Up to 2008, R&D investment accounted for 9.5 percent of revenue. Even though R&D investments more than doubled in the five years after 2008, when 6.9 trillion won (US$6.2 billion) was invested in R&D, Samsung's revenues grew much faster, causing the share of revenue represented by R&D to decline slightly. Since Samsung Electronics' R&D spending was approximately 2.4 trillion won (US$1.85 billion) in 2001, actual R&D spending increased by more than six times over 10 years. According to OECD data, Samsung's R&D spending in 2010 ranked seventh highest among all companies worldwide.[4] In a survey by global consulting firm Booz & Company, Samsung ranked sixth in R&D investment in 2012. In addition to Samsung Electronics, Samsung's other electronics affiliates invest 6 to 10 percent of their revenue in R&D every year, two to three times as much as any other Korean firm. More than half of Samsung Electronics' Korean employees, amounting to 69,000 people in 2013, are engaged in R&D. About 5,500 of its researchers have doctorate degrees.

Samsung Electronics' R&D investment has increased even more since it announced its preparatory technology management strategy in 2005. "Preparatory technology management" refers to gaining leadership by establishing a complete technology management system that can respond to any change. Chairman Lee has stressed that "Samsung must concentrate on setting global standards by growing its intangible assets over the next 10 years. Without independent technologies, Samsung may become beholden to industry leaders and permanently become a second- or third-tier enterprise."

As concrete strategies for realizing its plans, Samsung Electronics selected and implemented "strategic investment," "technology first management," "highly efficient R&D," and "technology talent management." "Strategic investment" focuses on preemptive investment in facilities to attain an overwhelming market share, while "technology first management" focuses on strengthening preemptive R&D from a long-term perspective. Samsung's goal with these two strategies was to increase its number one products from 8 in 2005 to 23 by 2010. "Highly efficient R&D" focused on establishing an integrated R&D infrastructure to achieve the highest development speeds while reducing costs. This strategy achieved its targets in late 2006. Finally, "technology talent management" concentrated on building a creative R&D culture that could foster globally competitive technology experts.

Samsung's emphasis on innovation culminated in Chairman Lee's declaration of creative management in 2006. The new declaration called for moving beyond evolutionary innovation by strengthening Samsung's soft capabilities, including creative technology, design, and branding. Samsung would thus focus on creative innovation, further strengthening its preparatory technology management and increasing its investment in next-generation technologies.

More recently, Samsung has been putting increasing emphasis on software, which has long been the company's weak point. Responding to the rapid rise of smart devices, where software is of critical importance, Samsung increased its number of software engineers, both domestic and overseas, from 23,000 in 2010 to 39,000 by the end of 2013. Consequently, almost 60 percent of Samsung's R&D workforce is now in software. In particular, Samsung has made an all-out effort to attract foreign software specialists because of the lower availability of domestic software talent. In 2013, some 19,000 people, or almost half of Samsung's total software workforce, were working in more than a dozen overseas institutions under the supervision of the DMC R&D Center.

Samsung's evolutionary innovation capabilities are amply reflected in the number of its U.S. patents (see Table 7.1). The company recognizes intellectual property as its most valuable corporate asset, and has aggressively sought patents both at home and abroad since the 1980s. As patent disputes have increased in frequency and impact, including a prolonged dispute with Apple, Samsung has devoted increasing attention to managing its patent portfolio.[5] In 2006, Samsung had obtained 2,665 patents from the United States Patent and Trademark Office (second only to IBM) and has maintained its second-place status since then. As shown in Table 7.1, Samsung acquired 4,676 U.S. patents in 2013, almost triple the number of patents it acquired in 2005.

Patents have given Samsung stronger bargaining power. In its early years in the semiconductor business, for example, Samsung had to pay massive amounts of royalties to Texas Instruments, as its weak technology assets made it vulnerable to patent claims. Today, however, Samsung is the second-largest holder of U.S. patents, and it can respond to patent disputes through cross-

Table 7.1   Number of Patents Obtained by Samsung Electronics in the United States

Year	2005	2006	2007	2008	2009	2010	2011	2012	2013
Number of Patents (ranking)	1,641 (fifth)	2,665 (second)	2,752 (second)	3,515 (second)	3,592 (second)	4,518 (second)	4,868 (second)	5,081 (second)	4,676 (second)

licensing (exchanging patents with other companies). At present, Samsung has a broad range of cross-licensing agreements with global companies, including IBM, Sony, Google, and Microsoft.

Advances in Technology Innovation Strategy

As a latecomer, Samsung had to invest massive amounts in R&D to catch up with leading companies. Since then, however, Samsung's R&D strategy has moved beyond quantity to emphasize speed, efficiency, and leadership. Examples of Samsung's R&D strategy include Lego-style R&D, long-term technology road maps, the product life-cycle management (PLM) system, value innovation, and TRIZ.

Lego-Style R&D   Samsung's basic principle for R&D is, "Research should lead to the development of products." Samsung's R&D process is akin to a jigsaw puzzle, or a model made of Lego bricks.[6] The process starts with planning a product and then gathering as many as possible of the necessary technologies internally. After that has been done, other needed technologies are secured from outside the company, then assembled into a final shape in conjunction with internal technologies. This Lego-style R&D thus avoids the waste caused by "research for research's sake" or "development for development's sake," a mistake that has been made even by famed institutions like Xerox's Palo Alto Research Center. Instead, Samsung focuses its R&D budget on developing marketable products and raising the speed of its technology development in order to catch up with advanced companies.

Long-Term Technology Road Maps   Since its declaration of preparatory technology management in 2005, Samsung has widely deployed new R&D management measures to extend its technology lead over its rivals. Samsung Advanced Institute of Technology, along with Samsung Semiconductor R&D Center and DMC R&D Center, has drafted a technology road map for the next 10 years. This road map is updated as needed and provides a template for Samsung's development of next-generation leading technologies. Particularly in memory chips, Samsung develops technologies not just for the next generation, but for three generations down the road. In addition to its long-term goals, Samsung updates its five- to ten-year technology targets on a quarterly basis as new issues emerge.

Samsung received considerable help from outside experts in the early stages of establishing its long-term road map. As it became a technology leader, however, it began to draft its road maps mostly on its own. The company now forecasts changes for the next five years in detail, before selecting next-generation technology items and developing them in phases.

PLM System Samsung has introduced product life-cycle management across the board to enhance efficiency in R&D and to respond to market changes effectively. PLM helps the company manage R&D status and results along product life cycles systematically, from initial planning to end of product life. Through the PLM system, project managers can manage development schedules and input human resources. Samsung's PLM system is designed to enable all participants in a project to share information online in real time. The shared information includes product designs, blueprints, and required parts. When a project is completed, data that are relevant to new products are sent to other projects. To prevent recurrence of mistakes, major problems that arose during the development process and their associated solutions are stored in the system. Developers of new products or technologies can then search for relevant records in the system, and records of the data that they accessed are left in the system.

In 2012, Samsung invested 20 billion won in hardware and 90 billion won in software to reconstruct its PLM system. By having integrated management of development data among departments, including basic, advanced, and product research, Samsung's PLM system allows it to release products at the right time, while reducing development times and quickly adapting to user needs.

Value Innovation Samsung has aggressively introduced value innovation centered on the customer.[7] To this end, in 1998, Samsung Electronics established a VIP Center to promote value innovation and engineering. Samsung then developed a process for producing innovative products through close observation of customer needs. Value innovation has helped Samsung increase its customer focus, which, in turn, has led to more successful products. Examples of Samsung's value innovation include compact and affordable color laser printers for the home (2005), HD-DVD Blu-ray combo players (2007), low-noise front-loading washing machines (2008), and the stylus for the Galaxy Note (2011).

TRIZ   TRIZ is an innovation methodology that consists of a "theory of inventive problem solving." It focuses on improving creative problem-solving capabilities. Developed by Soviet inventor Genrich Altshuller, TRIZ asks, "What should be solved?" and, "How should it be solved?" simultaneously. TRIZ uses its own unique methodology, including some 40 TRIZ principles, to solve problems that arise during product development. Thus, TRIZ not only helps to resolve problems, but also promotes innovative ways of resolving them.

Samsung Advanced Institute of Technology adopted TRIZ in 1999 and made performing a TRIZ review on all projects before they started mandatory. After being successful in improving DVD pickup technology, Samsung Electronics adopted TRIZ companywide. The center for the expansion of TRIZ throughout the company is the VIP Center. Samsung's successful Bordeaux TV line, for example, with its wineglass-shaped profile, was a result of TRIZ methodology. Other success stories include Samsung's inkjet printer line (now number two in the world after HP) and the redesign of Samsung's semiconductor production process for the development of ultradense circuits. In 2006, seven of Samsung's electronics-related affiliates jointly established the Samsung TRIZ Association. Since then, Samsung's affiliates have shared best practices in TRIZ every quarter at executive meetings.

Absorption of External Knowledge

Samsung aggressively absorbs external knowledge to build its evolutionary innovation capability. The company mixes internal and external technologies, secures external knowledge through open innovation, and absorbs foreign knowledge and talent through a global R&D network.

Mixing of Internal and External Technologies

As with its practice of Lego-style R&D, leapfrog R&D, and parallel development, Samsung gives strong priority to speed and efficiency in its technology development. Accordingly, Samsung did not insist on using only its own technologies, but often introduced external technologies and then adjusted and improved them to fit its needs.

Samsung's strong R&D capabilities have played an important role in this process. In September 1992, for example, Samsung Electronics reached a deal with the U.S. company Qualcomm to use its technology in Samsung's mobile phones. Some 6½ years after its first production of the core chip for code division multiple access (CDMA) mobile phones, Samsung developed its own chip.

When it was difficult to purchase or license advanced technologies, Samsung was willing to offer domestic and foreign engineers generous employment terms to develop these technologies internally. When Samsung first entered the memory chip business in 1983, for example, leading companies in the United States and Japan refused to transfer their technologies. Only Micron Technology, a U.S. firm that was suffering from financial problems at the time, was willing to transfer its chip design technologies. Even Micron, however, was unwilling to turn over all of its knowledge of the development and production process, leading Samsung to invest heavily to acquire the ability to develop the technology itself.

To this end, Samsung aggressively recruited Korean engineers who were working at leading foreign semiconductor makers. Samsung Electronics often had to make multiple offers through repeat visits, even offering salaries three times higher than that of its own CEO. In 1983, Samsung established Samsung Semiconductor Institute in California, a research facility, to attract talented Korean and foreign engineers living in Silicon Valley. Samsung took this bold step at a time when establishing a large overseas research institute seemed unimaginable even for U.S. and Japanese firms.

When Samsung needed technical advice, it invited experienced foreign engineers. Japanese engineers played a critical role in Samsung's early moves into the semiconductor industry. Recently, Samsung's recruitment has expanded to encompass more than 1,000 foreign engineers from the United

States, India, China, Russia, and Japan who work at Samsung's R&D institutes in Korea. Samsung's recruitment of foreign talent, combined with its introduction of foreign technology through licensing, ensured that it had access to the best outside technologies, even while it was simultaneously making aggressive investments in the development of its own technologies. Investment in internal R&D, moreover, was necessary if Samsung was to boost its "absorptive capacity," allowing it to better understand and incorporate external technologies. Samsung was thus able to build dynamic capabilities for innovation in a short time by combining external and internal technologies.

Securing External Knowledge Through Open Innovation

With Samsung now a leader in mobile phones and TVs, it has become more important than ever to harness open innovation. Through this, Samsung can secure competitiveness in the face of stiff competition and rapid changes in the industry. On the one hand, Samsung should pursue open innovation through M&A and equity investment in innovative start-ups to support Samsung's business. More important, Samsung should strive for open innovation through collaboration with outside organizations like universities, research institutes, and start-ups to seek out and incorporate promising seed technologies."

—*Kim Chang-Yeong, Executive Vice-President of Samsung Electronics*
and Head of the DMC R&D Center

In an age of fast environmental change and increasingly complex knowledge development, companies can no longer rely entirely on themselves for knowledge creation. Consequently, "open innovation," or the rapid acquisition of outside knowledge in collaboration with outside partners, has grown in importance. Moreover, open innovation puts a high priority on innovation in ecosystems, making cooperation with key suppliers and "complementers" more important. Open innovation also advocates user-based innovation by including "prosumers" (that is, professional-level consumers) in the innovation process.

Samsung strongly embraced open innovation in the late 2000s. The concept was first promoted by Professor Henry Chesbrough in the early 2000s, and it gained popularity worldwide when Procter & Gamble achieved success with its "connect and develop" method, which used open innovation.[8]

As discussed earlier, Samsung had been introducing and incorporating outside knowledge long before such techniques were called open innovation. In addition, since the late 2000s, Samsung has been building a culture and a system for open innovation through increased investment in industry-academia cooperation, strategic equity investments in start-ups, and strategic alliances with major companies. By doing so, Samsung hopes to overcome the limitations of relying solely on internal technology development.

Open Innovation in the Semiconductor Industry Samsung has actively pursued strategic partnerships with leading global companies to develop technologies. This has been especially true in system semiconductors, one of the company's traditional weak points. Samsung entered a strategic partnership with IBM to develop state-of-the-art logic technologies in 2004, and successfully built its large-scale integrated (LSI) circuit business to global levels. Through this partnership, Samsung and IBM succeeded in developing a 65-nm and 45-nm logic process for 300-mm wafers. For the 32-nm process, Samsung participated in development with global system semiconductor companies like Infineon, Chartered, and Freescale. Samsung was thus able to develop a foundation for leading the industry in system LSI as well as in memory.

In 2001, Samsung's system semiconductor division entered into an agreement on next-generation CPU technology with British semiconductor designer ARM, the world's leader in CPU core design. The deal allowed Samsung to apply ARM's new core technology—particularly in smartphone application processors, where Samsung became a major player. In particular, Samsung's Exynos 5 Octa processor, which has eight cores and was used in the Galaxy S4 smartphone, was developed in close cooperation with ARM and was the first processor to use a big/little architecture.

Open Innovation in the Set Division   Securing key technologies through strategic partnerships contributed greatly to increasing Samsung's market share in video devices, helping the company become a world leader. Samsung's Digital Natural Image engine (DNIe) technology, for example, was developed jointly by Samsung Advanced Institute of Technology and a Russian partner. Although Samsung was not able to commercialize the technology at first because digital TVs were not yet widely available, it later provided an important basis for Samsung's expansion into the world's top digital TV maker from 2006 onward.

Similar success stories can be found in Samsung's mobile phone business. Samsung's Galaxy Note, for example, was developed in a strategic partnership with Wacom, a Japanese maker of digital input tablets and styluses for desktop PCs. Samsung cooperated closely with Wacom to develop a pen solution that would use Wacom's Digitizer pen on the electrostatic panel of smart devices like smartphones and tablets. Samsung used this technology in the Galaxy Note, with rousing success. Samsung later acquired 5 percent of Wacom's equity, with Wacom agreeing to use 53 billion yen from the acquisition to strengthen development and supply systems for the products it provides to Samsung. Industry analysts predicted that the deal would make Samsung a nearly exclusive customer for Wacom's mobile pen technologies.[9]

In addition to its strategic alliances with leading firms, Samsung also actively seeks out partnerships with domestic start-ups and small and medium-sized enterprises. In developing the Galaxy Note, for example, Samsung cooperated with the domestic start-up Flexcom, which makes flexible circuit boards. As Samsung was developing the Galaxy Note, it found that capturing writing or a drawing from a stylus was more difficult than making the stylus itself. Samsung thus turned to Flexcom for its experience in manufacturing flexible boards, and Samsung engineers worked there three or four days a week. After 18 months of work, Flexcom developed a "digitizer" that recognizes 256 degrees of pressure from the S Pen, the stylus for the Galaxy Note.

Industry-Academia Cooperation   Samsung has actively cooperated with major universities at home and abroad in a spirit of open innovation.

Domestically, Samsung Electronics' DMC R&D Center, which oversees the development of consumer products, has conducted joint research with leading universities in Korea, such as Seoul National University, Korea Advanced Institute of Science and Technology, Pohang University of Science and Technology, Yonsei University, Korea University, and Sungkyunkwan University, to develop technology solutions. Overseas, Samsung runs an industry-academia program that in 2012 included one Russian university, two Asian universities, eight American universities, and eight European universities to discover and test innovative ideas. Samsung also sends its researchers to top engineering schools in the United States, including MIT, the University of California-Berkeley, Carnegie Mellon University, and the University of Maryland, through its Industrial Affiliate and Visiting Researcher programs. Samsung's DMC R&D Center, in turn, runs a technology advisory panel of leading experts to seek out and respond to new technologies, with localized "sensing organizations" at more than 10 overseas institutes.

Crowdsourcing   In addition to the methods just discussed, Samsung pursues open innovation through crowdsourcing on websites like InnoCentive. Crowdsourcing publicly solicits the suggestions of outside experts and ordinary people concerning the product development, thus allowing them to participate in that development. Profits from any ideas or solutions that are adopted are shared with those who originally provided them. Samsung Display Research Institute, for example, attempted to crowdsource ideas for the attachment and detachment of flexible OLED substrates. Among the ideas submitted was using nonlaser methods at low cost, which is expected to be of great assistance in the development of flexible displays.

Securing Foreign Knowledge and Talent Through a Global R&D Network

Samsung has recently expanded its global R&D network by establishing a network of overseas research institutes. By securing technologies and talent through this network, Samsung has been able to strengthen its capabilities in both creative and evolutionary innovation. In 2013, Samsung Electronics had

21,000 overseas researchers in 29 research institutes in 16 countries, including the United States, the United Kingdom, Russia, China, Japan, India, Israel, and Poland. Some of the institutes in advanced countries, like Samsung's research center in Austin, Texas, handle research on next-generation technologies like the design of CPU cores.

Samsung has also worked to bolster its software capabilities—historically one of the company's weak areas—through its network of overseas research institutes. Software development at Samsung's overseas research centers focuses on different characteristics for each region. For example, Samsung Research America in Silicon Valley develops advanced software like UX and cloud applications, while Samsung Research India in Bangalore develops software related to IT. Samsung's institutes in Russia and Ukraine, on the other hand, leverage those countries' strong basic science workforce to develop physics- and mathematics-based algorithms for graphics and security software.

Samsung also runs a global mobility program that allows talented researchers at overseas institutions to come to Korea for work experience. In 2013, a total of 337 overseas employees of Samsung Electronics were sent to Korea, and 97 of them were R&D personnel. Samsung's global mobility program helps foster unity and pride among overseas employees. The program also helps participants to become leaders in their own country by giving them a greater understanding of Samsung's corporate culture.

Infrastructure and Systems for Evolutionary Innovation

Samsung has successfully leveraged its evolutionary innovations to achieve the number one position worldwide in semiconductors, TVs, smartphones, and display panels. The company's evolutionary innovation capabilities, as refined through its consistent efforts and aggressive investments, are one of its inimitable core competencies. As Figure 7.3 indicates, Samsung's unique culture and values, and systems have provided the basis for its evolutionary innovation capabilities. Thus, this section covers the organizational culture and systems that enabled Samsung's evolutionary innovation. However, it

Figure 7.3 *Samsung's Evolutionary Innovation Enhancement Mechanism*

excludes factors like Chairman Lee's emphasis on technology and innovation, cooperation among affiliates, and clustering, which have been discussed earlier.

Sense of Crisis and Stretch Goals

In semiconductors, Samsung set a target of maintaining a three- to six-month lead in product and process development over Japanese competitors and a six-month lead over domestic competitors, and we have met the target for the last four years. By 2001, the gap had widened to one year, and Japanese firms gave up competing against us.

—Yun Jong-Yong, former Vice-Chairman and CEO of Samsung Electronics
in an interview conducted in 2004

Innovation brings change, and change inevitably brings resistance. Leaders of an industry in one era often lose out to up-and-comers in the next generation. This decline arises from hesitating to embrace structural change and innovation or failing to secure new capabilities when a disruptive technology appears. Moreover, a company's core competency, which acted as a source of competitiveness in the past, can become a source of "core rigidity" that obstructs change and innovation.

Accordingly, business leaders need to set challenging goals and instill a sense of crisis to continuously drive the creation of knowledge and innovation. Samsung's leaders enacted precisely this strategy to ward off negligence and complacency about previous success. Moreover, Samsung also regularly prepares for the worst-case scenario, and ensures that its employees are mindful of the competition. To this end, Samsung hosts a regular exhibition where employees can compare the company's products with leading products in the industry, in order to broaden their perspective and intensify their sense of crisis and challenge.

Samsung has now firmly established its practice of invoking a continuous sense of crisis and challenge. In the past, Samsung had adopted a more conservative and circumspect culture that prioritized organizational safety. However, after Chairman Lee took the helm, Samsung adopted a flexible, challenging, and innovative culture. In particular, Samsung's top management set stretch goals that are difficult to achieve using existing methods and technologies. By doing this, Samsung successfully spurred the formation of an organizational culture built around innovation.

Samsung applied the same strategy in its R&D. The company was a latecomer in technology-intensive areas like semiconductors, LCDs, and smartphones, but it caught up with and surpassed the industry leaders with remarkable speed.

Samsung's pursuit of challenging goals is well reflected in its "new growth theory for the semiconductor business." At the International Solid-State Circuit Conference, one of the world's three major semiconductor conferences, in 2002, Samsung announced a theory that can replace Moore's Law.[10] Samsung's theory holds that the density of semiconductors will double every year, with the increase being led by "non-PC" devices like mobile devices. Samsung has proved the theory for eight straight years, from 1999, when it developed its 256-megabyte NAND flash memory, to 2007, when it developed 64-gigabyte memory. This theory reflected both Samsung's confidence as a market leader and its need to establish challenging goals, as Samsung's semiconductor division would have the task of proving the theory every year.

Learning-Oriented Thinking and Culture

Learning is the basis of innovation, and Samsung has dedicated itself to promoting learning-oriented thinking and building a learning-oriented culture. Chairman Lee is well known for his diverse scholarly interests, which encompass film, broadcasting, history, semiconductors, golf, and automobiles. Lee's strong interest in machinery and state-of-the-art technologies has led to many late-night discussions with experts, and he has been known to personally disassemble and reassemble automobiles and electronics products to better understand their workings. Lee has stated, "If you ride on the subway without knowing its operating principles, you cannot say that you are riding it. You are just being carried by the subway." Lee has also said, "Anyone who has watched a TV more than five times but has never thought about looking inside it is not worthy of being called a manager."

Samsung's culture of learning served as a driving force for change and innovation and helped Samsung grow into a world-class learning organization. This learning-oriented mindset remains part of Samsung's culture today. Typical Samsung employees can expect to take regular examinations to assess their degree of learning. Every employee of Samsung Electronics at the director level or above, for example, must learn new management methods, techniques, and tools like supply chain management (SCM) and enterprise resource planning (ERP) that the company has adopted. Even if these practices are not directly related to their main duties, they are obliged to receive instructions and take examinations at the end of their training. As a result, Samsung employees can fully understand the company's operating systems and make suggestions about improving them.

Samsung has also put considerable effort into establishing a culture of respect for the individual and a culture of innovation from the bottom up. For example, Samsung's semiconductor personnel developed a production technology using a new material, High-K/Metal-Gate. This technology, with its dramatic power savings, has the potential to open a new era in the semiconductor industry. Initially, the considerable difference between High-K/Metal-

Gate and existing methods made it difficult to adopt, even for Samsung. By early 2011, however, one researcher at Samsung Electronics had proposed a solution, which led to the introduction of new methods and equipment that enabled mass production. Recognizing the novelty of this innovation, Samsung applied for patents on the related technology.

Systems for Securing Talent

Samsung recognizes that people are the agents of organizational learning and innovation, and that the company's evolutionary innovation capabilities lie primarily within the minds of its people. To build world-class innovation capabilities, Samsung recognized early on the need to secure and develop talent to build an organization that can lead innovation. As noted in Chapter 4, Samsung's "people first" policy is a core company value, and Samsung has long recruited world-class technology experts, both at home and abroad. On this front, Samsung has spared no expense, offering exceptionally high incentives to researchers who succeed in developing an outstanding patented technology or a successful commercial product. In November 2002, Samsung began its "Samsung Fellows" program to provide special treatment for technology experts. Researchers selected as Samsung Fellows can form a research team under their own name and supervision, and conduct research independently, without direction from the company.

Organizations Specialized in Learning

Samsung has established a tripartite R&D function. At the level of Samsung Group, Samsung Advanced Institute of Technology focuses on the development of "seed technologies" for new businesses. At the level of an affiliate, R&D institutes work on technologies to improve competitiveness of the affiliate core businesses, while R&D institutes established at the level of business divisions focus on the development of quickly commercializable technologies.

Samsung's Tripartite R&D Function

Samsung's R&D organization consists of three parts: the Samsung Advanced Institute of Technology for basic research; individual research institutions at electronic affiliates in charge of products, core components, and technology development; and development teams at different business divisions that research product and process improvements.

Samsung Advanced Institute of Technology works on a five- to seven-year time horizon with a focus on basic research and the development of "seed technologies" for new business. In particular, the institute focuses on basic technology projects that would be difficult for an affiliate to take on alone. The DMC R&D Center, on the other hand, works on a three- to seven-year horizon, while the Semiconductor R&D Center and the Display Research Center work on a three- to five-year horizon. These institutions focus on securing core product-related technologies. Research centers affiliated with business divisions have the shortest time horizon—one to two years—and focus on technologies that can be commercialized quickly.

Samsung Advanced Institute of Technology

Samsung Advanced Institute of Technology was established in 1987 as Samsung Group's primary research organization. It maintained 1,200 researchers in 2012, with more than 90 percent having master's or PhD degrees. With this talented workforce, the institute has played a pivotal role in giving Samsung evolutionary innovation capabilities.

Samsung Advanced Institute of Technology, in close cooperation with the DMC R&D Center, the Semiconductor R&D Center, and the Display Research Center, has had a hand in developing some of Samsung's most innovative technologies, including charge trap flash, LTE mobile data communications, OLED and LED displays, and DVD playback. The institute's research achievements also include DNIe, for enhanced video image quality, and multilayer ceramic capacitors, the centerpiece of many electronic components. Initially, Samsung Advanced Institute of Technology benchmarked AT&T's Bell Laboratories, but with few other private research institutes pursuing mid- and long-term technology development, Samsung Advanced Institute of Technology is now in a class of its own. To further boost Samsung's innovation capability, the institute is planning to establish branches in the United States, Japan, China, and India, and to participate in several industry-academia research projects.

After Samsung Electronics eliminated its chief technology officer position, Samsung Advanced Institute of Technology has acted as Samsung's control tower for R&D by coordinating projects among electronics affiliates and promoting collaboration and synergy between them. It also helps electronics affiliates develop long-term technologies rapidly by drafting Samsung's 10-year technology road map and updating it frequently.

The institute also acts as a central institution for technology information sharing and dissemination throughout the group. It provides the latest information on promising industries like nanotech and biotech and on global trends through the Samsung Tech Conference, which is held every year. Since 2004, Samsung Advanced Institute of Technology has hosted the Samsung Tech Conference, which is attended by research and development personnel, CEOs, and core technology talent at Samsung Group.

World-Class Manufacturing Process Technologies

As an enterprise, Samsung has traditionally increased its competitiveness based on its world-class manufacturing capabilities. Its main product categories, including semiconductors and display panels, require close cooperation between R&D and production. Accordingly, Samsung introduced concurrent engineering early on to encourage cooperation from the initial stages of technology and product development. As a result, Samsung has achieved continuous innovation in manufacturing technology and enhanced its ability to produce innovative products swiftly after the development stage.

In this era of mass customization, it is more important than ever for companies to develop and produce tailored solutions and products that can meet diverse consumer needs. To this end, companies need increasingly advanced manufacturing technology. Samsung Electronics' semiconductor division, for example, has been able to provide tailored solutions for its customers that create high added value. Samsung's world-class process and manufacturing technologies enable rapid production at low cost, while its introduction of flexible manufacturing has allowed different products to be manufactured simultaneously on one assembly line.

PART FOUR

SAMSUNG-STYLE PARADOX MANAGEMENT AND THE FUTURE OF THE SAMSUNG WAY

Part One discussed some of the reasons why Samsung's management deserves in-depth analysis and explained Samsung's process of growth and transformation. Part Two provided an analysis of Chairman Lee Kun-Hee's leadership and Samsung's corporate governance structure and management systems. Part Three examined Samsung's core competencies, including speed, synergy through convergence, and evolutionary innovation, and explained how these arose out of its management systems. Part Three also identified the culture, infrastructure, and mechanisms that underlie Samsung's core competencies, and explained how they gave Samsung a competitive advantage.

Part Four will reexamine the basic operating principles of the Samsung Way and suggest potential future directions for Samsung. Chapter 8 presents Samsung's principle of internal co-opetition and then analyzes how Samsung has succeeded in resolving the three management paradoxes of the Samsung Way. Chapter 9 will assess the sustainability of the Samsung Way, discuss the challenges ahead for Samsung as it develops into a premier world-class company, and summarize the major lessons from Samsung's remarkable success with the New Management initiative and the Samsung Way that companies all over the world can learn from.

CHAPTER 8

INTERNAL CO-OPETITION AND PARADOX MANAGEMENT

8

Previous chapters have described Samsung's growth into a world-class firm since the introduction of the New Management initiative in 1993. They provided an in-depth analysis of how Samsung surmounted the limitations of its birth as an emerging market–based company, the Asian currency crisis of 1997, and the global financial crisis of 2008.

This chapter provides a comprehensive discussion of the structure of the Samsung Way. It explains in detail Samsung's development of "internal co-opetition," that is, the company's unique combination of cooperation and competition. It also analyzes how Samsung was able to resolve its three paradoxes and use them as a source for its competitiveness, providing insight into the true nature of Samsung's paradox management. Such analysis provides useful lessons and implications for domestic and foreign companies that are hoping to benchmark the Samsung Way.

Structure of the Samsung Way

Companies that rise to world-class status and then maintain a sustainable and differentiated competitive advantage have their own unique management style and system. Examples include Toyota, with the Toyota Way, and GE, with the GE Way. Such management models are the result of a long history of evolution and the outstanding leadership of figures like Taiichi Ohno of Toyota and Jack Welch of GE. Likewise, the Samsung Way emerged from the knowledge and experience that Samsung accumulated over 60 years, as well as the push for qualitative growth led by Chairman Lee Kun-Hee.

The roots of the Samsung Way lie in the New Management initiative that Chairman Lee introduced. When Lee succeeded his father as head of Samsung Group in 1987, he emphasized that Samsung would need to embrace change. Although Samsung was number one in nearly all of its business lines at home, its product quality and management capabilities still lacked the ingredients needed to compete effectively in world markets. Moreover, Samsung Group was still made up of a range of disparate businesses that focused on quantitative growth. In particular, its main business lines, including Samsung Electronics, had still not achieved global-level competitiveness based on core competencies.

In addition, Samsung was not yet a strategically minded company, and it did not use a select-and-focus strategy to develop its core businesses and competencies. Instead, it was process-oriented and focused on the details. This business model proved unsuitable, however, for the fast-moving, fast-acting business that Samsung hoped to become. Samsung was stuck being an imitator, copying the technologies of advanced companies and using cheap labor to produce goods for the low-end and midrange markets.

It was under these circumstances that Chairman Lee introduced the New Management initiative at Samsung in 1993. Troubled by the upcoming risks facing Samsung's existing quantity-focused strategy, Lee pushed the New Management initiative intensively over a short period of time. Under this initiative, Samsung's vision was to become a "world-class company in the twenty-first century." In the service of this vision, all of Samsung's affiliates and employees were to shift their focus from indiscriminate quantitative expansion to a qualitative upgrade of Samsung's business structure.

Samsung's direction for the New Management initiative in large part originated from its successful experience with semiconductors, in which it became the world's number one producer in the early 1990s. Entering the semiconductor industry provided Samsung with an opportunity to combine American-style management practices with its existing Japanese-style practices to become a leading producer. The semiconductor business also provided the emphasis on quality that was to become a cornerstone of the New Management initiative. Likewise, other characteristics of the industry, including an emphasis on technology, preemptive seizure of opportunities, horizontal organization, a focus on speed, recruiting core talent, hefty monetary incentives, and a sense of crisis, would later find their way into Samsung's New Management doctrine.

The success of the semiconductor business motivated Samsung to drastically improve its soft competitiveness based on intangible assets. Quality in technology, brand, and design capability was addressed simultaneously with quality in management and people, strengthening Samsung's competitiveness. These measures allowed Samsung to shift its business model from being an imitator to being a market leader; and to revise its business strategy from unrelated diversification and quantitative expansion to upgrading of its business portfolio by enhancing the specialized competitiveness of each of its businesses.

Perhaps most important, Samsung's new direction, first in semiconductors and then in the New Management initiative generally, allowed it to establish a system of internal co-opetition that could lead to change in its management systems, as shown in Figure 8.1. This system of co-opetition allowed Samsung to increase the degree of internal fit between its strategy and the constituent factors of its management system.

Internal Co-opetition Is at the Core of the Samsung Way[1]

What I mean by "Single Samsung" is that everyone in Samsung Group should maintain the same values and comply with the same standards. "Single Samsung" does not mean affiliates give privileges to and receive privileges from each other. Whether we provide or purchase a service, we must create a level playing field of competition for affiliates and outside businesses. In this way, only capable firms can partner with us, enhancing our own competitiveness. This will truly create synergy for the group as a whole.

—*Chairman Lee Kun-Hee*

Figure 8.1 *Realignment of Samsung's Management System with the New Management Initiative*

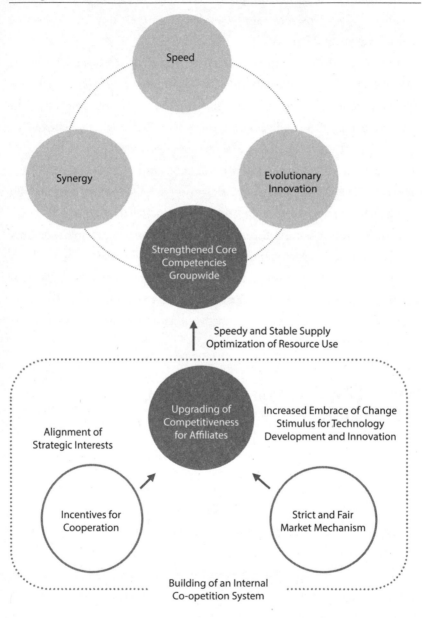

Samsung's unique internal co-opetition system has been an important catalyst for realizing its core competences, and it stands as a fundamental operating principle of the Samsung Way.[2] *Co-opetition* is a key term explaining the unusual type of tension—in which both cooperation and competition coexist—in the relationships between Samsung's affiliates and divisions that has evolved and been developed since the New Management initiative. Such competitive improvement mechanisms among these organizations have acted as a source for the creation of core competencies.

Why Was Internal Co-opetition Introduced?

Striking the right balance between cooperation and competition is the most critical task for any diversified business that is striving to realize synergies. Although in the past, Samsung focused more on cooperation, it has gradually introduced more market-style internal competition into its core business practices. These successful combinations of strategy have allowed Samsung to acquire greater capabilities for speed, convergence synergy, and evolutionary innovation.

Co-opetition, in particular, was the most distinguishing innovation introduced in the process of pursuing changes in the elements of Samsung's management system under the New Management initiative. Before the New Management initiative, Samsung largely favored cooperation, rather than competition, between divisions and affiliates in realizing synergies. This emphasis arose from the strong cohesion that emerged among employees who had the same organizational culture and values, centered around the owner-manager. However, such close relationships between affiliates invited a situation in which some affiliates were able to survive by depending on their stronger peers, even if they did little to increase their own competitiveness. This raised concerns over a downward spiral of competitiveness across all affiliates.

Such concerns proved to be justified with the arrival of the 1997 Asian currency crisis. Suddenly confronted by massive losses and impending failures, Samsung rapidly shifted its focus from fostering cooperation within the group to promoting internal competition. As a result, Samsung's unique structure for co-opetition emerged.

Mechanisms of Internal Co-opetition

As shown in Figure 8.2, Samsung's internal co-opetition system is made possible because of Samsung's owner-management and conglomerate structure, as well as its rigorous compensation and promotion systems. Samsung has pursued internal co-opetition in the form of dual sourcing and parallel investments in the same projects.

Owner-Management and Conglomerate Structure as the Basis for Co-opetition

Companies with an owner-manager and a conglomerate business structure have various well-known weaknesses. Samsung, however, was able to turn these seeming weaknesses into a source of competitive strength by simultaneously introducing vigorous internal competition and close cooperation.

At Samsung, cooperation and competition both are a result of strong leadership based on its owner-management structure. Chairman Lee and the Corporate Strategy Office have continuously striven to optimize Samsung's performance at the group level. They provide support for decision making by each affiliate's professional managers, and they help coordinate the optimization of each affiliate's performance. In particular, Samsung's owner-manager and the Corporate Strategy Office provide favorable treatment for executives who have contributed to optimization at the group level, resulting in simultaneous competition and cooperation among affiliates.

At Samsung, competition between affiliates is particularly intense because the affiliates are evaluated not only in absolute terms, but also in comparison with their peers. If Samsung had left decisions on the compensation and promotion of affiliates' executives to the boards of the individual affiliates, the company's current level of co-opetition would have been impossible to achieve. The results of these relative evaluations are critical factors in deciding on executives' compensation and career advancement. This rigorous

Figure 8.2   Structure of Samsung's Internal Co-opetition

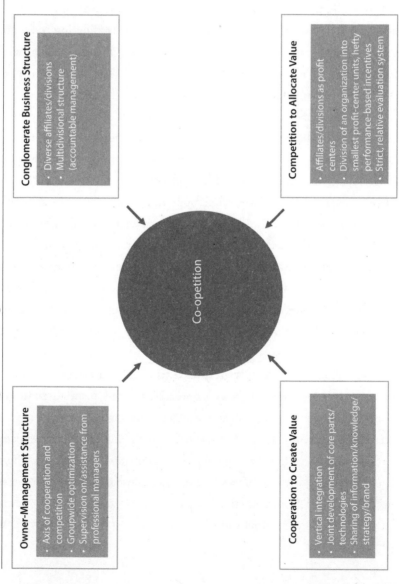

Conglomerate Business Structure
- Diverse affiliates/divisions
- Multidivisional structure (accountable management)

Competition to Allocate Value
- Affiliates/divisions as profit centers
- Division of an organization into smallest profit-center units, hefty performance-based incentives
- Strict relative evaluation system

Owner-Management Structure
- Axis of cooperation and competition
- Groupwide optimization
- Supervision on/assistance from professional managers

Cooperation to Create Value
- Vertical integration
- Joint development of core parts/technologies
- Sharing of information/knowledge/strategy/brand

Co-opetition

performance-based system enables Samsung to encourage close and voluntary cooperation when it can produce mutually beneficial outcomes, with the scope and degree of such cooperation being both broader and deeper than that of cooperation between independent companies. On the other hand, employees are likely to reject cooperation if they are asked to make sacrifices for the benefit of the whole, but receive only some benefit, or if benefits materialize only in the long-term. Such issues have hampered voluntary cooperation among Samsung's affiliates and divisions in developing innovative new products for the long-term. When cooperation would be mutually beneficial for affiliates, but still does not occur, Chairman Lee and the Corporate Strategy Office can intervene to coordinate action at the group level.

Samsung's conglomerate business structure has simultaneously helped facilitate interaffiliate cooperation to create value on the one hand, while facilitating competition to allocate value on the other. At the unit level, Samsung's conglomerate structure ensures independence for affiliates and divisions, encouraging them to practice autonomous and accountable management. At the group level, Samsung can perform relative evaluations of the performance of affiliates and divisions and use the results to determine the compensation and promotion of executives, resulting in both vigorous competition and cooperation. Unlike its foreign rivals in the electronics business, Samsung has built a vertically integrated business structure that spurs co-opetition, rapidly enhancing its competitiveness to world-class levels.

Introduction of Market Principles and Dual Sourcing

Since the late 1990s, Samsung has encouraged parts and materials divisions of its affiliates to raise productivity and product quality and cut costs by applying market principles to internal transactions while reducing the side effects of vertical integration. The company thus built a dual-sourcing system, where it would purchase parts and materials both externally and internally. For example, Samsung Electronics purchases panels for TVs from Sharp, a Japanese company, and other external suppliers in addition to those from its affiliate, Samsung Display.

Affiliates do not receive special treatment when they are making deals with other Samsung companies, and they must be prepared to lose out to external suppliers if they are not competitive in quality, price, and time to delivery. Samsung Electronics, for example, eliminated Samsung Electro-Mechanics from the bidding for electrolytic condensers in 2001. Shocked by this result, Samsung Electro-Mechanics used this setback as an opportunity to improve the quality of its high-value-added product, multilayer ceramic condensers (MLCCs), to world-class levels. Samsung Display produces its own color filters and also procures them from Dongwoo Fine-Chem, a local subsidiary of Japan's Sumitomo Chemical. Samsung Display then compares its own quality and price with those of Dongwoo, and issues reprimands and warnings if they are found to be inferior in either. Some employees have complained, "Samsung Electronics can feel more like a whip than an umbrella," and "Samsung Electronics is more demanding than external clients." Samsung has a firm purchasing guideline saying that more than 30 percent of parts and materials must come from external suppliers so that the company's affiliates can stay attuned to industry trends. This principle motivates affiliates that depend on Samsung Electronics for a significant portion of their revenue to avoid complacency regarding their sources of demand, and to pursue external markets vigorously.[3]

Parallel Investments in the Same Projects

At Samsung, affiliates and divisions sometimes directly compete with one another or enter the same business area simultaneously. When it is uncertain which technology or technique is best suited to a particular project, different units within the group can take on the same project, thereby spurring competition and increasing the speed of development. Samsung Electro-Mechanics and Samsung Techwin, for example, fiercely competed with each other to develop mobile phone camera modules. Moreover, before Samsung Mobile Display[4] was established as a joint venture in 2008, Samsung Electronic's liquid-crystal display (LCD) division competed intensely with Samsung SDI in the active-matrix organic light-emitting diode (AMOLED) market.

Samsung's "winner takes all" culture of providing extraordinary compensation to high-performing divisions means that internal competition is always a serious contest.

Sense of Urgency Created by Constant Restructuring

Samsung restructured extensively after the 1997 Asian currency crisis and the 2008 global financial crisis. The latter restructuring was not as well publicized, but it was nonetheless extensive, as nearly one-third of Samsung Electronics' executives were furloughed and put on standby. After the crisis, employees became increasingly aware of the constant restructuring, that is, that an uncompetitive business could be closed at any time, and thus that improving the competitiveness of one's own affiliate, rather than assisting other affiliates, was the chief priority. Samsung's affiliates thus were compelled to use market pricing in interaffiliate transactions, particularly when it came to transfer prices. As a result, a new culture emerged in which affiliates do not offer other affiliates special treatment if the transactions are not mutually beneficial.

Three Paradoxes Enhance Competitiveness

Samsung has continuously pursued changes in its management system since the launch of the New Management initiative. Such changes did not always completely replace past practices, and new methods were often grafted onto past practices to preserve the good points of the previous practices.[5] Accordingly, traditional management practices, such as a large organization, a diversified structure, and Japanese management styles, have coexisted with New Management practices like the pursuit of speed, soft competitiveness in each business unit, and American management styles. These are manifested in the form of the three paradoxes of Samsung management.

Against this backdrop, Samsung strove to achieve seemingly incompatible goals, such as maintaining high speed despite its vast size, enhancing the specialization of each business while maintaining diversification for convergence synergy, and leveraging the strengths of both Japanese and American management styles. Attempts to achieve such incompatible goals can easily blur a company's strategic focus and create imbalances, thereby undermining the company's overall competitiveness. However, Samsung successfully resolved its three paradoxes and turned them into the basis of the Samsung Way. Thus, it was able to differentiate itself from rivals who sought single goals to create sustainable competitive advantages. The rest of this chapter will explain how Samsung coped with the paradoxes.

Balance Between Size and Speed

At the end of 2013, Samsung had 75 affiliates employing 489,000 people worldwide. Its flagship Samsung Electronics alone recorded 228 trillion won (US$201 billion) in revenue. Speed is usually slow at a business entity that is this large. Decision making involves multiple layers of authority, and decisions may get bogged down in talks. Moreover, when the company is dealing with an entirely new issue, bureaucratic rules and regulations can hamper decision making. Even after a plan or idea is approved, executing it can take more time because the people who make decisions and the people who carry them out are different. Accurately conveying decision makers' intentions can be difficult, and carrying out those decisions can require the involvement of more business units and personnel. Thus, most companies are faced with the dilemma of choosing between enjoying the economies of scale that come with a large organization and benefiting from the speed and agility of a smaller organization.

In contrast, Samsung was able to achieve high velocity even as it grew in size, building a competitive advantage that its rivals could not easily imitate. Samsung's methods for increasing speed were elaborated in Chapter 5. This chapter will focus on how Samsung overcame the disadvantages of large size.

Strong Leadership from the Owner-Manager

Samsung's strong leadership from the owner-manager has enabled it to make and execute decisions faster than its rivals in Japan or America that are led solely by professional managers.

Samsung has been able to make and carry out large-scale investment decisions on facilities investment rapidly, as well as large investments in

R&D, branding, design, and other forms of intangible assets, thanks to the bold decision making of the owner-manager. The owner-manager, who was ready to take on risk, could make decisions from a long-term perspective more quickly than professional managers. This proved to be a critical factor allowing Samsung to gain a competitive advantage over Japanese firms in the semiconductor industry. In contrast to Samsung, Japanese chip makers had to spend time building consensus among the professional managers and being careful and circumspect in their decisions. In the meantime, Samsung's rapid and bold decision making allowed it to expand its production capacity at the right moment to develop successful new products. This system for making rapid investment decisions was later successfully employed in LCDs and other areas, allowing Samsung to achieve global competitiveness rapidly even in industries in which it was a latecomer.

Owner-managers have a high risk of making very bad choices if they indulge in autocratic decision making. At Samsung, however, this is difficult to do, as a system of checks and balances among Chairman Lee, the Corporate Strategy Office, and the CEOs of affiliates has emerged. When Samsung decides to enter a new business, the relevant division and any related divisions review its feasibility and potential. Simultaneously, Samsung Group's Corporate Strategy Office performs a strategic review, and the Samsung Advanced Institute of Technology and other Samsung research centers carry out technical reviews. For its part, the Samsung Economic Research Institute provides benchmarking and performs an economic feasibility review. Such multidimensional analysis of potential new lines of business lowers the potential for faulty decision making. At the same time, managers can be confident about entering a new business, allowing them to make even large investments rapidly.

Strong leadership from the owner-manager has also helped Samsung accelerate its execution. A prime example is Samsung's TV Advancement Committee. When Chairman Lee demanded that Samsung become the number one TV maker in the world, the affiliates came together and cooperated to become number one in a short period of time. Without the firm leadership of the owner-manager, affiliates and divisions would have wasted a significant amount of time discussing how responsibilities and profits should be divided. Instead, everyone concentrated on cooperating to achieve results and dealt with other tasks on an ad hoc basis, greatly increasing the company's speed of execution.

None of this is meant to imply that Samsung's decision making is solely concentrated in the owner-manager. In fact, even at its rapid pace, Samsung has achieved harmony between centralized and decentralized decision making. Samsung's owner-manager is responsible for long-term strategic decisions, while professional managers and working-level teams handle short-term strategy and operational decisions. In this way, Samsung has developed the ability to make rapid decisions based on on-the-spot specialized knowledge.

Speed-Oriented Culture and IT Infrastructure

Korea is well known for its "ppali ppali" culture and hurried pace, and this is even more true at Samsung. More than any other Korean company, Samsung is devoted to increasing the speed at which it does business. This is partly because Samsung's mainstay businesses, such as electronics, are all ones in which the pace of innovation is rapid, and partly because Samsung has set extremely challenging goals.

Samsung has made a variety of efforts to encourage its culture and values to prioritize speed. Samsung deliberately sets "stretch goals," setting ambitious targets to surpass industry leaders, and encouraging employees to join together to abandon existing conventions and embrace innovation and change. This has led to intensive activities like the all-out construction of semiconductor assembly lines at top speed and the use of seven-day workweeks to complete product development as quickly as possible.

In a large organization, collecting, processing, and distributing information to decision makers can be time-consuming and cumbersome. As was explained in Chapter 4, however, Samsung avoids these pitfalls by collecting data on production and sales from its worldwide business sites in near real time by using its world-class information technology (IT) infrastructure.

Methods and systems used to speed up technology development, management processes, and logistics were addressed in detail in Chapter 5.

Simultaneous Pursuit of Diversification and Specialization

Samsung is a diversified business with affiliates in manufacturing, finance, and services. As discussed earlier, however, the company's affiliates and divisions are in a paradoxical position of simultaneously being one another's foremost partners and fiercest competitors. Affiliates and divisions compete fiercely because their performance is evaluated against others when it comes to decisions on compensation and promotions of executives. Thus, affiliates and divisions will negotiate aggressively with one another on pricing when they are carrying out internal transactions. However, when they are confronted with a strong outside competitor or a project that can bring significant benefits for every participant, affiliates and divisions join forces and form a groupwide cooperation system through the formation of task forces and committees. Thus, although a diversified business like Samsung normally suffers from a lack of specialization, Samsung's co-opetition system allows it to use diversification as a means of increasing specialized competitiveness.

Samsung's co-opetition system also influences the company's business portfolio. When only competition is emphasized, individual affiliates may be reluctant to contribute to projects that are helpful to the group but not beneficial to them. Moreover, if it is already handling a similar project or business, an affiliate may even find itself subject to restructuring. From the group perspective, however, Samsung can optimize its business portfolio if affiliates invest in such projects jointly or pursue them even at the cost of short-term losses. On the other hand, emphasizing only cooperation can impede the restructuring process and weaken competitiveness in all business areas. Co-opetition resolves this problem by enabling Samsung to repeatedly realign the resources of its affiliates and adjust its business portfolio as needed. For example, when Samsung Electronics underwent restructuring during the 2008 global financial crisis, nothing was off limits for restructuring at any time.

Intensive investments in Samsung's soft capabilities or intangible assets (in R&D, design, and branding in electronics-related areas) were also key to enhancing the specialized competitiveness of Samsung's major business lines.

These investments owed a great deal to Chairman Lee's insightful leadership. In particular, focused and advanced investments in R&D helped Samsung acquire capabilities in evolutionary innovation, allowing it to build these capabilities to the world's best levels. Such investments were the motor that powered Samsung's rise to number one in the electronics industry.

Combination of Japanese and American Management Styles[6]

As Harvard Business School professor Michael Porter has noted, Japanese management styles, which gained sway in the 1980s, have strengths in operational management, but are weak on strategy, while the reverse is true of American management styles.[7] Companies with American management styles emphasize the creation of profit through a select-and-focus strategy that tries to advance business by focusing only on related areas. In doing this, American firms do not hesitate to restructure their business and product lines when necessary. American-style firms are also characterized by a tendency to outsource manufacturing or move it overseas, and to see technological innovation, brand marketing capabilities, and design as their core sources of competitiveness. In general, they have a more centralized structure than their Japanese rivals, and they put a high priority on core talent with differentiated competencies, rather than on employee loyalty. Accordingly, American-style firms depend heavily on the external labor market to fill their ranks. Employment contracts are often short-term, with high incentives and salaries for competencies and performance. Employees are typically skilled in specific functional areas.

Samsung has incorporated the strengths of both the Japanese and American styles into its own management system through vigorous benchmarking. After a lengthy process of research and experimentation, Samsung then tailored both management styles for its own management system to create a form of management that is unique to Samsung. This process has been an ongoing effort for decades as Samsung has grown. There is a saying at Samsung that "managing is education and learning," reflecting the depths of Samsung's commitment to learning from its competitors. As shown in Chapter 1, it is difficult to accommodate the elements of both the Japanese and American management styles into a single company. This is because the elements of each style are organically connected, and these elements cannot be easily disassembled and grafted onto the other.

Until it began manufacturing semiconductors, Samsung relied mainly on the Japanese management because of the preferences of its leaders, the characteristics of its business, and the culture and characteristics of Korea's labor market. Japanese management generally prioritizes the attainment of market share, unrelated diversification, vertical integration, manufacturing competitiveness, operational efficiency, internal development of human resources, and seniority-based promotion and compensation. At the time, Samsung's businesses needed strenuous efforts to raise the manufacturing productivity and quality, and this style served the company well.

When Samsung entered the chip business, however, it recruited core talent that had been trained in the United States. This proved to be an opportunity for the company to introduce American management styles. Practices that are typical at Samsung today, such as a far-reaching vision, taking bold risks, engaging in vigorous internal debate, engaging in rapid decision making and execution, providing large incentives, and recruiting core talent from outside, were first adopted in the semiconductor division. The experiment proved to be a huge success, and employees in Samsung Electronics' semiconductor division began filling higher positions elsewhere in the company. Eventually, their influence transformed the management practices and culture of Samsung Electronics as a whole. These changes then moved beyond Samsung Electronics and were spread throughout the group by the Corporate Strategy Office.

As the business environment became more uncertain, Chairman Lee, in his New Management initiative, encouraged Samsung's CEOs to think strategically and explore promising "seed" businesses. In the process, they would transform themselves from Japanese-style administrative leaders to American-style strategic leaders. In addition, the paradigm shift toward globalization and digitization beginning in the 1990s increased the role of strategic management, spurring Samsung to adopt a strategy-focused American management style comprehensively.

The turning point in Samsung's absorption and dissemination of American-style management was the 1997 Asian currency crisis. Facing serious threats to its survival, Samsung was able to successfully restructure itself by boldly introducing and practicing the core principles of American-style management. The currency crisis was thus an opportunity for Samsung to rapidly and boldly pursue the restructuring of its business lines and its workforce, a central feature of American management.

Intangible assets, including technology, branding, and design have grown in importance in the knowledge-based economy of the twenty-first century. Reflecting this change, Samsung has reduced its reliance on the Japanese models that it adopted in the past, including an emphasis on standardized talent and seniority-based compensation, while at the same time greatly increasing its use of American practices like an emphasis on core talent, competencies, and performance-based compensation and promotion.

However, rather than completely abandoning the Japanese method for the American one, Samsung combined the strengths of the two management styles. As a result, Samsung still maintains the virtues of Japanese management, including attention to detail, a disciplined organizational culture, high levels of employee loyalty, continuous workplace improvement based on human resource development and employee participation in decision making, strict quality control, and strategic emphasis on manufacturing competitiveness, product quality, and operational efficiency.

The coexistence of these two styles within Samsung stems directly from the fact that the company runs a business that has huge strategic uncertainty while maintaining massive manufacturing facilities. Its flagship IT business is in an industry that is noted for sharp swings in demand and rapidly changing technologies, thus requiring a high level of strategic foresight. To survive in such an environment, Samsung has adopted elements of the American management style, such as bold risk taking, securing core talent, strong performance-based incentives, a creative organizational culture, and high speed. At the same time, Samsung strenuously strives to reduce costs based on the massive manufacturing facilities that it has built around the world. Such efforts are powered by the Japanese management style, which Samsung used for decades before the New Management initiative. As a result, Samsung's strategic planning, which is focused on its CEO system, now mainly uses American management practices, while its operations mainly rely on Japanese practices.

Although Samsung introduced American management systems after thorough benchmarking, it did so only after a lengthy process of research on the affiliates who first introduced them, and rigorous research by Samsung Economic Research Institute. Experiments on a small scale allowed Samsung to tailor and improve on American management methods to fit Samsung's culture and management systems. Such efforts were well advised, as the main reason for failure in introducing external management innovations to a company is the indiscriminate imitation of a prominent company that has already done so. In contrast, Samsung first carefully studied and analyzed the best practices of global leaders, then in a process of experimentation, verified their effectiveness on a small scale. Only after doing so did Samsung expand these practices throughout the group under the leadership of the Corporate Strategy Office, thereby reducing the downsides of trial and error.

A key example of this is Six Sigma, a management-improvement methodology that was developed in the United States. Samsung SDI was the first affiliate to adopt this approach by benchmarking GE in 1996. Samsung Group then altered and improved it to suit Samsung's own culture and management system, to great effect. After Samsung SDI enjoyed the benefits of Six Sigma, Samsung's electronics affiliates followed suit. By 2002, Six Sigma was being applied groupwide under the instructions of the Corporate Strategy Office. While GE implemented Six Sigma solely at the manager level, Samsung promoted it for all employees groupwide, thus evolving and improving it and developing it into Samsung's own Six Sigma.

American-style performance-based incentives are another example. Samsung introduced performance incentives of profit sharing (PS) after benchmarking Hewlett-Packard. In the United States, however, performance-based pay is usually used to reward only those at the top levels of an organization. This was less suited to Korea's workplace culture, which prioritizes manufacturing competitiveness and maintains a strong emphasis on motivating all employees, and it also didn't fit with Korea's Confucian tendencies toward egalitarianism. Based on in-depth research and analysis by Samsung Economic Research Institute, Samsung modified the American system so that all employees working in the same profit center, either an affiliate or a business division, receive the same ratio of performance-based incentives. This contributed significantly to encouraging all employees to embrace Samsung's policy of "one direction."

As these cases suggest, it would be a mischaracterization to claim that Samsung's management is a simple mixture of American and Japanese management practices. Although Samsung benchmarked leading firms in both of these countries, it adopted only those features that suited it, and fundamentally recast them into a style suited for Samsung. Such mixing and modifying is analogous to Korea's national dish, *bibimbap*, a bowl of rice topped with vegetables and seasoned with red pepper paste. Rice and vegetables, although healthy, are unappealing if they are simply mixed together. Adding red pepper paste to the mix, however, makes the two elements delicious. Samsung's process of re-creating foreign management systems allowed it to achieve a strong internal fit with Samsung's own management systems, enabling it to build dynamic core competencies and greatly increasing its business performance. Table 8.1 illustrates how Samsung combined, transformed, and improved the strong points from both the Japanese management styles that prevailed in its early days, and the American management style that it adopted after the introduction of the New Management initiative.

Table 8.1   Japanese-, American-, and Samsung-Style Management[8]

	Japanese	American	Samsung
Strategy	• Diversification into multiple products • Vertical integration	• Select and focus • Frequent business restructuring	• Diversification and vertical integration + concentration on a small number of products
Core competency	• Continuous improvement to enhance operational efficiency • Emphasis on manufacturing capabilities and product quality	• Focus on innovation, marketing, and design to establish strong brands and premium pricing	• Focus on continuous improvement and applied R&D, but also on innovation, marketing, and design to establish strong brand and premium pricing
Personnel	• Dependence on the internal labor market, which results in long-term employment • Promotion and compensation based on seniority • Emphasis on employee loyalty	• Dependence on the external labor market: recruitment of experienced workers • Merit-based promotion and compensation • Emphasis on core talent	• Coexistence of open recruitment for entry-level positions and recruitment of experienced workers • Coexistence of seniority- and merit-based compensation • Emphasis on both employee loyalty and core talent
Supply network management	• Sourcing based on long-term partnerships	• Sourcing based on competitive bidding	• Dual sourcing • Market-based internal transactions (co-opetition)

CHAPTER 9

THE FUTURE OF THE SAMSUNG WAY

9

This chapter examines the internal and external fit of the Samsung Way and evaluates its prospects for being sustainable. It also analyzes future tasks for the Samsung Way, and presents the authors' opinions on the steps that Samsung can take to reach the next level as a world-class firm. Finally, the authors conclude by suggesting what other companies, especially non-Korean companies, can learn from the Samsung Way.

Is the Samsung Way Sustainable?

To answer this question, we must examine the internal and external fit of the Samsung Way. Raymond Miles and Charles Snow have argued that companies that succeed do so because of the external fit that comes from devising new strategies in response to environmental change, and also the internal fit that comes from restructuring their organization in accordance with these new strategies.[1] Likewise, David Nadler and Michel Tushman have emphasized that companies need to secure an external fit by pursuing strategies that can lead change, while securing internal fit by ensuring consistency between the newly adopted strategies and management systems.[2]

As these theorists have noted, Samsung succeeded because it improved both its external and its internal fit through the New Management initiative. To improve its external fit, Samsung introduced strategic changes in response to major shifts in the environment, including digitization, globalization, and the rise of the knowledge-based economy. These strategic changes resulted in Samsung's shift to quality-driven management, its successful drive to become a market leader, and its successful upgrading of its business portfolio. To achieve an internal fit with its newly adopted strategies, Samsung improved its talent management, introduced new management techniques, and pursued innovation in its organizational culture and values. Through this process, Samsung was able to reorganize its management systems and create its three core competencies successfully. In particular, Samsung introduced its co-opetition system during this time. In short, Samsung's rise to world-class status over the 20 years since the New Management initiative has been the result of its ability to improve the external and internal fit of its businesses to reach world-class levels.

Achieving the External Fit of the Samsung Way

With the launch of the New Management initiative, Samsung aggressively pursued quality-driven management, market leadership, and an upgraded business portfolio. In particular, the arrival of the twenty-first century's "winner takes all" digital economy heightened the company's urgent need to shed its fast follower status and become a market leader. Samsung thus mounted an all-out effort to increase the speed of its decision making and business execution.

The company recognized, moreover, that competitiveness in a knowledge economy depends on intangible assets and intellectual property, including technology, design, branding, and the ability to provide solutions. To thrive in this environment, not only do companies need to develop best-in-class products, technologies, and processes, but they also need to develop them faster than others. Thus, Samsung devoted all its efforts to strengthening its evolutionary innovation capabilities and bolstering its soft competitiveness in branding and design. By doing this, Samsung was able to effectively leverage the synergy arising from horizontal diversification, vertical integration, regional clustering, and convergence of products and services to gain a competitive advantage over specialized firms and overcome its status as a latecomer and a challenger. From this perspective, Samsung achieved a high degree of external fit for the strategies, core competencies, and management systems that it adopted under the New Management initiative (see Table 9.1).

Samsung also benefited greatly from the foresight of Chairman Lee, who anticipated paradigm shifts before his rivals did. His prediction that the electronics industry would migrate entirely from analog to digital, for example,

Table 9.1 *Samsung's Three Core Competencies and Five Elements of Management*

	Speed	Synergy	Evolutionary Innovation
Leadership and governance	• Stretch goals • Bold decision making • Delegation and empowerment	• Collaboration centered on the owner-manager • Coordination by the Corporate Strategy Office	• Stretch goals • Creating a sense of crisis • Knowledge transfer and diffusion by the Corporate Strategy Office
Strategy	• Preemptive investment • Select-and-focus strategy	• Vertical integration • Sharing of knowledge, information, and brand	• Emphasis on technology and innovation • Being first to market • Focus on quality
HR management	• Employee loyalty and commitment • Diligence • Group incentive schemes	• CEO and executive rotation (sharing the DNA for success) • Collaboration as a criterion in CEO evaluations	• Scouting of core talent • Recruitment of outstanding foreign talent (overseas research institutes) • Performance-based evaluation and compensation • Group incentive schemes
Management control	• Macromanagement • Innovation in IT processes (SCM and ERP) • Regional clustering • Lego-style, leapfrog, and preemptive R&D; parallel development	• Collaborative R&D among divisions and affiliates in pursuit of convergence • Regional clustering • Coordination by the Corporate Strategy Office and Samsung Advanced Institute of Technology • Interaffiliate committees	• Regional clustering • Lego-style, leapfrog, and preemptive R&D; parallel development • Collaborative R&D among divisions and affiliates
Culture and values	• Pursuit of excellence • Sense of crisis • Leading innovation • Embracing change	• Single Samsung	• Pursuit of excellence and leading innovation • Pursuit of rationality • Sense of crisis • People first

proved to be entirely true, allowing Samsung to invest heavily in digital technologies and beat competitors like Sony to the market. As a result, Samsung produced the first entirely digital TV in 1998, then went on to dominate the industry. Chairman Lee also predicted that as product differentiation through technology became increasingly difficult, intangibles like design and branding would play a larger role in consumer purchases. As a result, Samsung has now raised its design and brand status to world-class levels.

Even when Samsung failed to predict changes accurately, it has been able to rely on its rapid execution ability to catch up with and surpass market leaders. When Apple's iPhone became a runaway hit in 2008, all of the phone manufacturers that were then in the lead, including Nokia, Motorola, LG Electronics, and Samsung, suffered from "smartphone shock." However, only Samsung, with its uniquely fast execution speed, was able to catch up with Apple. This was possible because of the owner-manager's constant exhortations to embrace change and innovation, and the speed, convergence synergy, and evolutionary innovation capabilities that Samsung had developed over time as its core competencies.

Achieving the Internal Fit of the Samsung Way

Samsung pursued change management to improve the internal fit between the strategies that it used to respond to change and its core competencies and management systems. Chapters 3 and 4 of this book explained how Samsung restructured its leadership and governance, HR management, management control, and culture and values to achieve an internal fit with its strategies of market leadership and upgrading of its business portfolio. As shown in Table 9.1, Samsung's three core competencies were formed and developed based on changes in its leadership and governance. Samsung succeeded in growing into a world-class firm because of the high internal fit between its dynamic core competencies, its leadership and governance, and its management systems. Chapter 8 showed how Samsung promoted speed and evolutionary innovation simultaneously through its co-opetition system, while reducing the dependence of weaker affiliates on stronger ones, which can arise when a company is pursuing synergy. Samsung's three core competencies were thus able to propel it to world-class status.

Sustainability of the Samsung Way

Will the Samsung Way continue to generate strong results? To continuously demonstrate high performance, companies need to dynamically improve and then maintain their external fit with the environment, while simultaneously increasing the internal fit among their strategies, management systems, and core competencies. To gain and sustain competitive advantage, companies need to deliver differentiated customer value and maintain organizational resources that their competitors cannot imitate. In light of this, it seems likely that Samsung can sustain its competitive advantage and maintain its high performance as long as the paradigms that are currently prevailing continue.

Viewed in terms of external fit, the management systems and dynamic core competencies that Samsung built as it developed the Samsung Way are well suited to the major paradigm shifts of the 2010s. In particular, Samsung's capacity for speed has grown in importance as product life cycles have shortened, and as the business environment has grown more complex with the arrival of smart devices. At the same time, the borders between industries are falling and convergence is increasing, making Samsung's conglomerate business structure and the resultant synergies all the more useful. Samsung's evolutionary innovation capabilities, moreover, are especially appropriate for the current knowledge-based economy, which depends on the creation of knowledge through innovation.

Just as important, Samsung's strategies, management systems, and core competencies have achieved a strong and consistent internal fit under the New Management initiative, leaving little chance that its rivals will be able to imitate Samsung and achieve similar results. This is similar to what Toyota has done. Toyota allows employees from rival companies to visit its automobile plants, and almost all automakers worldwide have adopted its techniques. However, none of them have yet succeeded in achieving equivalent results.

If a company's competitive edge is limited to a particular technology or function, it can be imitated relatively easily. However, if a company's competitiveness arises from its overall systems, as in Samsung's case, it can be difficult for competitors to fully comprehend its advantages. Even if its rivals pass this hurdle, they are unlikely to reap similar performance simply by imitating a few practices, but not deploying the whole system. In fact, imitating outside practices can even worsen performance if those practices conflict with the existing culture and values. Accordingly, there is high potential for the Samsung Way to be a source of sustainable competitive advantage.

However, this does not mean that the Samsung Way can simply be maintained as is. Although Samsung has become a world-class company, it still has numerous weaknesses. Shifts in the business environment can erode the basis of the Samsung Way at any time, while the appearance of any cracks in Samsung's leadership, governance, or management systems can cause the whole structure to buckle. Hence, Samsung must always continue to evolve and develop the Samsung Way.

Tasks Ahead for the Samsung Way

The years since 2000 have been some of Samsung's best ever. In 2013, Samsung Electronics' operating profit topped 36 trillion won (US$34 billion), the best performance among global manufacturers. However, even record performance can signal the onset of a crisis. Moreover, companies that are leading in one era often fall into a competency trap if they fail to understand paradigm shifts and embrace change, leading to their decline or collapse.

Most companies that have experienced a peak tend to adhere to their existing methods and products in the belief that they can enjoy uninterrupted leadership. However, it is at such times that companies are most in need of the "creative destruction" described by Joseph Schumpeter. As happened to Sony and Nokia, many leading companies fall behind because they are afraid of cannibalizing their existing businesses and consequently fail to embrace creative destruction. Such firms are toppled by competitors that have products, technologies, services, business models, and management systems with a better fit with a new business paradigm. For latecomers in particular, paradigm shifts provide the perfect opportunity to upend leading firms through disruptive innovation. In a stable environment, the existing leaders can leverage economies of scale, brand image, and other factors that favor first movers, making it difficult for latecomers to catch up. A shift in the paradigm, however, can not only neutralize such advantages but turn them into a barrier to embracing change.

Samsung Electronics has achieved the world's highest levels of performance by securing core competencies and a competitive advantage that its rivals cannot easily match. However, to sustain its competitive edge and fully achieve creative management, Samsung needs to embrace constant change and innovation and continuously develop the Samsung Way. As Chairman Lee Kun-Hee recently warned, Samsung still has a long way to go to be a premier world-class company, and all of Samsung's core business lines can disappear in the long term.

The more I hear about our record performance, the more I get worried. Samsung still has a long way to go to become a premier world-class company, and this is no time for us to relax or return to old habits.

—*Chairman Lee Kun-Hee*

Now is the real crisis. Top global companies are collapsing. This could happen to Samsung as well. The businesses and products that represent Samsung today will be gone within the next 10 years. We will have to start all over again. There is no time to lose. We have to focus and march ahead."

—*Chairman Lee Kun-Hee*

A premier world-class company is a company that dominates source technology and industry standards to create new categories, products, or businesses. It sets the pace for industry growth and sustains stable business performance based on its strong market dominance. It leads creative innovation and carries out creative destruction that encroaches on its own products and businesses so that it is constantly re-creating them for the future.[3] In addition, a premier world-class company is not dependent on the abilities of a single CEO, but has the institutions that can deliver outstanding performance well after that CEO is gone. It is a company that has built a unique and superior management system that provides it with a long-term competitive edge.[4]

In this chapter, the authors analyze the tasks that Samsung needs to carry out if it is to become a premier world-class company, and suggest directions in which the Samsung Way can evolve and develop in the future. Table 9.2 summarizes the tasks and potential solutions that the authors believe are needed if Samsung is to reach the next level as a premier global company.

Tasks in Strategy

To be a premier world-class company, Samsung needs to change its strategic directions. We suggest that the company should secure market leadership through creative innovation, transform itself into a total solution provider and platform leader, reduce the gap among affiliates, transform itself into a transnational corporation, and establish a co-prosperity business model to become a loved company.

Market Leadership Through Creative Innovation

Since the New Management initiative, Samsung has transformed itself from a fast follower and imitator to a first mover and innovator. It has succeeded in doing so by constantly pursuing a strategy of constantly becoming the "world's best through quality." This strategy paid off when Samsung leveraged evolutionary innovation—improvement and differentiation in existing products and technologies to increase customer value—to become number one in semiconductors, liquid-crystal displays (LCDs), TVs, mobile phones, rechargeable batteries, and shipbuilding. More recently, Samsung has taken

Table 9.2   *Long-Term Tasks for the Samsung Way*

Classification	Task	Solution
Strategy	Strengthen market leadership through creative innovation	• Evolution into an ambidextrous organization • Investment in M&A and real options
	Become a total solution provider and platform leader	• Provision of product-related solutions • Achievement of platform leadership in an industrial ecosystem
	Reduce the gaps in competitiveness among affiliates and upgrade the business portfolio	• Improve the competitiveness of the financial and service businesses • Restructure affiliates that have fallen below global standards
	Become a transnational corporation	• Optimization through a global network • Resource procurement through a global network
	Establish a co-prosperity business model	• Establish a favorable corporate image through harmonization of competitiveness and co-prosperity • Establish a mutually cooperative business model
Management of HR and organizational culture	Acquire high-caliber global talent	• Presentation of a career path for foreign talent • Creation of a foreign talent–friendly management system
	Create an open culture that acknowledges diversity	• Promote a culture of openness and respect for the individual • Decentralization, horizontal structure, and networking
	Develop a creative culture	• Horizontal and decentralized operations • Rewards based on long-term performance • Promotion of a culture with greater tolerance for risk and failure
	Maintain cohesion as "Single Samsung"	• Promotion of groupwide common values and culture

its innovativeness to the next level by moving beyond improvements in existing products and introducing wholly new product categories.

Since 2009, Samsung has increased its market share in digital TVs by leading the industry in the development of light-emitting diode (LED) TVs, 3D TVs, and smart TVs. In semiconductors, Samsung has reinvented the industry by tapping fusion memory and leading the market in developing solid-state drives (SSDs), the next generation in data storage. In smartphones, Samsung's Galaxy Note launched a new category of "phablets" based on Samsung's unique pen solution. In displays, Samsung was the first to commercialize flexible models based on its success in building active-matrix organic LED (AMOLED) panels. In shipbuilding, Samsung was the first in the world to build an icebreaking tanker and to develop offshore floating dock technology. By launching entirely new categories of products, Samsung has raised its evolutionary innovation capabilities to the highest levels.

Recently, Samsung has intensified its efforts to lead global technology standards by strengthening its patent management. Many of Samsung's technologies, including Moving Picture Experts Group-4 (MPEG-4) video, digital TV (DTV), and International Movile Telecommunication 2000 (IMT-2000), have been chosen as global standards, with MPEG-4 in particular bringing in substantial royalties every year.

Nonetheless, Samsung's current level of innovation, which now consists of introducing new categories within existing products and technologies, still falls short of being called "creative innovation." From a management theory perspective, Samsung's innovation can be seen as a highly developed form of evolutionary innovation or, more generously, as a stage midway between evolutionary innovation and creative innovation. Samsung has yet to develop new products, business models, or source technologies whose like has never been seen in the market before—that is, creative innovation. Even when it has introduced new categories of products, it has mostly relied on outsiders for its source technologies. This has resulted in a situation in which Samsung is paying increasing royalties as its revenue grows.

With the recent trend toward aggressive use of patents and intellectual property rights, building technologies through reverse engineering has become difficult, and licensing costs have soared. The number of intellectual property rights–related suits for source technologies has grown steeply in recent years, including Apple's lawsuits against Samsung concerning smartphones and tablet PCs. Settlements and compensation paid for patent infringement can amount to billions of U.S. dollars, and basic technologies are becoming increasingly difficult to buy at any price, particularly in the high-tech industry.

To become a premier world-class business, Samsung needs to continue pursuing evolutionary innovation that improves on existing products and technologies, and also efficient innovation that decreases production costs significantly. At the same time, Samsung needs to develop creative innovation that can disrupt existing industries and create new ones. In this vein, Chairman Lee's declaration of creative management in 2006 proved remarkably prescient.

To achieve creative innovation, Samsung will need to greatly increase its preemptive investments in core source technologies, based on a strategy of preparatory R&D management. To this end, Samsung has greatly increased its investment in developing core source technologies through Samsung Advanced Institute of Technology. This has already led to results like the successful development of the world's first graphene semiconductors, which are expected to become a breakthrough technology. Further efforts to develop and secure such core technologies will be needed in the future.

However, creative innovation need not be limited to developing source technologies. In the iPhone, Apple achieved creative innovation by reassembling existing technologies from both inside and outside the company, then adding a pioneering business model in the Apple App Store. As noted by Joseph Schumpeter, an early theorist on innovation, most innovation consists of taking existing knowledge and using it in new ways—and creative innovation is no exception. Thus, in addition to source technologies, Samsung also needs business model innovations that can take existing knowledge and reconfigure it in creative ways that add value for customers. To this end, the Samsung Way needs to continuously evolve in the following directions.

Evolution into an Ambidextrous Organization   Samsung's search for creative management pursues creative innovation to develop products, technologies, services, and business models that have never existed before. For Samsung, which has long focused on operational efficiency and cost cutting, along with imitation of and improvement on existing products and technologies, establishing new capabilities, systems, and culture suitable for creative innovation will be a highly challenging task.

Successful firms have a strong tendency toward complacency, resistance to change, and hostility to creative innovation. Such organizations are characterized by a bureaucratic culture that is focused on maintaining the status quo, and R&D that is focused on incremental innovation, short-term performance, and easily visible results. Likewise, some organizations suffer from the "not invented here" syndrome, where people and technologies arriving from outside are regarded with distrust, and only internal technologies and R&D are accepted. Indeed, Samsung cannot be regarded as being free of these short-term performance and status quo-oriented tendencies.

Samsung has several characteristics that arise out of Korea's position as a Confucian culture with a history of Japanese management and military rule. These include a tendency toward a homogenized workforce, a work ethic arising from an agricultural past, centralized control and hierarchical organization, micromanagement that is intolerant of failure, and a closed organizational monoculture. These characteristics matched well with strategies that were focused on cost-effectiveness and advancement through imitation, helping Samsung rapidly catch up with global leaders.

Samsung has experimented with several different ways to encourage creative innovation. For example, the company has launched "IDEA Open Space" to more actively seek out creative ideas within the organization, and to develop them through collective intelligence. To turn these ideas into reality, Samsung has begun operating and supporting C-Labs (creative labs) in each business division and a Creative Development Center to oversee the C-Labs. To spread a more creative culture and mindset throughout the company, Samsung opened a "Creative Academy" and declared a "C-Lab Day," where the results of C-Lab research are exhibited. The Creative Development Center, for its part, functions as a control tower for Samsung's creative work;

it is responsible for seeking out and realizing creative ideas, and spreading a culture and a mindset of creativity throughout the group.

In its research organizations, Samsung has long pursued a balance between long-term explorative research from the Samsung Advanced Institute of Technology and short-term exploitative research at individual business divisions. The institute has grown in importance as Samsung has pursued creative management. In particular, the creative management advocated by Chairman Lee has allowed Samsung to rapidly increase the share of its research that is focused on creative innovation projects, including the development of entirely new materials like graphene.

However, these efforts were not strong enough to enable Samsung to pursue creative innovation. Samsung must now evolve into an "ambidextrous organization" that can realize creative innovation, while at the same time maintaining its existing capabilities in operational efficiency and evolutionary innovation.[5] Samsung currently has very strong "right-handed" organizations, which are existing business divisions that are gradually improving their competitiveness while maintaining their existing capabilities, systems, and culture. However, Samsung needs to add separate "left-handed" organizations to be an ambidextrous organization.

As they are existing business divisions, right-handed organizations focus on enhancing already proven products, business models, and technologies through incremental or evolutionary innovation to provide short-term gains, better operational efficiency, and cost savings. These organizations do not have the ability to take on very ambitious new businesses or to initiate creative innovation, and they characteristically avoid long-term projects with high financial requirements and high failure rates. Naturally, trying to impose creative innovation on such organizations will probably fail.

Creative management, however, requires a very different workforce, skill set, culture, and managerial system. It is thus desirable for Samsung to establish separate left-handed organizations, or task force organizations that seek out new growth engines through creative innovation. Left-handed organizations are made up of specialized people with a strong sense of creativity and challenge. These organizations must have a culture that respects diversity, openness, and flexibility, and that accepts and learns from failures.

M&A and "Real Options" Investment   All of the world's major businesses, including Samsung, face an uncertain environment in which creative innovation can unleash discontinuous change at any time. Given these circumstances, Samsung needs more flexible strategic thinking and investing if it is to adapt to and lead these changes. It is thus time for Samsung to consider the "real options" strategy that firms like Hewlett-Packard, Intel, Microsoft, GlaxoSmithKline, and Merck use to cope with uncertainty.

If Samsung is to lead the future, it needs to step up its creative innovation efforts. However, it is risky for a company to try to develop every new technology and product in-house, or to continuously bet the company on uncertain new technologies. Accordingly, a "real options" strategy of investing in start-ups and acquiring companies that have core technology, either at home or overseas, merits consideration. Compared with its rivals, Samsung has typically been averse to acquisitions. This stems from its experience when it purchased U.S. PC manufacturer AST Research in the 1990s, on which it lost nearly US$1 billion. However, if Samsung hopes to secure advanced technologies from overseas, particularly technologies with the potential to become global standards, it needs to seriously consider making equity investments in a number of firms as a means of dealing with uncertainty. Samsung also needs to strengthen its open innovation efforts and expand its alliances with companies that have complementary technologies, or with start-ups that have potential core technologies. It also needs to secure basic technologies through cooperation with research universities and major public and nonprofit research institutes.

Samsung now recognizes these needs, somewhat belatedly, and has begun to strengthen its worldwide open innovation activities through strategic equity investments. The company opened its Strategy and Innovation Center and its Open Innovation Center in Silicon Valley in November 2012. The former focuses on finding new parts and components technologies, while the latter seeks out and invests in start-ups focusing on consumer products like smartphones and smart TVs. Both centers are authorized to make small-scale acquisitions to obtain not only promising companies, but also promising core talent. Underneath these organizations, Samsung runs Samsung Accelerator, which acts as an "incubation center" for start-ups. Samsung has also set up related task force organizations at its domestic business divisions and research institutes to cooperate closely with these organizations.

Both centers seek out and assess local innovations through a variety of open innovation activities, including strategic equity investments, small-scale M&A, and business incubation. They can then transfer any relevant technologies that they have acquired to Samsung's business divisions. Particularly advanced and important technologies can be internalized through Samsung's domestic research institutes. Samsung has assembled its own fund in connection with the two centers, strengthening its M&A and equity investments in Silicon Valley's next-generation technology start-ups. Although Samsung is a latecomer in this area, this is a promising new direction for the company.

Although Samsung was skeptical about acquisitions for a long time after its failure with AST Research, it broke this habit when its System LSI division successfully acquired Israel's TransChip in 2007. Based on the confidence it gained through this relatively small acquisition, Samsung pulled off a string of M&A deals to secure complementary technologies and products, centering on the System LSI division and the newly established medical equipment division.

However, Samsung's investments in M&A are still negligible when we consider Samsung Electronics' huge cash reserves and operating income. Going forward, Samsung will need to overcome its fear of failure, and actively pursue acquisitions and alliances to secure technologies, products, talent, and brands. Since the success rate for acquisitions is only 30 to 40 percent at best, even for experienced firms, Samsung is likely to start by focusing on making small deals, then consider larger acquisitions later, when it has more experience and where the need presents itself.

Transformation into a Total Solution Provider and Platform Leader

Samsung's history is rooted in its strong manufacturing competitiveness. Since the New Management initiative, however, Samsung has greatly strengthened its soft competitiveness in technology, marketing, brand power, and design. Such efforts will need to be redoubled if Samsung wishes to become a premier world-class firm. In particular, the twenty-first century has seen a marked tendency to erode the role of manufacturing and hardware in the value chain through developments like the modularization of parts and system-on-a-chip circuitry. Value creation is now rapidly migrating to "soft" areas like technology, core parts, content, software, marketing, branding, design, services, and solutions. In effect, we are now seeing "soft industry," with an increasing role for services; "soft products," where software creates most of the value; and "soft consumers," who prize a product's emotive aspects.[6] For example, in the recent smartphone revolution, Apple's operating profit–to–sales ratio was almost twice as high as Samsung's in 2012, thanks to its superiority in software, design, and branding. This was achieved despite Apple's outsourcing all of its manufacturing to Taiwan's Foxconn, which operates massive assembly lines in China.

To rise to premier world-class status, Samsung must go beyond simply boosting the individual aspects of soft competitiveness and become a customer-oriented total solution provider like IBM or GE. In the early 1990s, IBM drastically shifted its strategy and culture from a focus on products and technologies to a focus on customers. Instead of simply providing products for customers, IBM became a total solution provider that provides both products and product-related solutions and services. GE, for its part, did not stop with the sale of high-priced products like power generation facilities, medical equipment, and aircraft engines, but also connected these sales to its financial service arm.

Today, Samsung has a roster of high-end clients thanks to its leadership in electronics—from core parts to consumer products—and is well positioned to become a total solution provider. If the company can provide its current clients with integrated systems, services, and solutions, it can raise switching costs and improve customer retention. This strategy can also provide an escape from the "commodity trap," where product differentiation becomes more difficult and price competition intensifies as an industry matures. By doing this, Samsung can sustainably enjoy both high levels of value added and high margins.

From this perspective, it is encouraging that Samsung has already become a total solution provider in some areas. The leading example is the company's semiconductor business. To avoid the commodity trap in memory chips, Samsung has developed fusion memory, a total solution product that integrates dynamic random access memory (DRAM) and flash memory with nonmemory logic. The company has developed and provided custom fusion memory to different customers, enabling it to reinvent itself as the world's best total mobile chip solution provider. Samsung is currently trying to transform itself into a total solution provider in many business areas, and it will need to strengthen these efforts as it fends off Chinese rivals who are commoditizing its main lines of business.

Of course, none of this should be taken to mean that Samsung must directly develop, produce, and provide all the products and services that it sells. Any company that attempts to directly develop and provide all the products and services that customers need, even in areas where it is not competent, is bound to disappoint. Accordingly, as a total solutions provider, Samsung will benefit from seeking out "complementors" who can handle areas in which Samsung is lacking.

For platform products like smart TVs, smartphones, game consoles, and MP3 players, however, Samsung will need to go beyond total solutions and demonstrate "platform leadership," or the ability to manage and nurture its own industrial ecosystem. Platforms like smartphones and DVD players have value only as a means of gaining access to content. As with the TV industry, which is rapidly migrating toward smart TVs, many industries are undergoing a shift to a platform-based ecosystem.

Platform products are characterized by a phenomenon in which having more customers on a platform causes more products to be available for that platform, which in turn leads to even more customers and more value for that platform. In economic parlance, this phenomenon is called "indirect network effects from complementary goods." During the 1980s home video format war, for example, Sony introduced a superior videotape standard with its Betamax machines. Nonetheless, Sony lost to the rival VHS standard, largely because of its inability to create indirect network effects. Another example was the MP3 player market, which at one time was dominated by Samsung and other Korean firms. These companies were rapidly overtaken by Apple when it leveraged indirect network effects through its iPod player and iTunes music service. Apple's success, which it repeated on an even greater scale in smartphones, is attributable to its accurate understanding of the nature of platforms, its platform leadership through cooperation with content providers, and its ability to create network effects.

Samsung has made a few attempts to gain control of international standards and secure industry leadership by releasing a string of "world's first" products or technologies such as WiBro, the world's first mobile broadband technology. However, Samsung lacks a strategic understanding of the nature of platform leadership and the way it can make products into global standards. Platform leadership cannot be achieved simply by emphasizing functionality, or by being the world's first or best. Platform leadership, as in Apple's case, requires an accurate understanding of industrial ecosystems and a willingness to forgo profits on occasion in order to support developers and partners. In short, healthy platforms must be based on the principle of co-prosperity. This process may even require cooperation with competitors. Companies that aspire to be platform leaders should thus refrain from engaging in autocratic behavior and focusing only on one's own short-term profits. Such behavior violates the principle of co-prosperity with partners, and it impairs the formation of a healthy industrial ecosystem.

Analysis of Samsung's past strategies shows that it has considerable work ahead of it if it is to become a platform leader. While it made little sense for Samsung to pursue platform leadership when it was still a fast follower, now that it is the world's number one provider of smartphones and TVs, the company needs to devise platforms aggressively and form its own industrial ecosystem. By doing this, Samsung can become a genuine global leader.

Fortunately, Samsung has recognized the need to both build platform leadership and become a total solutions provider. This recognition is already visible in the changing direction of its smartphone and TV business. In particular, Samsung Electronics recently established a separate Media Solution Center to draft long-term platform service road maps for the mobile business, and to devise business models in services. With the advent of an "N Screen" era, in which TVs, mobile phones, and computers are all connected to one another, the center is also focusing on establishing an integrated service platform strategy that connects Samsung's various business areas. To this end, the Media Solution Center has recently formed an "ecosystem integration team."

As a result of the Media Solution Center's efforts, Samsung has joined with Intel to develop Tizen, Samsung's own web-based operating system (OS), that will challenge Google's Android and Apple's iOS. It makes sense for Samsung to reduce its reliance on Android and to secure platform leadership based on its own OS. However, in light of the network effects that are inherent in platform competition, the prospects that a new platform will succeed without the introduction of a disruptive new technology or business model are not so bright.

Accordingly, if Tizen is to compete effectively with the Google and Apple platforms, Samsung needs to have deep insight into the nature of platform leadership and use impeccable judgment in its strategy and execution. Above all, Samsung needs to attract developers, telecommunications carriers, and even competitors into the Tizen camp. To this end, Samsung must show a more open and mutually beneficial attitude, including a willingness to sacrifice its own interests and provide Tizen developers with greater profits than Apple and Google do.

Samsung Electronics' business portfolio includes TVs, smartphones, and PCs, and among these, it is number one in TVs and smartphones. This means that Samsung has a strong potential to achieve unique competitiveness if it can organically connect its products into an ecosystem. Now is the time for Samsung Electronics to invest heavily in developing platforms to realize this potential.

Reducing the Gap Between Affiliates

Although Samsung is now a household name worldwide, its global success has continued to be limited to Samsung Electronics and its electronics-related affiliates. As a result, this book has focused on Samsung Electronics' success, and on the core competencies and management systems that made that success possible. In the other areas in which Samsung does business, including finance and services, the company is a leading firm domestically, but is still relatively unknown on the global stage. Its financial affiliates in particular are dealing with challenges from new global competitors even in their home market.

Since the 1997 Asian currency crisis, Samsung has upgraded its business portfolio through regular restructuring of its electronics business and the building of a co-opetition system between affiliates and divisions. However, Samsung Group overall still exhibits a large degree of unrelated diversification; in particular, there is a substantial gap between the competitiveness of its electronics and non-electronics-related affiliates. Accordingly, serious consideration must be given to the group's future business portfolio.

To this end, Samsung needs to either greatly increase the competitiveness of its finance and service affiliates or, in the long term, restructure any uncompetitive affiliates and divisions through spin-offs and divestitures. If Samsung selects the former path, it will need to find a way to create win-win synergy through cooperation between strong and weak affiliates that leverages the "Single Samsung" spirit. GE, for example, enhanced its competitiveness and performance through cooperation between its manufacturing, finance, and service divisions in the process of becoming a total solutions provider. However, such tactics can weaken the company's overall competitiveness if strong affiliates provide unilateral support to weaker ones. This phenomenon must be guarded against.

Transformation into a Transnational Corporation

Today's global leaders are transforming themselves from "multinational corporations" into "transnational corporations."[7] Multinational corporations have their head office and their main business in a particular country, with financial capital, human resources, technology, and information flowing unilaterally from headquarters to the company's overseas subsidiaries. As a result, headquarters functions as the company's absolute source of competitiveness, with overseas subsidiaries acting as subordinates. For transnational companies, on the other hand, headquarters and the home country are preeminent, but competitive advantage comes from the whole global network.

Thus, instead of a unilateral flow from headquarters outward, resources like outstanding employees can move from overseas subsidiaries to headquarters or to another overseas subsidiary in a multilateral flow.

Companies that are making the transition to transnational corporations create competitiveness by relocating activities like production, marketing, and call centers in the most optimal place. In this process, even headquarters functions can move overseas. At the same time, nationality, gender, and race are no longer important factors when securing and appointing talented human resources. Even the most "native" functions like R&D have been distributed to global R&D networks overseas.

In fact, 90 percent of Samsung Electronics' total revenue comes from overseas, and this share is growing. Samsung mobile phones dominate the world's high-end smartphone market, and its international brand value has soared to eighth place through efforts like its Olympic sponsorship. However, compared to its worldwide presence, Samsung's global management capabilities are still significantly lacking. Although its level of localization and its ability to secure technology and human resources through global networks have improved, Samsung still lags considerably behind European and U.S. firms in terms of being a global concern. It will be very difficult for Samsung to become an elite global firm if it continues to rely heavily on its domestic resources and personnel. Thus, Samsung must become more aggressive in sourcing talent and technology from its global network.

Above all, the head office and its Korean personnel must have a more open and global mindset, and must establish management systems and practices that can be effective in other countries. Treating the employees of overseas subsidiaries and foreign employees in Korea as migrant workers, and showing favoritism toward Korean workers, will make it difficult for Samsung to secure top global talent and develop roots overseas. The company must establish a more locally rooted global network if it is to become a transnational company. Since Samsung's future competitiveness depends upon its securing the best technology talent, the company needs to strengthen the role and function of its overseas research centers and expand its global R&D network.

Establishing a Co-prosperity Business Model
and Becoming a Loved Company

Being number one induces strong feelings of admiration, even as it invokes feelings of rivalry and envy. In Korea in particular, the prevailing feeling is that even though Samsung deserves respect for being number one in many areas, it still lacks emotional ties to the community. Rationally speaking, Samsung's products, services, human resources, and technological innovations are all well regarded; however, emotionally speaking, Samsung does not enjoy equivalent goodwill. As emotional concerns come to have increasing influence in the global marketplace, it will become more difficult for a company to achieve continuous growth solely on the basis of functionality.

Accordingly, Samsung needs to move away from its preoccupation with being a "strong company" and establish a co-prosperity business model that values the interests of its partners, consumers, and local society. By doing so, Samsung can reinvent itself as a company that is both respected and loved. In particular, Korean *chaebols* like Samsung are now facing a tougher regulatory environment, with trends like economic democratization and corporate governance reform rising as major political issues in Korea because of the very high level of concentration of economic power in the hands of a small number of *chaebols*. Thus, Samsung must strengthen its efforts at responsible community membership. To this end, the company can practice ethical and environment-friendly management and promote co-prosperity with its partners. To make this possible, Samsung must win social trust from its employees, partners, and customers, as set forth in the New Management initiative.

Likewise, Samsung has to pay more attention to its role as a global citizen. While expanding its business on the global stage, Samsung has greatly increased both its number of overseas employees and its share of production and sales that takes place overseas. Simultaneously, Samsung's brand value as assessed by Interbrand has also risen. Accordingly, expectations about Samsung's social responsibility at its overseas locations are growing, and the company needs to do more to become known as a respected local presence. In particular, Samsung needs to practice ethics that exceed local standards by practicing IBM's policy of "abiding by company codes of conduct even if local laws are more lenient, and abiding by local laws when they are more rigorous than company codes." The company can then encourage its partners to follow suit. Finally, Samsung needs to practice corporate citizenship activities that are compatible with the circumstances of local society and that contribute to its development.

To sum up, Samsung needs to find an appropriate balance between competitiveness and co-prosperity to become a loved and respected business, both at home and abroad.

Tasks for Management of Human Resources and Organizational Culture

To be a premier world-class company, Samsung needs to change its human resource management and organizational culture to accommodate the new strategic directions we elaborarated above. We suggest that Samsung should secure the world's best talent, develop an open culture that recognizes diversity, develop a creative culture, and maintain "Single Samsung" internal solidarity.

Securing the World's Best Talent

Samsung has long recognized the role of outstanding human resources through its "people first" policy. The company's success in areas like semiconductors is due in large part to its ability to secure, foster, and utilize talented people. More recently, Samsung has reemphasized the importance of core talent, and has boosted the recruiting of "S-class" talent. The company must strengthen these efforts further, without regard to nationality, gender, or race. Samsung works in an industry that is based on knowledge and innovation, where a single genius can feed 100,000 people. This makes the competition for talent akin to a war, and securing talent akin to a victory. Samsung thus needs to hire the best people from around the world who can make it a premier world-class corporation.

Thus far, few foreigners have become executives at Samsung's headquarters or presidents of overseas subsidiaries. It will thus need to make more of an effort to persuade worldwide talent to consider Samsung over top domestic firms. Foreigners must be given career paths that will allow them to become executives at headquarters, heads of overseas subsidiaries, or even CEOs. Since foreign talent is likely to be reluctant to move to Korea, management of overseas subsidiaries must also be changed. For example, the existing practice of using expatriate Koreans as intermediaries in the process of coordinating overseas branches must be abandoned in favor of using official channels. Likewise, Samsung needs to strengthen the autonomy of overseas subsidiaries to enhance their capabilities.

Recruiting a large number of outstanding foreign talent and appointing these people to management positions, however, can weaken Samsung's core strengths of speed, efficiency, and organizational cohesion. To resolve the problem, the company will need to do more to support promising local talent by transferring people to headquarters in Korea and building networks with executives. Samsung can also consider providing short-term intensive training at the Samsung Human Resources Development Center to help overseas talent develop a more "Samsung" identity and feeling of belonging.

Development of an Open Culture That Recognizes Diversity

Establishing a culture that enables talented people to demonstrate their skills is just as important as finding and hiring those people in the first place. In the past, Samsung's strong reliance on internal hiring led to an entrenched corporate culture that did not tolerate diversity. However, today, a "closed" culture would be very detrimental to creative innovation, as talented people who are hired from outside or who are minorities will have a hard time collaborating with other employees. A case in point is that despite improvements, S-class employees, whose pay often exceeds that of CEOs, still frequently leave Samsung. Their unfamiliarity with Samsung's culture leads to difficulties when they are working with other employees. Also, these employees do not get enough support from other employees or enough opportunities to demonstrate their capabilities. To fully utilize and retain outstanding overseas talent, Samsung's headquarters and its Korean workforce must demonstrate more openness and adopt global mindsets, practices, management systems, and values.

An open corporate culture fosters fluid communications and turns the organization into a melting pot in which employees with varying backgrounds and from diverse countries get together, share their ideas and know-how, and find creative solutions by recombining those ideas and know-how. This is because innovation arises when an organization's knowledge is both heterogeneous and complementary. In Samsung's case, however, it is undeniable that in the past, homogeneity and internal solidarity have prevailed over diversity. Despite increased efforts to increase diversity by actively recruiting abroad, Samsung still lags considerably behind European and U.S. companies in this regard. It is thus becoming more important for the company to establish a culture that respects openness and diversity.

Recently, Samsung has increased its hiring of women, young people, and R&D workers, and these groups are increasing as a share of Samsung's core personnel. Nonetheless, old customs that demand conformity from young people and impose rigid rules on R&D personnel still persist. These customs are not suitable for young people, who value individuality and autonomy. These new core personnel may not be strongly motivated by Samsung's performance-based incentive schemes, and thus they will hesitate to work long hours because they value work/life balance. Samsung thus needs to design a new work system that can raise productivity to a level that is equivalent to or higher than the current level, even if it follows a regular eight-hour work schedule.

For all their advantages, increased diversity and openness can weaken Samsung's core strengths of speed, efficiency, and organizational cohesion. Accordingly, efforts to strengthen teamwork and loyalty must be made at the same time as efforts to increase diversity and openness.

Developing a Creative Culture

Chairman Lee's emphasis on creative management has inspired Samsung to pursue a creative organizational culture. However, creativity has yet to become the prevailing culture at Samsung. In order to become a creative organization, the company needs to pursue horizontal and decentralized management, increase compensation for long-term performance, and develop a culture that accepts failure. While this is an especially urgent task for units that are operating in new and innovative businesses, the entire organization will eventually have to accommodate a creative organizational culture.

To this end, Samsung must begin by abandoning working practices that are rooted in the agricultural past and overemphasize diligence and hard work. Those of Samsung's executives and managers who are in their forties and fifties have placed work and the company above all else. Competitiveness in a knowledge-based economy, however, depends more on creativity than on simple persistence. As Chairman Lee stressed, we have entered an era in which a single genius can feed tens of thousands of people.

Second, Samsung needs to move beyond top-down management and consider introducing a decentralized organization that delegates more power and responsibility to lower-ranking workers. This can enable these lower-ranking employees to seek out more useful ideas. Furthermore, when confronting conflicts between organizational units, Samsung needs to increasingly utilize horizontal negotiation and coordination, which incorporate input from multiple interests, rather than vertical management, which relies solely on the decisions of senior managers. Horizontal decisions can produce integrative, creative solutions. Likewise, Samsung needs to put more effort into developing a trusting and supportive relationship between organizational units, as these kinds of relationships foster creative and cooperative decision making.

Third, Samsung needs to increase the share of its compensation that is based on long-term performance. Samsung Electronics' employees can receive performance incentives of up to 50 percent of their annual salary based on the financial performance of their divisions during the previous year. This system is a very powerful way for Samsung Electronics' division heads to concentrate the capabilities of the entire organization for achieving their yearly financial goals. However, it may lead to an excessive focus on short-term performance rather than on creative work that delivers long-term gains. While Samsung pays long-term performance incentives to executives on the basis of the performance of their affiliates over the past three years, this is not enough to encourage executives to pursue creative management. Samsung should consider reducing short-term performance incentives and increasing longer-term incentives instead. Providing stock options to executives and long-term incentives to ordinary employees would be more persuasive alternatives.

Fourth, Samsung needs a culture that accepts failure. Creative innovation and new businesses by definition involve a high risk of failure. As a result, if Samsung is to become an innovation-driven organization that seeks out new growth engines, it needs to develop a cultural acceptance of failure. As creative innovation grows in importance, "learning from failure," an ability that Samsung has often lacked in the past, has become increasingly critical. If people are harshly reprimanded for failures, few of them will be willing to take on challenges, and valuable knowledge that could be gained from mistakes will be concealed and forgotten. This is a major obstacle to creative innovation, which is often the result of numerous failures.

One example of a situation in which failure led to later success is in Samsung's successful system semiconductor line. This resulted from the transfer of technical know-how from the Alpha chip, a highly innovative microprocessor that had previously failed in the market. Knowledge gained from the development of the Alpha chip helped Samsung upgrade its system semiconductor designs, production processes, and reliability. Another example was the failed attempt to develop charge trap flash (CTF) semiconductor technology. Knowledge gained during the development process helped Samsung develop a 3D structure in NAND flash memory. Nevertheless, fear of failure and a reluctance to explore new directions are still pervasive at Samsung. Employees often wait for orders from their superiors rather than taking initiative. Accordingly, a culture of learning from failures needs to grow, particularly in left-handed organizations.

Maintaining "Single Samsung" Internal Solidarity

Samsung's cohesion, as embodied in the "Single Samsung" spirit, has spearheaded its rapid growth, and it remains a key to the company's competitiveness today. However, signs of strain began to appear after the 1997 Asian currency crisis, when Samsung pursued intensive restructuring. As the company has introduced profit sharing, internal competition, performance-based rewards, and the recruiting of core talent, its cohesion as an organization has faced significant challenges. Recent developments, including business diversification, decentralization, globalization, and a more diverse workforce, have created further issues for the Single Samsung spirit. The feeling of solidarity among affiliates, among employees within affiliates, and among employees and the organization has begun to erode. As a result, there is the potential for affiliates to lose their sense of identifying with Samsung and other affiliates, weakening its ability to create convergence synergy.

As noted earlier, Samsung needs to strengthen its openness and diversity, both within the organization and among individual members, and it must increase management autonomy for affiliates and major divisions, while maintaining healthy internal competition. However, those efforts can seriously erode the Single Samsung spirit. Samsung's employees should not discard their sense of solidarity and cohesion as part of the company's group structure. Samsung's common groupwide organizational culture and language, shared values, and voluntary mutual cooperation have a great deal of potential to create further valuable synergy. Accordingly, the simultaneous pursuit of solidarity based on the group's common culture and of openness and diversity is one of the most important tasks for the future of the Samsung Way.

As government regulations on corporate governance and business groups are becoming stricter, affiliates are finding it increasingly necessary to maintain independent management. Interaffiliate integration based on fiats issued by the Corporate Strategy Office has become increasingly constrained. In the future, as a substitute for formal integration through the Corporate Strategy Office, Samsung needs to maintain its spirit of Single Samsung to foster informal interaffiliate integration. To maintain this spirit, Samsung needs to adopt universal human values and a shared brand that will embrace employees from diverse countries and cultures.

The Samsung Way Must Continuously Evolve

Although Samsung has achieved world-class performance, its path to achieving premier world-class status remains uncertain. In particular, Samsung must avoid the trap of being number one and the complacency that this often entails. Samsung is at risk of falling into the trap of arrogance and complacency, as Chairman Lee has previously warned.

> What we have achieved today is partly due to our abilities, but it is mostly due to the carelessness of leading companies, a lot of luck, and the sacrifices of our predecessors.

Samsung's main business lines, including electronics, finance, and services, are in no position to be complacent. Samsung Electronics in particular has many obstacles to overcome on its way to reaching premier status. At the same time, Samsung's finance and services businesses are only treading water by protecting their positions in their home market, while facing serious challenges from local and global rivals. These threats have prompted Chairman Lee to warn, "Samsung may lose all of its number one products after 10 years."

In the twenty-first century in particular, being number one is no guarantee that a company can rebound from any serious setback. If Samsung cannot evolve, it is likely to suffer an irrecoverable decline. Failing to acknowledge this reality will ensure that opportunities that are within reach now will turn into threats later.

If Samsung's outstanding performance continues in the future, the unique and inimitable nature of the company's management style will be validated. However, Samsung's future path cannot rely on imitation or learning from others. Although following in others' footsteps has been enough for Samsung until now, its future as a premier world-class firm will be different.

> As professional climbers must experience the agony of altitude sickness when climbing Mt. Everest, climbing to the world's top position requires the same perilous path.
>
> —*Chairman Lee Kun-Hee*

The time has come for Samsung to blaze its own path through creativity, not imitation. This will be both a difficult and a dangerous process. The competitors that will seek to topple Samsung in the future are all top-ranked global firms. Only victory over these competitors can achieve the goals that the New Management initiative set forth some 20 years ago.

As paradigm changes become more frequent and more destructive, Samsung must attempt to lead these changes, and when this is not possible, respond to them swiftly. To this end, the CEO's insight and strong leadership and management systems must be well connected. Up until now, Samsung has been able to rely on Chairman Lee's ability to leverage paradigm shifts and become a world-class company. However, from this point on, Samsung must devise a next-generation governance structure and management system for when Chairman Lee retires.

Through this process, Samsung will be able to upgrade its paradox management, the engine that has powered its success. In particular, Samsung must develop into a transnational corporation that pioneers new markets and industries by discovering new growth engines based on creative innovation. At the same time, however, the increasing racial, religious, and cultural diversity of its workforce and a growing spirit of openness can compromise the company's ability to pursue speed and efficiency, which have long been among its core competencies. Samsung thus needs to develop a new form of paradox management that can overcome the conflict between speed and efficiency on the one hand, and diversity and creative innovation on the other.

What Are the Major Lessons from the Samsung Way?

To conclude this book, we summarize the major lessons from Samsung's remarkable success with the New Management initiative and the Samsung Way that companies all over the world can learn from.

First, Samsung's dramatic ascent as a world-class company illustrates the importance of strategic agility in response to major paradigm changes. Samsung emerged as a global electronics firm when it seized opportunities that arose during the shift from analog to digital technology. Sony was a dominant industry leader in the analog era, but it was too complacent and feared cannibalization too much. As a result, Sony was slow to make the transition to being a digital company. This is why Sony lost to Samsung even in its core TV business. The reversal of fortune between Sony and Samsung clearly tells us that major paradigm changes can provide latecomers like Samsung with golden opportunities to catch up with incumbents by leveraging the emerging paradigm shifts early on, whereas the same paradigm shift can pose a serious threat to incumbents because of competency traps and fear of cannibalization.

Samsung's performance took off during the recent smartphone revolution that Apple led. Samsung entered the smartphone industry after Apple seriously threatened its mobile phone business. However, based on its strong strategic agility, it bounced back quickly and became a world leader in only four years, capturing 32 percent market share in 2013 as opposed to 15 percent for Apple. Thus, Samsung's remarkable success in the past two decades shows that companies all over the world should enhance their strategic agility based on strategic foresight and a speedy and flexible management system in an era of major paradigm changes.

Second, if they are to survive and prosper in this hypercompetitive world, companies that aim to be global leaders should seek paradox management by pursuing seemingly contradictory goals, such as global-scale economies and speed, differentiation and low-cost leadership, or innovation and efficiency. As we have discussed Samsung's paradox management throughout this book, we will not explain it further here. We believe that other companies can learn how to manage paradoxes to create multiple sources of competitive advantage in this hypercompetitive and uncertain global economic environment, if they thoroughly investigate Samsung's success.

Third, Samsung's success through paradox management highlights the importance of creating an ambidextrous learning organization, and also making long-term investments in core talent and intangible assets such as technology, brand, and design. Samsung actively benchmarked global leaders such as GE and Toyota and then carefully modified those companies' practices to make them more appropriate for its unique culture. Samsung has also been very aggressive in securing globally minded core employees. For example, since 1990, Samsung has sent about 5,000 core employees abroad for one year without any assignment through the regional specialist program. This core talent could later serve as global growth leaders or key change agents in Samsung's transformation.

Such long-term investments in core talent and intangible assets to make Samsung a learning organization were possible because of the presence of an owner-manager with long-term vision. To gain and sustain competitive advantage, striking the appropriate balance between a long-term perspective and long-term investments and a short-term performance orientation is very important. Harmony between a long-term-oriented owner-manager and more short-term-oriented, yet competent, professional managers has led to amazing success at Samsung.

Of course, not all companies have an owner-manager with such a long-term vision; in fact, many have only professional managers. Since the 1990s, moreover, as the priority given to shareholder value has increased worldwide, pressure for corporate performance has increased. More and more companies—particularly publicly traded companies run by professional managers—have moved toward pursuing short-term gains rather than innovating and investing in intangible assets from a long-term perspective, as Samsung did. Such tendencies were particularly pronounced at companies whose CEO's term was short or whose company status was unstable. Therefore, in order to maintain and strengthen investments in core talent and build a learning organization to obtain long-term competitiveness, it is necessary to build a governance system that enables long-term investment under professional managers. A key example is GE, which appointed a CEO after a thorough verification and well-managed management succession. When it appointed a CEO, GE guaranteed that person a 10-year term in principle and allowed a second succession term. This allowed the CEO to focus on investment, innovation, and change management from a long-term perspective.

Many companies worldwide are impressed with Samsung's performance up to now and are trying to learn from the company. In particular, latecomer companies in emerging economies like China that are growing rapidly are aspiring to become the next Samsung by benchmarking it. Samsung was an emerging market latecomer 20 to 30 years ago, but it transformed itself into a world-class company. We hope this book serves as a useful guide for foreign companies that want to learn from Samsung.

NOTES

Chapter 1

1. J. Liker, *The Toyota Way: 14 Management Principles from the World's Greatest Manufacturer* (New York: McGraw-Hill, 2003).
2. M. Porter, *Competitive Advantage: Creating and Sustaining Superior Performance* (New York: Free Press, 1985).
3. Lee Kun-Hee, "Essay," *Dong-A Daily*, 1997.
4. This is often referred to as *X-inefficiency*. For detailed information on X-inefficiency, refer to C. Markides, *Diversification, Refocusing, and Economic Performance* (Cambridge, MA: MIT Press, 1995).
5. G. F. Davis, K. A. Diekmann, and C. H. Tinsley, "The Decline and Fall of the Conglomerate Firm in the 1980s: The Deinstitutionalization of an Organizational Form," *American Sociological Review*, 59 (1994): 547–570.
6. R. M. Grant, *Contemporary Strategy Analysis*, 6th ed. (Malden, MA: Blackwell Publishing. 2007).
7. This section is based on W. Ouchi, *Theory Z: How American Business Can Meet the Japanese Challenge* (New York: Avon Books, 1980); J. Abegglen and G. Stalk, *Kaisha: The Japanese Corporation* (New York: Basic Books, 1985); M. Aoki and R. Dore, *The Japanese Firm: The Sources of Competitive Strength* (New York: Oxford University Press, 1988); and P. Milgrom and J. Roberts, "Complementarities and Systems: Understanding Japanese Economic Organization," *Estudios Economicos*, 9 (1994): 3–42.

Part Two

1. R. E. Miles and C. C. Snow, *Organizational Strategy, Structure, and Process* (New York: McGraw-Hill, 1978) and R. E. Miles and C. C. Snow, *Fit, Failure and the Hall of Fame* (Free Press, 1994).
2. L. G. Hrebiniak and W. F. Joyce, *Implementing Strategy* (New York: Macmillan, 1984).
3. J. R. Galbraith, *Designing Organizations* (San Francisco: Jossey-Bass, 1995).

Chapter 3

1. When Chairman Lee was installed in 1987, he said, "We should increase the group's profits up to 1 trillion won and double or triple the wages of employees." Given that Samsung's profits stood at around 200 billion won at that time, it was not easy even to imagine profits of 1 trillion won. Samsung, however, achieved the 1 trillion won (about US$1.25 billion) level in profit, the first Korean company to do so, in 1994, six years after Chairman Lee acceded.

Chapter 4

1. Interview with Samsung Electronics Executive Vice-President Gee Wan-Goo.
2. *Samsung's 60-Year History* (Samsung Chairman Secretary Office, 1998), p. 190.
3. Ibid., p. 185.

Part Three

1. Samsung defines certain characteristics of each business. For example, it defines the semiconductor business as a "time industry" or "conscience industry," the watch business as a "fashion industry," home appliances as a "mass production and assembly industry," and hotels as an "installation and real estate industry."
2. J. R. Barney, *Gaining and Sustaining Competitive Advantage*, 4th ed. (Upper Saddle River, NJ: Prentice Hall, 2010).

Chapter 5

1. B. Gates, *Business @ the Speed of Thought: Using a Digital Nervous System* (New York: Warner Books, 1999).
2. F. Cairncross, *The Death of Distance* (Boston: Harvard Business School Press, 1997).
3. R. A. D'Aveni and R. E. Gunther, *Hypercompetition* (New York: Free Press, 1994). For more recent studies, see R. A. D'Aveni, G. B. Dagnino, and K. G. Smith, "The Age of Temporary Advantage," *Strategic Management Journal* 31, no. 13 (2010): 1371–1548.
4. "Learning curve effect" refers to an increase in efficiency or skills as a result of increasing production and the accumulated experience of an individual worker or an organization. The learning curve effect reduces

the number of workers needed for production. "Network effects" refer to an increase in benefits for customers when an increasing number of customers buy the same product or service. Strong network effects can lead to a "winner takes all" market for first movers. For more details about the source of the first-mover advantage, see M. B. Liberman and D. B. Montgomery, "First Mover Advantage," *Strategic Management Journal* 9, no. S1 (1998): 441–458 (1998); F. Zhu and M. Iansiti, "Entry into Platform-Based Markets," *Strategic Management Journal* 33, no. 1 (2012): 88–106; and S. K. Ethiraj and D. H. Zhu, "Performance Effects of Imitative Entry," *Strategic Management Journal* 29, no. 8 (2008): 797–817.

5. G. Stalk, "Time: The Next Source of Competitive Advantage," *Harvard Business Review* 66, no. 4 (1998): 41–45.

6. K. M. Eisenhardt, "Speed and Strategic Choice: How Managers Accelerate Decision Making," *California Management Review* 32, no. 3 (1990): 39–54; W. Q. Judge and A. Miller, "Antecedents and Outcomes of Decision Speed in Different Environmental Contexts," *Academy of Management Journal* 34, no. 2 (1991): 449–463; and J. R. Baum and S. Wally, "Strategic Decision Speed and Firm Performance," *Strategic Management Journal* 24, no. 11 (2003): 1107–1129.

7. *Weekly Diamond*, February 23, 2002.

8. Many studies have demonstrated that owner-managers are more aggressive than professional managers in making mid- to long-term investments, including those in R&D. See R. C. Anderson and D. M. Reeb, "Founding-Family Ownership and Firm Performance: Evidence from the S&P 500," *Journal of Finance* 58, no. 3 (2003): 1301–1328; and H. Kim, H. Kim, and P. M. Lee, "Ownership Structure and the Relationship Between Financial Slack and R&D Investments: Evidence from Korean Firms," *Organization Science* 19, no. 3 (2008): 404–418.

9. S. Wally and J. R. Baum, "Personal and Structural Determinants of the Pace of Strategic Decision Making," *Academy of Management Journal* 37, no. 4 (1994): 932–956.

10. A. Toffler, *The Third Wave* (New York: Bantam, 1984).

11. For details, see K. M. Eisenhardt and S. Brown, "Time Pacing: Competing in Markets That Won't Stand Still," *Harvard Business Review* 76, no. 2 (1998): 59–69; G. Lynn and R. Reilly, *Blockbusters: The Five Keys to Developing Great New Products* (New York: HarperCollins,

2002); and B. Davidson, *Breakthrough: How Great Companies Set Outrageous Objectives and Achieve Them* (Hoboken, NJ: John Wiley & Sons, 2004).

12. B. Arthur, "Increasing Returns and the New World of Business," *Harvard Business Review* 74, no. 4 (1996): 100–109; and C. Shapiro and H. Variana, *Information Rules* (Boston: Harvard Business School Press, 1999).

13. Located near Seoul, Giheung has advantages in attracting talent, as well as an ample water supply, clean air, and less noise and vibrations. Rent is relatively affordable, and the location is convenient for importing raw materials and exporting finished goods.

14. Also referred to as process integration, or PI.

15. In 2003, Samsung planned to build its 13th fabrication plant in Onyang, a two-hour drive from Seoul, as there was no more space for another plant in Giheung. However, Chairman Lee ordered that the line be built in Giheung, and Samsung changed its plan to use a former parking lot in Giheung. Behind the decision was an understanding that the benefits from clustering were significant.

16. As Samsung sold all of its equity to its joint-venture partner Corning in 2013, the name of the company is now Corning Precision Materials.

Chapter 6

1. Excerpt from Sam Grobart, "How Samsung Became the World's No. 1 Smartphone Maker," *Bloomberg Businessweek*, March 28, 2013.

2. Vertical integration occurs when a company owns and simultaneously conducts interrelated activities at different stages in its value chain. A typical form is a firm that makes both finished goods and parts and materials for those goods. For details, see J. Barney, *Gaining and Sustaining Competitive Advantage*, 4th ed. (Upper Saddle River, NJ: Prentice Hall, 2010).

3. R. M. Kanter, *When Giants Learn to Dance* (New York: Simon & Schuster, 1989).

4. There are in fact more conglomerates that create negative synergy than there are conglomerates that create positive synergy; see M. Goold and A. Campbell, "Desperately Seeking Synergy," *Harvard Business Review* 76, no. 5 (1998): 131–143; M. Sirower, *The Synergy Trap: How Companies Lose the Acquisition Game* (New York: Simon & Schuster, 2000); and E. Rawley, "Diversification, Coordination Costs, and Organizational

Rigidity: Evidence from Microdata," *Strategic Management Journal*, 31, no. 8 (2010): 873–891.

5. Rumelt classified types of corporate diversification and verified the relationship between diversification and economic performance. (See R. Rumelt, *Strategy, Structure, and Economic Performance*, [Boston: Harvard University Press, 1974]). Since then, many empirical studies have been conducted in Korea and abroad. For those done abroad, see C. Markides, *Diversification, Refocusing, and Economic Performance* (Cambridge, MA: MIT Press, 1995); and J. Barney, *Gaining and Sustaining Competitive Advantage*.

6. For the development stages of digital convergence, see Samsung Electronics, *Four Decades of Samsung Electronics: History of Taking Challenges and Creation*, (Seoul, Korea: Samsung, 2010), p. 289.

7. Ibid., pp. 291–292.

8. For positive effects of business groups in developing countries, see N. H. Leff, "Industrial Organization and Entrepreneurship in the Developing Countries: The Economic Groups," *Economic Development and Cultural Change* 26, no. 4 (1978): 661–675; T. Khanna and K. Palepu, "Why Focused Strategies May Be Wrong for Emerging Markets," *Harvard Business Review* 75, no. 4 (1997): 3–10; and T. Khanna and J. Rivkin, "Estimating the Performance Effects of Business Groups in Emerging Markets," *Strategic Management Journal* 22, no. 1 (2001): 45–74.

9. M. Goold, A. Campbell, and M. Alexander, *Corporate-Level Strategy: Creating Value in the Multibusiness Company* (New York: John Wiley & Sons, 1994).

10. Excerpts from Parmy Olson, "Samsung's Secret to Innovating: An Extraordinary Grip on Components," *Forbes*, March 20, 2013.

11. Cost reductions from vertical integration are not guaranteed. On the contrary, costs may increase if companies develop a dependent relationship, ignoring both quality and price, and unconditionally purchase from each other. Samsung broke away from such dependent partnerships and established an economic cooperation system that optimized the positive functions of vertical integration.

12. Samsung Corning Precision Materials became Corning Precision Materials when Samsung divested the joint-venture entity in 2014.

13. T. Levine, "The Walt Disney Company: The Entertainment King," Harvard Business School Case 9-701-035, 2001.

14. Major benefits of agglomeration economies include skilled workers and engineers with professional knowledge, securing of suppliers, and knowledge spillover. For the benefits of agglomeration, see P. Krugman, *Geography and Trade* (Cambridge, MA: MIT Press, 1991); E. Malecki, *Technology and Economic Development*, 2nd ed. (Essex, U.K.: Addison Wesley Longman Limited, 1997); and M. Porter, *On Competition* (Boston: Harvard Business School Press, 1998).

Chapter 7

1. For the concept of incremental innovation and radical innovation, refer to R. Leifer, C. McDermott, G. O'Connor, L. Peters, M. Rice, and R.Veryzer, *Radical Innovation* (Boston: Harvard Business School Press, 2000). For continuous innovation and discontinuous innovation, refer to T. S. Robertson, "The Process of Innovation and the Diffusion of Innovation," *Journal of Marketing* 31, no. 1 (1967): 14–19; and M. L. Tushman and P. Anderson, "Technological Discontinuities and Organizational Environments," *Administrative Science Quarterly* 31, no. 3 (1986): 439–465. For exploitative innovation and exploratory innovation, refer to M. Benner and M. Tushman, "Process Management and Technological Innovation: A Longitudinal Study of the Photography and Paint Industries," *Administrative Science Quarterly* 47, no. 4 (2002): 4676–4707. For sustaining innovation and disruptive innovation, refer to C. M. Christensen, *The Innovator's Dilemma: When New Technologies Cause Great Firms to Fail* (Boston: Harvard Business School Press, 1997).

2. Digital Times. "Mobile AP, Age of Two Powers Samsung-Qualcomm." March 12, 2013. Survey results of Strategy Analytics reported on this article were quoted.

3. To learn more about research on long-term tendencies and the accompanying aggressive R&D investment of Korean companies' owner-managers, refer to H. Kim, H. Kim, and P. M. Lee, "Ownership Structure and the Relationship Between Financial Slack and R&D Investments: Evidence from Korean Firms," *Organization Science* 19, no. 3 (2008): 404–418. For foreign research on the same issue, refer to B. D. Baysinger, T. D. Kosnik, and T. A. Turk, "Effects of Board and Ownership Structure on Corporate R&D strategy," *Academy of Management Journal* 34, no. 1 (1991): 205–214; R. E. Hoskisson, M. A. Hitt, and C. W. L. Hill, "Managerial Incentives and Investment in R&D

in Large Multiproduct Firms," *Organization Science* 4, no. 2 (1993): 325–341; and M. Tushman, P. Anderson, and C. O'Reilly, "Technology Cycles, Innovation Streams, and Ambidextrous Organizations: Organization Renewal Through Innovation Streams and Strategic Change," in *Managing Strategic Innovation and Change* (New York: Oxford University Press, 1997), pp. 3–23.

4. Kwon Soon-Woo et al., "2012 SERI Outlook," Samsung Economic Research Institute, 2011.

5. Samsung Electronics declared patent management connecting technology strategies, R&D, and management strategies for the mid-to long term in 2005. In 2006, the company introduced a new post, chief patent officer, for the first time in Korea, strengthening its system to strategically respond to patent issues.

6. STEPI (Science and Technology Policy Institute), *Case Study on Technological Innovation of Korean Firms* (Washington, DC: STEPI, 2002).

7. To learn more about value innovation, refer to W. C. Kim and R. Mauborgne, *Blue Ocean Strategy: How to Create Uncontested Market Space and Make Competition Irrelevant* (Boston: Harvard Business School Press, 2005).

8. To learn more about the concept and example of open innovation, refer to H. Chesbrough, *Open Innovation* (Boston: Harvard Business School Press, 2009).

9. "Will S Pen Become Samsung's Exclusive Property?," *Financial News*, January 31, 2013.

10. Gordon Moore, a founder of Intel, said in 1965, "The integration degree of semiconductors doubles every year and a half."

Chapter 8

1. This section was written based on J. Song, K. Lee, and T. Khanna, "How Did Samsung Outcompete Apple in the Smartphone Industry? A Dynamic Capabilities Framework," unpublished manuscript prepared for the *California Management Review*, 2014.

2. The term *co-opetition* was first used by B. J. Nalebuff and A. Brandenburger, based on game theory economics. It refers to a competitive situation in which a rival business is both a competitor and a complementor. B. Nalebuff and A. Brandenburger, *Co-opetition* (New York: Doubleday Publishing Group, 1996).

3. Another unwritten rule at Samsung is not to build relationships with companies run by executives' relatives, which reflects the strong commitment of top management to fair transactions.

4. Samsung Mobile Display merged with Samsung Display in July 2012 and the name of new entity is Samsung Display.

5. T. Khanna, J. Song, and K. Lee, "The Paradox of Samsung's Rise," *Harvard Business Review* 89, no. 7–8 (2011): 142–147.

6. For the combination of Japanese management styles and American management styles at Samsung, see Khanna, Song, and Lee, "Paradox of Samsung's Rise."

7. M. Porter, "What Is Strategy?," *Harvard Business Review* 74, no. 6 (1996): 61–78.

8. Khanna, Song, and Lee, "Paradox of Samsung's Rise."

Chapter 9

1. R. E. Miles and C. C. Snow, "Environmental Fit Versus Internal Fit," *Organization Science* 3, no. 2 (1992): 159–178; R. E. Miles and C. C. Snow, *Fit, Failure and the Hall of Fame* (New York: Free Press, 1994).

2. D. Nadler and M. Tushman, *Strategic Organizational Design: Concepts, Tools, and Processes* (Glenview, IL: Scott Foreman and Company, 1988).

3. Samsung Electronics has designated innovative products, speed, superior cost competitiveness, the fastest processes, ability to attract global customers, and organizational dynamism as preconditions to becoming a premier world-class enterprise. To realize these conditions, Samsung is pursuing innovation in products, technologies, marketing, cost cutting, global operations, and corporate culture. Samsung has also selected the following seven factors as essential for becoming a premier world-class enterprise:

   - A dream, vision, and goals
   - Insight and distinction
   - Constant change and innovation
   - Creativity and a sense of challenge
   - High regard for technology and data
   - Speed
   - Trust

4. In their bestselling book of the late 1990s, *Built to Last* (New York; HarperBusiness, 1994), Jim Collins and Jerry Porras defined premier

world-class companies as "visionary companies." The CEOs of these companies, they emphasized, are not "time tellers" but "clock builders." Clock builders build long-lasting management systems.

5. M. Tushman and C. O'Reilly, "Ambidextrous Organization: Managing Evolutionary and Revolutionary Change," *California Management Review* 38, no. 4 (2004): 8–30; and C. Gilbert and J. Bower, "Disruptive Change: When Trying Harder Is Part of the Problem," *Harvard Business Review* 80, no. 5 (2002): 94–101.

6. Yun Jong Yong, "Ways of Thinking Towards World-Class," Samsung Electronics' in-house data, 2004.

7. C. Bartlett and S. Ghoshal, *Managing Across Borders: The Transnational Solution*, 2nd ed. (Boston: Harvard Business School Press, 1999).

INDEX

7 to 4 working system, 47
20 (twenty) years to the top, 1
21st century, 131–133
1938 to mid-1950s, 23–25
1950s to late 1960s, 25–26
1960s to late 1980s, 26–27
1980s to present, 27–29
1985 Plaza Agreement, 6
1996 (Year of Design Innovation), 67
1997 Asian currency crisis
    co-opetition and, 207–208, 242
    collapse of Korean business groups
      in, 152
    digital corporate culture after, 139
    in history of Samsung, 49–54
    Lee's leadership during, 70
    management style and, 219
    New Management initiative and,
      49–54, 115, 118
    restucturing during, 70, 76, 83
    sense of urgency and, 212
    synergy after, 165
2008 global financial crisis
    aftermath of, 149
    creative organizational culture and,
      114
    ERP systems and, 109, 149
    opportunities in, 8–9, 80
    R&D and, 182
    restructuring and, 139, 212, 216

A-level employees, 87
academia, 191–192
Accelerator, 237
active-matrix organic light-emitting
    diodes (AMOLEDs)
    competition over, 211
    development of, 160
    innovation and, 232

    market leadership and, 84
    vision leadership and, 64
Advanced Institute of Technology. *See*
    Samsung Advanced Institute of
    Technology
affiliates
    competition and, 212
    diversification vs. specialization
      and, 216
    dual-sourcing and, 210–211
    new product development and, 99
    reducing gaps between, 241–242
    size vs. speed and, 213
agency problems reduction, 76
agglomeration, 262
Alpha chips, 249
Altshuller, Genrich, 187
ambidextrous organizations, 233–236
American vs. Japanese management
    styles
    in Korean firms, 9–10
    in paradox management, 16–17,
      217–222
AMOLEDs (active-matrix organic
    light-emitting diodes). *See*
    active-matrix organic light-
    emitting diodes (AMOLEDs)
Ankuk Fire & Marine Insurance, 25
Apple
    App Store of, 233
    iPhone by, 226, 233
    lawsuits of, 233
    manufacturing and, 78–79
    network effects at, 240
    operating profit–to–sales ratio of,
      238
    smartphone leadership of, 253
    smartphone shock and, 9
application processors (APs), 83

ARM, 190
Asian currency crisis. *See* 1997 Asian currency crisis
assembly industry, 258
AST Research, 236–237
AT&T, 198

batteries
  innovation and, 230
  manufacturing of, 83–84
  market share in, 4, 151
Baum, J. Robert, 137
Bell Laboratories, 198
best practices, 164
bibimbap, 221
block cell production, 102
Bloomberg Businessweek
  on Chairman Lee's role, 61
  on Galaxy S4, 151
  on Samsung's brand ranking, 5
Booz & Company, 183
Bordeaux TV line, 187
brand power, 68
brand sharing, 164–165
Broadcasting Center, 167
Bundang, 169
business portfolios upgrades, 82–84, 122–123

C-Labs (creative labs), 234
C&T Corporation, 74–75
CAD (computer-aided design), 43
CAE (computer-aided engineering), 43–44
CAM (computer-aided manufacturing), 43
Campbell, Andrew, 157
carbon nanotube field-emission display (CNT-FED), 178
casual dress code, 113–114
cathode-ray tube (CRT) TVs, 83, 161
CDMA (code division multiple access), 188
CE (Consumer Electronics), 144
cell production, 102

chaebols, 244
Chairman Lee. *See* Lee Kun-Hee (Chairman)
change, as core value, 110–112
charge trap flash (CTF) semiconductors, 179, 249
Cheil Industries, 25
cheil ("number one"), 116
CheilJedang, 25
Cheonan, 143–145
Chesbrough, Henry, 190
China
  benchmarking Samsung, 254
  recruiting talent from, 91, 189
  regional headquarters in, 103
  research institutes in, 193, 199
Choi, Chi-Hun, 75
Citizens' Coalition for Economic Justice, 74
clock builders, 265
cloud computing, 132
clustering
  New Management initiative and, 224–225
  for R&D, 142–144
  for synergy, 169–170
CNT-FED (carbon nanotube field-emission display), 178
co-opetition
  conglomerate structure and, 208–210
  constant restructuring and, 212
  as core of Samsung, generally, 205–207
  definition of, 263
  diversification vs. specialization and, 216–217
  dual sourcing in, 210–211
  enhancing competitiveness in, 212–221
  in evolution of Samsung, 74
  introduction to, 203
  IT infrastructure and, 215
  Japanese vs. American management styles and, 217–222

market principles in, 210–211
mechanisms of, 208–212
owner-managers in, 208–210,
   213–215
parallel investments in, 211–212
reasons for, 207–208
size vs. speed in, 213–215
structure of Samsung and,
   203–205
vision leadership and, 64–65
co-prosperity, 110–112, 244–245
code division multiple access (CDMA),
   188
compensation policy, 92–94, 248–249
competitiveness, 212–221
computer-aided design (CAD), 43
computer-aided engineering (CAE),
   43–44
computer-aided manufacturing
   (CAM), 43
computers. *See also* phablets
   digital convergence and, 81
   domestic leadership and, 26
   employee skills in, 43–44
   laptops, 165
   N Screen era of, 241
   speed and, 131–132
   tablets, 132
   ubiquitous era of, 155
concept of business, 127
concurrent engineering, 147–148
conferences, 169–171, 195, 199
conglomerates
   diversified business structures and,
     152
   paradox management and, 14–15,
     208–210
   synergy through convergence and,
     153
conscience industries, 258
Constitution of Samsung, 44–45
Consumer Electronics (CE), 144
continuous evolution, 250–252
control by management. *See* management control

convergence. *See* synergy through
   convergence
core competencies
   evolutionary innovation. *See* evolu-
     tionary innovation
   introduction to, 127–130
   overview of, 225
   speed. *See* speed
   synergy via convergence. *See* synergy
     through convergence
core management control processes,
   98–105
core talents, 67–69, 86–87
core values, 109
corporate culture community, 166–167
Corporate Strategy Office
   affiliates and, 122
   in evolution of Samsung, 74–75
   introduction to, 71–72
   Management Consulting Team at,
     76
   owner-management and, 208–210
   "Single Samsung" spirit and, 250
   Six Sigma and, 220
   strategic reviews by, 214
   synergy through convergence and,
     167–168
cost reduction, 163
CPU technology, 190
creative culture, 113–114, 247–249
Creative Development Center, 234–235
creative labs (C-Labs), 234
crisis
   currency. *See* 1997 Asian currency
     crisis
   financial. *See* 2008 global financial
     crisis
   healthy sense of, 66, 109, 116,
     120–122
CRM (customer relationship management), 104
crowdsourcing, 192
CRT (cathode-ray tube) TVs, 83, 161
CTF (charge trap flash) semiconductors, 179, 249

cultlike culture, 140
cultural values
    core, 109
    core competencies and, 225
    creative organizational culture and,
        113–114
    definition of, 109
    dominant, 115–116
    in future of Samsung Way,
        245–250
    introduction to, 109
    "people first" policy in, 119–120
    pursuit of excellence in, 116–118
    pursuit of rationality in, 118–119
    sense of crisis in, 109
    "Single Samsung" spirit in,
        114–115
    trinity of, 109–113
Culture and Values Team, 113
culture, definition of, 109
currency crisis. See 1997 Asian
    currency crisis
current status, 175–179
customer relationship management
    (CRM), 104, 107–108

Daewoo, 152
debt reductions, 53
decision-making
    about investments and opportunity,
        135–138
    increasing speed of, generally,
        134–135
    on-the-spot, 138–139
democratization, 6
Device Solutions (DS), 139
DHL, 103
digital convergence, 81
digital management
    Lee on, 134
    market leader strategy and, 80
    principles of, 138–139
Digital Media & Communications
    (DMC) R&D Center, 139, 142,
    192

Digital Natural Image engine (DNIe),
    142, 162, 191
digital revolution, 131–132
digital TVs (DTVs)
    innovation and, 232
    market share in, 4
    speed management and, 134, 137
digital video devices (DVDs), 81,
    178–179
Disney's Synergy Group, 168
Display, 160, 163, 211
display panels
    AMOLED, 64, 84, 160, 211, 232
    CNT-FED, 178
    evolutionary innovation in,
        177–178
    LCD. See LCDs (liquid-crystal
        displays)
    LED, 134, 136–137
    plasma, 83, 146
    synergy and, 160
    thin-film-transistor LCD. See
        TFT-LCDs (thin-film-transistor
        liquid-crystal displays)
Display Research Institute, 192
diversification
    of business structures. See diversi-
        fied business structures
    of product line, 261
    specialization vs., 216–217
diversified business structures
    conglomerates and, 152
    in era of convergence, 152–154
    in history of Samsung, 155–157
    synergy through convergence and,
        152
diversity, 114
divestures, 53
DMC (Digital Media &
    Communications) R&D Center,
    139, 142, 192
DNIe (Digital Natural Image engine),
    142, 162, 191
dominant cultural values, 115–116
Dongwoo Fine-Chem, 211

DRAM (dynamic random access
    memory)
    concurrent engineering and, 148
    era of, 176
    in history of Samsung, 32–34
    introduction to, 4, 7
    market share in, 4
    speed management and, 135–136,
        146
    strategic decision making and, 69
DS (Device Solutions), 139
DTVs (digital TVs). See digital TVs
    (DTVs)
dual sourcing, 210–211
DVD Combo, 81
DVDs (digital video devices), 81,
    178–179
dynamic random access memory
    (DRAM). See DRAM (dynamic
    random access memory)

Economic Research Institute, 162, 214,
    220–221
economic value added (EVA), 94
ecosystem integration teams, 241
education of workforce, 85
Electro-Mechanics, 163, 211
enterprise resource planning (ERP).
        See ERP (enterprise resource
        planning)
era of convergence, 154–155
era of DRAM, 176
ERP (enterprise resource planning)
    global, 97
    IT-based innovations and, 148–149
    management control and, 106
    SCM and, 108–109
EVA (economic value added), 94
Everland, 73
evolution of Samsung Way
    to ambidextrous organization,
        233–236
    innovation and. See evolutionary
        innovation
    long-term, 179

to a loved company, 244–245
of management systems. See man-
    agement systems
of Samsung Way, 57–59, 61
to total solution provider/platform
    leader, 237–241
to transnational corporation,
    242–243
evolutionary innovation
    Advanced Institute of Technology
        and, 198–199
    as core competency, generally,
        128–130
    crowdsourcing in, 192
    current status of, 175, 176–179
    definition of, 175–176
    in digital video devices, 178–179
    in display panels, 177–178
    external knowledge and, 187–192
    foreign knowledge/talent in,
        192–193
    formation of, generally, 179
    global R&D network for, 192–193
    industry-academia cooperation in,
        191–192
    infrastructure/systems for, 193–200
    internal innovation in, 180–181
    introduction to, 173–175
    learning-orientation and, 196–197
    Lego-style R&D in, 185
    long-term technology road maps in,
        185–186
    management elements and, 225
    manufacturing process technolo-
        gies and, 199–200
    mixing internal/external technolo-
        gies in, 188–189
    in mobile phones, 178
    open innovation for external
        knowledge in, 189–192
    PLM systems in, 186
    R&D in, 181–185
    in semiconductors, 177, 190
    sense of crisis in, 194–195
    in set division, 191

evolutionary innovation (*continued*)
  stretch goals in, 194–195
  systems for securing talent in, 197
  technology innovation strategy in,
    185–187
  in telecommunications, 178
  tripartite R&D function in, 197–198
  TRIZ in, 187
  value innovation in, 186–187
  world-class manufacturing and,
    199–200
execution, speed of, 139–141
external knowledge, 187–192
external technologies, 188–189
Exynos 5 Octa processors, 177, 190

failure, 249
Fair Trade Commission, 74
Fairchild Semiconductor, 70
fashion industry, 258
fast-track promotion policy, 95
Fellows program, 197
financial crisis. *See* 1997 Asian cur-
    rency crisis; 2008 global finan-
    cial crisis
Financial Supervisory Service, 74
Fine Chemicals, 83
"first, fast, on time, and frequent,"
    138–139
flat-screen TVs, 65
Flexcom, 191
flexible work schedules, 113–114
flying geese strategy, 82–83
foreign experts, 90–92, 192–193
Fortune, 3, 61
Foxconn, 238
Frankfurt, 38–39
Frankfurter Allgemeine Zeitung,
    9–10
fruit trees, 84
fusion memory chips, 177
future of Samsung Way
  co-prosperity in, 244–245
  continuous evolution in, 250–252
  creative culture in, 247–249

evolving to a loved company in,
    244–245
evolving to ambidextrous organiza-
    tion in, 233–236
evolving to total solution provider/
    platform leader in, 237–241
evolving to transnational corpora-
    tion in, 242–243
human resource management in,
    245–250
introduction to, 223
lessons from Samsung Way and,
    252–255
M&A and "real options" invest-
    ments in, 236–237
market leadership via creative
    innovation in, 230–233
open culture recognizing diversity
    in, 246–247
organizational culture in, 245–250
overview of, 201
reducing gaps between affiliates in,
    241–242
securing world's best talent in,
    245–246
"Single Samsung" internal
    solidarity in, 249–250
strategy tasks in, generally, 230
sustainability in, 223–228
tasks ahead for, generally, 228–230
values and, 109

G-ERP (global enterprise resource
    planning), 97
G-SCM (global supply chain manage-
    ment), 97
Galaxy Camera, 81
Galaxy Note, 79, 191, 232
Galaxy S4, 79, 151–152, 163
Galbraith, Jay R., 57
gaps between affiliates, 241–242
Gates, Bill, 132
GE (General Electric)
  benchmarking of, 16
  co-opetition and, 203

customer orientation of, 238
divisions/affiliates at, 27
future and, 242, 254
recruiting talent from, 75
synergy creation strategy at, 157
Way of, 9
generational shifts, 45–46
genius-level talent, 174
"gigabyte dynamic random access
  memory (DRAM)" era, 176
Giheung, 143, 260
global enterprise resource planning
  (G-ERP), 97
global financial crisis. *See* 2008 global
  financial crisis
Global Help Desk, 91
global logistics system (GLS), 107
global manufacturing execution
  system (GMES), 107
Global Operations Center (GOC)
  IT-based innovations and, 149
  manufacturing and, 102
  parts procurement and, 100
  process integration and, 104–105
  SCM and, 105, 107–108
Global Strategy Group (GSG), 90
global supply chain management
  (G-SCM), 97
globalization
  in New Management initiative,
    43–44
  of R&D networks, 192–193
  of workforce, 88–92
GLS (global logistics system), 107
GMES (global manufacturing
  execution system), 107
goal-driven R&D (research and
  development), 146–149
GOC (Global Operations Center).
  See Global Operations Center
  (GOC)
Goold, Michael, 157
governance
  agency problems reduction in,
    76

Chairman Lee and. *See* Lee Kun-
  Hee (Chairman)
changes in, 71–73
core competencies and, 225
core talents in, 67–69
Corporate Strategy Office in, 74–75
far-reaching vision in, 63–65
healthy sense of crisis in, 66
insight leadership in, 66–70
introduction to, 61
leadership by professional managers in, 75–76
leadership/governance, changes in,
  71–73
nurturing talent in, 75
opportunities/incentives in, 75–76
owner-managers vs. professional
  managers in, 70–76
ownership structures in, 73–74
recruiting in, 75
soft competitiveness in, 67–69
strategic decision making in, 69–70
synergy through convergence and,
  166–167
triangular, 72
vision leadership in, 61, 63–66
graphene chips, 179
Great Work Place program, 113
greenfield investments, 16
groupwide committees, 168–169
groupwide dissemination, 123–125
groupwide vision, 130
growth of Samsung
  in 1938 to mid 1950s, 23–25
  introduction to, 23
  in late 1960s to late 1980s, 26–27
  in late 1980s to present, 27–29
  in mid 1950s to late 1960s, 25–26
GSG (Global Strategy Group), 90

H-level employees, 87
Harvard Business Review, 3
healthy sense of crisis. *See* sense of
  crisis
Heavy Industries, 83

hesitation of employees, 31–32
HEVC (high-efficiency video coding), 81, 179
Hewlett-Packard (HP), 9, 94, 220
high-efficiency video coding (HEVC), 81, 179
High-K/Metal-Gate, 196–197
history of Samsung
    1938 to mid 1950s, 23–25
    1997 Asian currency crisis in, 49–54
    business group structure in, 155–157
    Chairman Lee's leadership in. See Lee Kun-Hee (Chairman)
    characteristics of transformation in, 54–56
    dynamic random access memory (DRAM) business in, 32–34
    generational shift in, 45–46
    growth in, 23–29
    hesitation of employees in, 31–32
    introduction to, 23
    late 1960s to late 1980s, 26–27
    late 1980s to present, 27–29
    mid 1950s to late 1960s, 25–26
    New Management initiative in. See New Management initiative
    Second Foundation in, 29–32
    semiconductors in, 32–37
    shock therapy in, 46–49
    summary of, 54–56
home appliances, 258
Hong Won-Pyo, 131
hotels, 258
HP (Hewlett-Packard), 9, 94, 220
Hrebiniak, Lawrence G., 57
human resource management
    compensation policy in, 92–94
    core competencies and, 225
    core talent emphasis in, 86–87
    foreign experts in, 90–92
    in future of Samsung Way, 245–250
    globalization of workforce in, 88–92

introduction to, 84–85
New Management initiative and, 86
performance-based policy in, 92–95
principles for, 27
promotion policy in, 94–95
recruitment from outside in, 87–88
regional specialists in, 88–90
select-and-focus policy and, 122–123
systems for securing talent in, 197
workforce structure in, 85
Human Resources Development Center
cultural values and, 113
"Single Samsung" and, 89
synergy and, 163
syngery and, 167
Hwang Young-Key, 53
Hwaseong, 143

IBM
conduct policy of, 244–245
customer orientation of, 238
DRAM trench design at, 69
patents of, 5, 184–185
policies of, 244–245
recruiting talent from, 86
strategic partnership with, 190
IDEA (International Design Excellence Awards), 67
"IDEA Open Space," 234
IF (International Forum) design awards, 67
IM (Information Technology and Mobile Communications) divisions, 144
IMT-2000 (International Mobile Telecommunications), 81, 232
India
recruiting talent from, 91, 189
research institutes in, 193, 199
indirect network effects, 239–240
Industrial Design Excellence awards, 5
industry-academia cooperation, 191–192

information sharing, 163–164
Information Technology and Mobile
    Communications (IM)
    divisions, 144
information technology (IT). *See* IT
    (information technology)
infrastructure
    for evolutionary innovation,
      193–200
    for IT, 105–109, 148–149, 215
    for speed management, 141–149
    for synergy through convergence,
      165–171
InnoCentive, 192
insight leadership. *See also* leadership,
    66–70
installation and real estate industry,
    258
Intel, 241
intellectual property. *See also* patents
    competitiveness and, 224
    knowledge management and, 170,
      233
    lawsuits over, 232–233
    as most valuable corporate asset,
      184
Interbrand's 2013 Global Brand
    Rankings, 5, 68
internal co-opetition
    conglomerate structure and,
      208–210
    constant restructuring and, 212
    as core of Samsung, generally,
      205–207
    diversification vs. specialization
      and, 216–217
    dual sourcing in, 210–211
    enhancing competitiveness in,
      212–221
    introduction to, 203
    IT infrastructure and, 215
    Japanese vs. American manage-
      ment styles and, 217–222
    market principles in, 210–211
    mechanisms of, 208–212

    owner-managers in, 208–210,
      213–215
    parallel investments in, 211–212
    reasons for introducing, 207–208
    size vs. speed in, 213–215
    structure of Samsung and, 203–205
internal innovation, 180–181
internal technologies, 188–189
International Design Excellence
    Awards (IDEA), 67
International Forum (IF) design
    awards, 67
International Mobile
    Telecommunications (IMT-
    2000), 81, 232
International Olympic Committee
    (IOC), 62
International Solid-State Circuit
    Conference, 195
investments seizing opportunity,
    135–138
IOC (International Olympic
    Committee), 62
iPhone, 226, 233
IT (information technology)
    in evolution of management
      systems, 105–109
    in New Management initiative,
      43–44
    paradox management and, 215
    R&D and, 148–149
    speed management and, 132, 140

Japan
    management style in. *See* Japanese
      vs. American management styles
    recruiting talent from, 189
    regional headquarters in, 103
    research institutes in, 193, 199
Japanese vs. American management
    styles
    in Korean firms, 9–10
    in paradox management, 16–17,
      217–222
Joyce, William F., 57

Kanter, Rosabeth Moss, 152
Katsuya Okumura, 135–136
Kiheung, 169–170
Kim Chang-Yeong
    on innovation, 129, 173, 189
    on preparedness, 142
Kim Hak-Sun, 146
Kim Ki-Nam, 148
knowledge management, 89, 170–171
Korea
    after 1960s, 154–155
    after 1997 Asian currency crisis, 165
    Asian currency crisis in, 8, 152
    Chairman Lee's life in, 62
    Confucian culture of, 234
    Confucian tendencies in, 221
    democratization of, 6
    employees from, 85–86, 88–91
    Japanese vs. American manage-
        ment styles in, 9–10
    management styles in, 9–10
    ppali ppali spirit of, 139–140
    Samsung culture and, 57
    training in, 193
    universities in, 192
Korea Economic Daily, 152
Kwon Oh-Hyun, 128

large-scale integration (LSI), 81, 190
LCDs (liquid-crystal displays)
    development of, 64
    speed management and, 134,
        136–137, 145–146
    synergy and, 157, 158, 162
    thin-film-transistor. *See* TFT-LCDs
        (thin-film-transistor liquid-
        crystal displays)
leadership
    of Chairman Lee. *See* Lee Kun-Hee
        (Chairman)
    changes in, 71–73
    core competencies and, 225
    core talents and, 67–69
    Corporate Strategy Office and,
        74–75

far-reaching vision of, 63–65
    healthy sense of crisis of, 66
    insight, 66–70
    introduction to, 61
    nurturing talent of, 75
    opportunities/incentives for, 75–76
    owner-managers vs. professional
        managers in, 70–76
    ownership structures and, 73–74
    by professional managers, 75–76
    recruiting, 75
    soft competitiveness and, 67–69
    strategic decision making by, 69–70
    vision of, 61, 63–66
leapfrog R&D (research and develop-
    ment), 146–147
learning curve effect, 258–259
learning orientation, 173, 196–197
LEDs (light-emitting diodes)
    active-matrix organic. *See* active-
        matrix organic light-emitting
        diodes (AMOLEDs)
    innovation and, 232
    market leadership and, 84
    organic, 4, 81, 162
Lee Byung-Chull
    as founder of Samsung, 23–25, 62
    management roles under, 72
    on putting people first, 119
    son of, 27
Lee Kun-Hee (Chairman)
    on being number one, 117
    biography of, 62–63
    on core talent, 86
    on core talents, 67–69
    foresight of, 224–226
    on future, 77
    healthy sense of crisis of, 66,
        108–109
    insight leadership of, 66–70
    introduction to, 4, 6–9
    on learning, 196
    on New Management initiative,
        203–204
    on paradox management, 12

on profits and wages, 258
on putting people first, 119–120
on R&D, 180, 183
on "Single Samsung," 205
on soft competitiveness, 67–69
on speed management, 133–134
strategic decision-making of,
    69–70
on strategic issues, 82
on synergy through convergence,
    152–153, 166
vision leadership of, 61, 63–66
warnings of, 229, 251
Lee Sun-Woo, 129
Lee Won-Shik, 143
"left-handed" organizations, 235–236
Lego-style R&D, 185
lessons from Samsung Way. See also
    Samsung Way, 252–255
Life Insurance, 73
light-emitting diodes (LEDs). See LEDs
    (light-emitting diodes)
Liker, Jeffrey, 9
line stops, 47–48
liquid-crystal display (LCD) panels. See
    LCDs (liquid-crystal displays)
logistics, 102–103
long-term evolution (LTE), 179
long-term technology road maps,
    185–186
Los Angeles, 37–38
loved companies, 244–245
LSI (large-scale integration), 81, 190
LTE (long-term evolution), 179

M&A (mergers and acquisitions), 16,
    52, 236–237
macro management, 96–98
management
    control by. See management control
    micro vs macro, 96–98
    by numbers, 97–98
    paradox in. See paradox
        management
    quality of, 42–43

systems for. See management
    systems
Management Consulting Team, 76
management control
    core competencies and, 225
    core processes in, 98–105
    IT infrastructure in, 105–109
    logistics in, 102–103
    management by numbers in, 97–98
    manufacturing in, 100–102
    marketing/sales/service in, 103–104
    micro vs macro approaches to,
        96–98
    new product development in, 99
    parts procurement in, 99–100
    process integration via SCM in,
        104–105
Management Principles Steering
    Committee, 113
management systems
    aligning components of, 120–125
    business portfolios upgrades in,
        82–84, 122–123
    compensation policy in, 92–94
    core management control processes
        in, 98–105
    core talent emphasis in, 86–87
    core values in, 109
    creative organizational culture in,
        113–114
    culture/values in, generally, 109
    dominant cultural values in,
        115–116
    foreign experts in, 90–92
    globalization of workforce in,
        88–92
    groupwide dissemination of,
        123–125
    human resources in, generally,
        84–85
    introduction to, 77
    IT infrastructure in, 105–109
    for knowledge, 170–171
    logistics in, 102–103
    management by numbers in, 97–98

management systems (*continued*)
  manufacturing in, 100–102
  market leader strategy in, 79–82,
    120–122
  marketing/sales/service in, 103–104
  micro vs macro management
    controls in, 96–98
  new product development in, 99
  parts procurement in, 99–100
  "people first" policy in, 119–120
  performance-based policy in, 92–95
  process integration via SCM in,
    104–105
  promotion policy in, 94–95
  pursuit of excellence in, 116–118
  pursuit of rationality in, 118–119
  quality-focused strategy in, 78–79
  quantity vs. quality in, generally,
    77–84
  recruitment from outside in,
    87–88
  regional specialists in, 88–90
  sense of crisis in, 109
  "Single Samsung" spirit in, 114–115
  for talent, 68–69
  trinity of values in, 109–113
  workforce structure in, 85
manufacturing
  in evolution of management
    systems, 100–102
  in-house, 78–79
  technologies for, 199–200
map of new management, 39–40
market leader strategy
  aligning management systems and,
    120–122
  creative innovation and, 230–233
  quality-focused strategy and,
    79–82
market principles, 210–211
marketing/sales/service, 103–104
mass production and assembly
    industry, 258
material requirement planning (MRP),
    107

Media Solution Center, 240–241
memory chips
  DRAM. *See* DRAM (dynamic
    random access memory)
  fusion, 177
  market leader strategy and, 80–81
  NAND, 69–70, 249
  PRAM, 81, 176
  speed and, 135–136
mergers and acquisitions (M&A), 16,
    52, 236–237
micro management, 96–98
Micron Technology, 188
Miles, Raymond E., 57, 223
Milgrom, Paul, 17
MLCCs (multilayer ceramic condens-
    ers), 211
mobile phones
  code division multiple access,
    188
  concurrent engineering and,
    147–148
  innovation and, 178, 191
  market leader strategy and, 80
  market share in, 4
  N Screen era of, 241
  speed management and, 134, 145
  synergy and, 160–163
Mobile Solution Forum, 82
monitors. *See also* display panels, 4
Moore's Law, 195
Motor, 83
Moving Picture Experts Group-4
    (MPEG-4), 232
Moving Picture Experts Group
    (MPEG), 81
MPEG-4 (Moving Picture Experts
    Group-4), 232
MPEG (Moving Picture Experts
    Group), 81
MRP (material requirement planning),
    107
multifaceted integration, 43–44
multilayer ceramic condensers
    (MLCCs), 211

Nadler, David, 223
NAND flash memory, 69–70, 177, 249
nature of business, 127
network convergence, 152–154
"new growth theory," 195
New Management initiative
    7 to 4 working system in, 47
    1997 Asian currency crisis and,
       49–54
    compensation and, 92
    core values and, 113, 116–117,
       119–121
    debt reductions in, 53
    declaration of, 37–39
    dissemination of, 46
    divestures in, 53
    fast-track promotion policy and, 95
    in Frankfurt, 38–39
    future and. *See* future of Samsung
      Way
    generational shift and, 45–46
    globalization in, 43–44
    governance under. *See* governance
    human resource management and,
      86
    implementation of, 39–45, 49–51
    introduction of, 204–205
    introduction to, 37
    IT-based reorganization in, 43–44
    IT infrastructure and, 105
    leadership under. *See* leadership
    line stops in, 47–48
    in Los Angeles, 37–38
    macromanagement and, 96–97
    management quality in, 42–43
    management systems under. *See*
      management systems
    map of new management in, 39–40
    mergers in, 52
    multifaceted integration in, 43–44
    organizational restructuring
      through, 52
    people quality in, 42–43
    performance-based policy and, 92
    product quality in, 42–43
    public burning of defective prod-
      ucts in, 48–49
    quality-driven management in,
      41–44
    quantity vs. quality in, 41
    reasons for, 6
    reporting nonperforming assets
      in, 48
    restructuring through, 51–54
    sale of noncore businesses in, 52
    Samsung Constitution and, 44–45
    shock therapy in, 46–49
    speed and, 133–134
    spin-offs in, 53
    transformation of Samsung via,
      54–56
    unprofitable businesses and, 52
    vision of world-class company in,
      41
new product development, 99
nonperforming assets, 48
"not invented here" syndrome, 234
"number one" (*cheil*), 116
nurturing talent, 75

OEMs (original equipment manufac-
    turers), 5, 79
Office for Culture and Values, 113
old trees, 84
OLEDs (organic light-emitting
    diodes). *See also* active-matrix
    organic light-emitting diodes
    (AMOLEDs), 4, 81, 179
Olympic sponsorship, 62, 68
on-the-spot decision-making, 138–139
"One Design" styling, 162
One NAND, 177
"one product, one company"
    campaign, 117–118
open competitive recruitment, 25
open culture recognizing diversity,
    246–247
open innovation
    crowdsourcing in, 192
    for external knowledge, 189–192

open innovation (*continued*)
  industry-academia cooperation in,
    191–192
  introduction to, 189–190
  in semiconductors, 190
  in set division, 191
Open Innovation Center, 236
operating systems (OS), 241
opportunity management, 75–76, 138
organic light-emitting diodes
    (OLEDs). *See also* active-matrix
    organic light-emitting diodes
    (AMOLEDs), 4, 81, 161
organizational culture. *See also* cultural
    values, 166–167, 245–250
organizational restructuring, 52
original equipment manufacturers
    (OEMs), 5, 79
OS (operating systems), 241
Ouchi, William, 17
owner-managers
  agency problems reduction and, 76
  aggressiveness of, 259
  Corporate Strategy Office and,
    74–75
  in evolution of Samsung, 70–76
  future of, 254
  leadership/governance changes and,
    71–73
  nurturing talent of, 75
  opportunities/incentives and, 75–76
  ownership structures and, 73–74
  in paradox management, 208–210,
    213–215
  professional managers vs.,
    generally, 70, 75–76
  recruiting, 75
  in synergy through convergence,
    166
ownership structures, 73–74

PA (process architecture), 143
paradox management
  conglomerate structure and,
    208–210

constant restructuring and, 212
diversification vs. specialization in,
    14–16, 216–217
dual sourcing in, 210–211
enhancing competitiveness in,
    212–221
future of, 253
internal co-opetition and, 203,
    205–212
introduction to, 11–13
IT infrastructure and, 215
Japanese vs. American manage-
    ment styles in, 16–17, 217–222
largeness vs. speed in, 13–14
market principles in, 210–211
overview of, 201
owner-managers in, 208–210,
    213–215
parallel investments in, 211–212
size vs. speed in, 213–215
structure of Samsung and, 203–205
summary of, 20
parallel development, 146
parallel investments, 211–212
parts procurement, 99–100
Patent and Trademark Office, 4–5, 184
patents
  for digital video devices, 178
  evolutionary innovation and, 184
  introduction to, 4–5
  leadership in, 263
patriarchal leadership, 57–59
PDPs (plasma display panels), 83, 146
"people first" policy. *See also* human
    resource management
  as core value, 110–112
  emergence of, 155–156
  introduction to, 84–85
  in management systems, 119–120
  securing talent and, 197, 245
people quality, 42–43
People's Solidarity for Participatory
    Democracy, 74
performance-based policy, 92–95
personnel reductions, 53

phablets, 175, 178, 232
phase-change random access memory (PRAM), 81, 176
PhD holders, 182
phones. *See* mobile phones
PI (productivity incentives), 94
plasma display panels (PDPs), 83, 146
platform leadership, 237–241
PLM (product life-cycle management), 107, 185–186
Plus One TV, 161
Porter, Michael, 11, 217
ppali ppali spirit, 139, 215
PRAM (phase-change random access memory), 81, 176
process architecture (PA), 143
process innovation, 147–148
process integration, 104–105
product life-cycle management (PLM), 107, 185–186
product quality, 42–43
productivity incentives (PI), 94
professional managers
    at affiliates, 72–73
    agency problems reduction and, 76
    Corporate Strategy Office and, 74–75
    in evolution of Samsung, 70–76
    leadership/governance changes and, 71–73
    leadership of, 75–76
    nurturing talent of, 75
    opportunities/incentives and, 75–76
    owner-managers vs., generally, 70
    ownership structures and, 73–74
    recruiting and, 75
profit-sharing (PS) bonuses, 94, 220
promotion policy, 94–95
prosumers, 190
PS (profit-sharing) bonuses, 94
public burning of defective products, 48–49
pursuit of excellence, 116–118
pursuit of rationality
    in cultural values, 118–119

introduction to, 24–25
management by numbers in, 97

quality-driven management
    globalization in, 43–44
    introduction to, 41
    IT-based reorganization in, 43–44
    management quality in, 42–43
    multifaceted integration in, 43–44
    people quality in, 42–43
    product quality in, 42–43
    quantity vs. quality in, 41
quality-focused strategy
    market leader strategy and, 79–82
    quantity vs., 41
    shifting to, generally, 77–78
    summary of, 78–79
    upgrading business portfolios in, 82–84
quantity vs. quality, 41
"quickly, quickly" spirit, 140

R&D (research and development)
    clustering for, 142–144
    Digital Media & Communications, 139, 192
    in evolutionary innovation, 181–185
    global network for, 192–193
    goal-driven, 146–149
    importance of, 142
    insight management and, 67
    IT infrastructure and, 148–149
    leapfrog, 146–147
    Lego-style, 185
    parallel development in, 146
    process innovation and, 147–148
    Semiconductor, 142
    tripartite, 197–198
    upgrading of, 147–148
    vertical integration for, 144–146
    workforce for, 85
R5 building, 169
real estate industry, 258
"real options" investments, 236–237
rechargeable batteries, 4

recruitment
    evolutionary innovation and, 197
    in future of Samsung Way,
        245–246
    human resource management and,
        87–88
    of leadership, 75
regional specialists, 88–90
reporting nonperforming assets, 48
Research America, 193
research and development (R&D).
        See R&D (research and
        development)
Research India, 193
Rhee Pil-Gon, 156
"right-handed" organizations, 235
Roberts, John, 17
Russia, 91

S-level employees, 87, 245–246
sales
    management systems for, 103–104
    of noncore businesses, 52
    synergy and, 160–162
Samsung
    Accelerator, 237
    Advanced Institute of Technology.
        See Samsung Advanced Institute
        of Technology
    Broadcasting Center, 167
    C&T Corporation, 74–75
    Constitution of, 44–45
    Consumer Electronics division, 144
    Display, 160, 163, 211
    Display Research Institute, 192
    domestic/foreign environments
        and, 3–9
    Economic Research Institute, 162,
        214, 220–221
    Electro-Mechanics, 163, 211
    Electronics. *See* Samsung
        Electronics
    Everland, 73
    Fellows program of, 197
    Fine Chemicals, 83

    future of. *See* future of Samsung
        Way
    Group. *See* Samsung Group
    growth of. *See* growth of Samsung
    Heavy Industries, 83
    history of. *See* history of Samsung
    Human Resources Development
        Center, 89, 113, 167
    Life Insurance, 73
    Motor, 83
    paradigm shifts and, 5–9
    performance of, 3–9
    Research America, 193
    Research India, 193
    SDI, 83, 163, 211
    Semiconductor Institute, 146, 188
    Single. *See* "Single Samsung"
    Tech Conference, 199
    Technology Exhibitions, 171
    Techwin, 211
    Values portal site of, 113
    Way. *See* Samsung Way
Samsung Advanced Institute of
    Technology
    evolutionary innovation and,
        198–199
    innovation of, 179
    speed management and, 142, 145
    synergy and, 163
    technical reviews by, 214
    in tripartite R&D, 198–199
    TRIZ at, 187
Samsung Electronics
    awards of, 5
    clustering at, 143
    concurrent engineering at, 148
    core competencies at, generally,
        128
    dual-sourcing and, 211
    foreign experts at, 91
    future of, 251
    innovation of, 264
    insight management and, 67–68
    Japanese vs. American manage-
        ment styles in, 218

liquid-crystal display division of, 211
management by numbers at, 97
manufacturing by, 100–102
market leader strategy and, 79–81, 83
marketing at, 103–104
memory chip division of, 12
new product development at, 99
operating profits of, 228
overseas revenues of, 243
parts procurement at, 99–100
profit-sharing bonuses at, 94
R&D workforce at, 85
regional specialists at, 89–90
revenue of, 3
sales/service at, 103–104
Samsung Life Insurance and, 73–74
SCM system at, 106
Six Sigma Academy of, 98
smartphones by, 79
speed management at, 139
TRIZ at, 187
Samsung Group
affiliates of, 72–73
business group structure at, 155–156
Chairman Lee's history with, 62
internal market mechanism of, 155–157
largeness vs. speed in, 13
New Management initiative and, 204–206
profits of, 66
revenue of, 4
Samsung Semiconductor Institute (SSI), 146, 188
Samsung Way
competitiveness and, 9–10
core of. See leadership
diversification vs. specialization in, 14–16
evolution of, 57–59
future of. See future of Samsung Way
introduction to, 1

Japanese vs. American management styles in, 16–17
largeness vs. speed in, 13–14
organization of, 18–21
paradoxes of management and, 11–17
reasons for, 3–9
relatives and, 264
structure of, 203–205
Schumpeter, Joseph, 228, 233
SCM (supply chain management). See supply chain management (SCM)
SDI, 83, 163, 211
Second Foundation, 29–32, 180
secretariat, 25–26
seed businesses, 84
select-and-focus policy, 122–123
Semiconductor Institute, 146, 188
Semiconductor R&D Center, 142
semiconductors
charge trap flash, 179, 249
as conscience industry, 258
development of, 64
domestic leadership and, 26
evolutionary innovation in, 177
Fairchild Semiconductor and, 70
in history of Samsung, 32–37
human resource management and, 88
innovation and, 232
market leader strategy and, 79–80
New Management initiative and, 205
open innovation in, 190
speed and, 136
synergy and, 154–155, 160
as time industry, 258
sense of crisis
in cultural values, 109
in evolution of Samsung, 66
in evolutionary innovation, 194–195
market leader strategy and, 120–122
pursuit of excellence and, 116

Seoul, 169
Seremban Industrial Complex, 170
service, 103–104
set division, 191
sharing information, 163–164
Sharp, 210
Shin Jong-Kyun, 128, 151
ship building, 232
shock therapy, 46–49
shutter glass 3D TVs, 179
"Single Samsung"
  as core value, 109
  future of, 249–250
  management systems and, 114–115
  Samsung, 89
  speed management and, 140–141
  synergy and, 167
Six Sigma
  adoption of, 220
  as quality control process, 98
  speed management and, 141
  synergy and, 164
size vs. speed, 213–215
smart age, 132
"smartphone revolution," 253
"smartphone shock," 9
smartphones
  Samsung producing, 14, 79
  speed management and, 131–132, 142
  synergy and, 151–152
Snow, Charles C., 57, 223
SoC (system-on-chip) technology, 145
social networking, 132
soft competitiveness, 67–69, 163–165
software, 184
solid-state drives (SSDs), 232
Sony
  cross-licensing agreements with, 185
  customer orientation and, 239
  in future, 252–253
  surpassing of, 179
speed
  in 21st century, 131–133
  advanced development and,
    142–149

advanced IT infrastructure and,
    148–149
  clustering for, 142–144
  as core competency, generally,
    127–130
  of decision-making, 134–139
  of execution, 139–141
  goal-driven R&D for, 146–149
  infrastructure/systems for,
    141–149
  leapfrog R&D for, 146–147
  management elements and, 225
  New Management initiative and,
    133–134
  parallel development and, 146
  preparedness and, 142–149
  process innovation and, 147–148
  upgrading R&D for, 147–148
  vertical integration for, 144–146
  spin-offs, 53
SRAM (static RAM), 177
SRM (supplier relationship
    management), 107
SSDs (solid-state drives), 232
SSI (Samsung Semiconductor
    Institute), 146, 188
stack design, 69
Stalk, George, 133
static RAM (SRAM), 177
strategic partnerships, 190
strategy
  core competencies and, 225
  in decision-making, 69–70
  management elements and, 124
  tasks for. See strategy tasks
Strategy and Innovation Center, 236
strategy tasks
  co-prosperity business model in,
    244–245
  evolving to a loved company,
    244–245
  evolving to ambidextrous
    organization, 233–236
  evolving to total solution provider/
    platform leader, 237–241

evolving to transnational
corporation, 242–243
future of, generally, 230
M&A and "real options" investments in, 236–237
market leadership via creative
innovation, 230–233
reducing gaps between affiliates,
241–242
stretch goals, 194–195, 215
success factors
evolutionary innovation as. *See*
evolutionary innovation
introduction to, 127–130
speed as. *See* speed
synergy as. *See* synergy through
convergence
supplier relationship management
(SRM), 107
supply chain management (SCM)
customer service and, 104
global, 97
IT-based innovations and,
148–149
manufacturing and, 100–101
process integration via, 104–105
purchasing information systems
and, 99
sustainability, 223–228
Suwon, 143–144, 169
Synergy Group, 168
synergy through convergence
best practices in, 164
brand sharing in, 164–165
business group structure and,
155–157
clustering for, 169–170
conglomerates and, 152–153
as core competency, generally,
127–130
corporate culture community in,
166–167
Corporate Strategy Office and,
167–168
cost reduction and, 163

diversified business structures and,
152–157
in era of convergence, 152–155
governance structure and, 166–167
groupwide committees in, 168–169
increased sales and, 160–162
infrastructure/systems for, 165–171
introduction to, 151–152
knowledge management systems
and, 170–171
LCD business success and, 160
management elements and, 225
means for creation of, 157–165
mobile phone business success and,
160–162
organizational culture and, 166–167
owner-managers in, 166
sharing information in, 164
soft competitiveness and, 163–165
synergy and, 159
systems for, 167–171
task force teams in, 168–169
TV business success and, 162
System LSI division, 237
system-on-chip (SoC) technology, 145

Taiichi Ohno, 203
talent management systems, 68–69
task force teams, 168–169
TBC (Tongyang Broadcasting
Company), 62
Tech Conference, 199
Technology Exhibitions, 171
technology innovation strategy,
185–187
Techwin, 211
telecommunications, 178
televisions (TVs). *See* TVs (televisions)
TFT-LCDs (thin-film-transistor liquid-
crystal displays)
innovation and, 178
introduction to, 7
speed management and, 137
strategic decision making and, 69,
79–80

three-day finalization, 99–101

Time, 61

time industry, 258

Tizen, 82, 241

ToC (Touch of Color) TVs, 179

Toffler, Alvin, 137

Tongyang Broadcasting Company (TBC), 62

topical management, 66

Toshiba, 69–70

total solution providers, 237–241

Touch of Color (ToC) TVs, 179

Toyota, 9, 203

TransChip, 237

transnational corporations, 242–243

trench design, 69

triangular governance structure, 72

trinity of values, 109–113

tripartite R&D function, 197–198

TRIZ, 187

Tushman, Michael, 223

TV Advancement Committee, 214

TVs (televisions). *See also* display panels

  Bordeaux line of, 187

  cathode-ray tube, 83, 161

  digital, 134, 137

  flat-screen, 65

  LED, 232

  market leader strategy and, 79–81

  N Screen era of, 241

  Plus One, 161

  shutter glass 3D, 179

  speed management and, 145–146

  synergy and, 161

  Touch of Color, 179

twenty (20) years to the top, 1

ubiquitous era, 155

UHD (ultra-high-definition) broadcasting, 179

United States

  management style in. *See* Japanese vs. American management styles

  recruiting talent from, 189

  regional headquarters in, 103

  research institutes in, 193, 199

U.S. Patent and Trademark Office, 4–5, 184

value innovation, 186–187

values. *See* cultural values

Values portal site, 113

vertical integration

  cost reduction and, 261

  quality-focused strategy and, 83–84

  for R&D, 144–146

VIP Center, 186–187

vision leadership, 41, 61–66

Wacom, 191

Wally, Stefan, 137

watches, 258

Way of Samsung. *See* Samsung Way

Welch, Jack, 203

WiBro (wireless broadband), 81, 240

Woo Nam-Sung, 131

workforce. *See* human resource management

world-class company

  as goal, 58, 117, 130

  manufacturing by, 199–200

  rise to, 3–9

"World's Most Admired Companies," 3

worldwide trade network (WTN), 108–109

Year of Design Innovation (1996), 67

Yun Jong-Hong, 68, 75, 194

ABOUT THE AUTHORS

Professor Jaeyong Song

Jaeyong Song is Amore Pacific Professor of Strategy and International Management at Seoul National University (SNU) Business School. He received his PhD at the Wharton School of the University of Pennsylvania. Before joining SNU, he was a Professor of strategy at Columbia Business School and Yonsei University. He has served as the associate dean of SNU Business School. He has also served as vice president of the Korea Academy Society of Business Administration (KASBA) and president of the Association of Korean Management Scholars (AKMS). He is a Korea Chapter Chair of the Academy of International Business (AIB) and an editor of the *Journal of International Business Studies* (*JIBS*), which is a *Financial Times* top 45 business journal. Professor Song has also served as an adjunct consultant to both the World Bank and Medley Global Advisors in New York. He has worked as a visiting research fellow for the Asian Development Bank Institute and the Long-Term Credit Bank Research Institute in Japan.

He won both the Richman Best Dissertation Award of the Academy of Management and the Hedlund Best Dissertation Award from the European International Business Association in 1999. He also won the Chazen Teaching Innovation Award at Columbia Business School in 1999 and the SNU Teaching Award (2009). He also received the KASBA SERI Best Researcher Award (2014).

Professor Song was chosen as one of the top 10 business/management gurus in Korea by *Maeil Economic Daily*. He was a keynote speaker for GE's Global Leadership Meeting in 2014. He has been involved in executive education programs for such major corporations as Samsung, Hyundai-Kia Motors, LG, SK, POSCO, Lotte, Hanjin, Hanwha, and KT. He has also served as an advisor and/or a board member of major corporations, such as Samsung,

Hyundai-Kia Motors, SK Holdings, Lotte Confectionary, POSCO, Amore Pacific, Nongshim, and Hanmi Parsons.

His research has appeared in top-tier journals, including *Management Science*, *Strategic Management Journal*, *Organization Science*, *Journal of Management*, *Journal of International Business Studies*, and *Research Policy*. His article on Samsung's paradox management, coauthored with Kyungmook Lee, was also published in the *Harvard Business Review* (July–August 2011). His book *Smart Management* became a bestseller in Korea, selling more than 30,000 copies. He is on the editorial board of *Long Range Planning and Global Strategy Journal*.

Professor Kyungmook Lee

Kyungmook Lee is Youngone Corporation Professor of Organizational Behavior and Human Resource Management at Seoul National University Business School, where he currently serves as senior associate dean for academic affairs. He did his undergraduate work in business administration at Seoul National University and received his PhD in management from the Wharton School, University of Pennsylvania.

His current research interests cover the management of Korean companies and Confucian leadership. His earlier research focused on the social capital of organizations and institutional changes. His research has been published in *Academy of Management Journal*, *Strategic Management Journal*, *Long Range Planning*, and *Harvard Business Review*.

His work on the institutional changes in large American law firms won the award for the best paper published in the *Academy of Management Journal* in 2002. His work on Confucian leadership won the Baekbum Leadership Research Award for the best paper published in *Leadership Research* in 2005. He was selected as the Professor of the Year in 2003 by the Alumni Association of the College of Commerce, Seoul National University. He was the recipient of the KASBA SERI Best Researcher Award in 2013.